THINKING BEYOND TECHNOLOGY

THINKING

BEYOND

TECHNOLOGY

Creating New Value in Business

Joseph A. DiVanna

First published 2003 by
PALGRAVE MACMILLAN
Houndmills, Basingstoke, Hampshire RG21 6XS and
175 Fifth Avenue, New York, N.Y. 10010
Companies and representatives throughout the world

PALGRAVE MACMILLAN is the global academic imprint of the Palgrave
Macmillan division of St. Martin's Press, LLC and of Palgrave Macmillan Ltd.
Macmillan® is a registered trademark in the United States, United Kingdom
and other countries. Palgrave is a registered trademark in the European
Union and other countries.

ISBN 1–4039–0255–0 hardback

This book is printed on paper suitable for recycling and made from fully
managed and sustained forest sources.

A catalogue record for this book is available from the British Library.

Library of Congress Cataloging-in-Publication Data

DiVanna, Joseph A.
    Thinking beyond technology : creating new value in business/
    Joseph DiVanna.
        p. cm.
    Includes bibliographical references and index.
    ISBN 1–4039–0255–0

    1. Technological innovations. 2. Organizational behavior. 3. Value. I. Title.

HD45 .D55 2002
658.4'06—dc21

                                                                    2002031739

Editing and origination by Aardvark Editorial, Mendham, Suffolk

10   9   8   7   6   5   4   3   2   1
12 11 10 09 08 07 06 05 04 03

Printed and bound in Great Britain by
Creative Print & Design (Wales), Ebbw Vale

To my grandmother Nellie DiCanto, who has witnessed ninety years of technological change and continues to keep an optimistic outlook on life; to my wife Isabel, whose pragmatic views on technology make each day an adventure; to my son Frank, who I used in many early experiments with technology; and to my grandson Salvatore, whose technology journey has just begun.

CONTENTS

LIST OF FIGURES AND TABLES

Figures

Tables

PREFACE

To my colleagues in medieval history, I once again must beg forgiveness for making sweeping generalities on the nature of medieval society to bring modern management messages to light. This book does not in any way pretend to be a scholarly work on medieval history; it merely borrows the metaphorical richness of the Middle Ages to weave a tapestry of concepts that lend themselves to contemporary business strategies, showing continuity between the practices of managers or people in the position of managers in the Middle Ages and today. The comparison of instances found in the past which exhibit similarities to events in today's society is intended to demonstrate the cyclical nature of business and social behaviour regarding technology. The historical references are intended to be a baseline for discussion on the nature and structure of work, business practices, society, commerce, government, taxation, geopolitical limits and the self-imposed boundaries that today's society has placed on the current process of globalization.

To my associates in business, I wish to express my most sincere thanks for allowing me the latitude in constructing the business lessons learned during the past 20 years, loosely applying them across ten centuries of history. The intent is to stimulate the readers' thinking and promote the radical redesign of business processes by engaging technology in the true spirit of reengineering. The business case studies used in this book are organizations trying to make massive changes in their business cultures, influence the markets they serve, cater to the attitudes of society and alter the very nature of work itself. In many cases, the true names of the organizations have been omitted to protect information that was shared in confidence or that may reveal data which would be detrimental to their competitive advantage.

JOSEPH A. DIVANNA

Acknowledgements

So many people have made kind suggestions that it is a pleasure to acknowledge their contribution. First of all, I would like to express my continued thanks to my wife Isabel for her vigilance in reviewing drafts of the manuscripts, help in researching companies and consistent attention to detail in the development (and typing) of this text.

I have had the privilege to work with many talented individuals over the years, many of whom broke new ground in the field of technological innovation. I would like to acknowledge the contributions of those whose names have not been in the limelight as often as they should have been. The early pioneering efforts of Scott Shultz, Adrian Merryman, Deborah Pulak and Kitsie Holcumb at Dupont Information Engineering Associates radically altered the approach to computer software development and resulted in the creation of the Rapid Iterative Prototyping Process which became the foundation for many software development methodologies such as joint application development and ultimately reengineering laboratories. Additionally, Eric Dubiner, Richard Thomas, John Saboliauskas, Dr Tony Picardi, Ted Osetek and the many dedicated employees of the CORTEX Corporation who provided long hours of debate on the concept of portals in the 1980s. Many thanks to Warrant Officer John Eget of the Philadelphia Naval Station whose vision of how technology could be applied to military administration was at least ten years ahead of its time in the 1980s.

Special thanks to Jeff Morgan of Computer Sciences Corporation in the United Kingdom for his insights on project management, and to my colleague and friend Ian Head of Head-e Designs Ltd, London, a former CSC Index associate, for his efforts in converting my feeble attempts at drawing into graphs. Additionally, heartfelt thanks to Jim Baxter, Clelland Johnson, Jim Ettwein of the national practice of Computer Sciences Corporation who bridged the gap between business process reengineering and technology transformation. I am especially grateful to another CSC Index veteran Jay Rogers, a friend, sounding board, and longtime confidant who exemplifies the concept of a thought partner. I would also like to acknowledge Harry L. Freeman from the Mark Twain Institute, Simon Bragg from Arc-Web, Mike Killingly from HSBC Bank, Daragh O'Byrne and Martin Dolan from Misys International Banking Systems, and Margot Silva for their comments on the unedited version of this book.

I would like to give special recognition to Professor Patrick Bateson, Provost of King's College, Cambridge, whose kindness and friendship made possible the continuation of my research into the ways of medieval craftsmen. A continued thanks to the fellows of King's College for granting me access to King's College Chapel, which acts as a catalyst for my research on medieval buildings. Special thanks to Dr Frank Woodman, from the Board of Continuing Education, University of Cambridge, for so many interesting insights into the construction of medieval churches.

Once again, I am grateful to my publishing editor Stephen Rutt for his willingness to take the ideas found in my lectures and formulate them into this text. It should also be noted that this book could not have been developed without the interaction, dialogue and exchange of ideas of the countless people who have attended my lectures.

In addition, I am forever grateful to Richard Buckminster Fuller, whose writing continues to inspire my research in architecture, history, business and science.

I would also like to acknowledge C. Stabell and fl. Fjeldstad for their work on Value Configurations and offer my most sincere apologies for overlooking their contribution in my first book *Redefining Financial Services: The New Renaissance in Value Propositions*. The error was not intended to diminish their intellectual property, but was merely an oversight due to the research method used.

INTRODUCTION

The evolution of technology, if stripped from contemporary marketing hype and media coverage, is a silent, steadfast process which invokes the following question: Is society shaping technology or is technology shaping society? In *Thinking beyond Technology: Creating New Value in Business*, I intend to introduce the readers to the parallelism between the value proposition of new technologies such as the Internet and the birth of the Renaissance in medieval Europe. Examining technology's effect on modern culture, one realizes that it presents striking similarities to the behaviours of society and business at the end of the Middle Ages. The reason for using examples from history is to provide insights into today's challenges by placing them in a framework that allows us to compare them over a greater socio-technological context. As Rochlin put it: 'History is possessed of an inherently inverse perspective: the closer in time an event is, the less able we are to perceive it clearly.'[1]

It is within a historical context that the journey of this book begins by demonstrating that society's relationship with technology is not a product of modernity, but an inherent part of human nature, as Rochlin noted:

> Medieval Europe had been a domain of lord and serf, town and feud, with one great universal Church serving as a central, coherent force. Reformation Europe saw the emergence of nation-states possessed of pre-eminently national interest, state religions, and primarily mercantile economies based largely on technology.[2]

Looking back at medieval history – even if just metaphorically – can thus help us to understand better the developments of the application of technology in the world of today. History provides clarifying lenses through which contemporary society can examine the roots of how value is created, and the synergistic role that technology has played in the development of modern business.

The reader is invited to consider a series of possible conclusive states that can be drawn from the actions of today's corporate behaviour. Using medieval history as a backdrop for thinking, I collected contemporary ideas on how individuals and corporations are using technology in the development of new value propositions with customers. This book provides a series of lessons learned and alternate ways of thinking for individuals to participate actively in the digital world and corporations to conduct business. I compiled my observations from client engagements, individuals and other anecdotal sources ranging from simple technology start-up firms to large corporations. Additionally, the text explores the composition of digital communities and their members seeking to trade, communicate and interact with individuals having similar interests.

In Chapter 1, the invention of technology and its relationship with society's ability to adopt it into the mainstream of everyday life is explored as a foundation to discuss how technology affects society and what factors influence technological innovation. Innovation is undergoing an evolution from technological improvements originating as a continuous process found in the medieval guild system to an individualistic endeavour by inventors of the nineteenth and twentieth centuries. This chapter explores the question: Is technological innovation the product of an elite group of thinkers, or is it the result of a compound process of many people labouring to fulfil the dreams of previous generations?

The central theme of Chapter 2 is the application of technology as a mechanism for improving productivity. Because of its implementation, technology often reinforces the inefficiencies inherent in business bureaucracies. When technology is applied to business, the traditional objective has been to increase productivity, decrease specific operating costs or improve access to markets and customers. However, in many cases the implementation of technology has led to the reinforcement of existing bureaucracies or the establishment of new ones by creating a need for stringent rules to be followed. This chapter examines the questions: Do technologies bring order to an unordered business? Are different technologies needed as organizations mature and grow?

The third chapter reveals the effects of technology on the mediation of business transactions. Additionally, it investigates how technology is redefining the social contract between employer and employee, government and taxpayer, and how social cultures sometimes conflict with business values. The role of intermediaries from the time of the Medici in medieval Europe to the dot-coms of the 1990s has not changed, adding value in the facilitation of commerce as a simple timeless formula. The transactions of commerce are enhanced by technology, which plays a pivotal role in reducing costs and increasing the performance of the markets, companies and the transactions themselves. This chapter asks the question: What is the relationship between technology and disintermediation and the role of technology in influencing consumer buying, business transactions and government regulation?

Chapter 4 seeks to develop an understanding of the relationship between technology and customers, markets and products by analysing the behaviour of social adoption. The iconography of the Middle Ages and its eventual path to today's advertising demonstrates the intrinsic nature of technology as a vehicle for product awareness and an instrument to formulate customer demand. This chapter probes the side effect of the Internet's influence on products, brands and demographics and puts forward the questions: Is the Internet merely the next generation of technologies that enable communication and facilitate transaction? Can social responses and consumer behaviour be anticipated globally?

The final chapter is dedicated to thinking beyond the boundaries of traditional technology design by investigating how connective technologies are changing the way in which an organization functions, how products are designed and how commerce is transacted. This chapter asks the question: Is the role of the Internet simply to allow the global coordination of decentralized and complex activities?

The closing chapter presents perspectives on what lies ahead from a variety of sources. These views are not intended to predict specific instances of what is to become of technology in the coming decades; rather, the intention is to provide a lens with which to view scenarios of the future state of the relationship between technology, business and society. The historical information provided in previous chapters, coupled with our prognosis, provide the reader with elements from which to think about the issues facing today's business, the use of technology and the greater context of value generation.

This book does not pretend to be a scholarly work on history or a definitive guide to developing business strategy; it does, however, expose the reader to a broad range of issues, using examples and case studies that are not necessarily considered but are vital when constructing corporate strategies.

CHAPTER I

Technology Evolution, Invention and Transformation

In the post-dot-com business climate, a growing number of organizations are adopting a more conservative approach to purchasing, implementing and applying technology to service customers. The technologies used to introduce new products and optimize the process of business now meet with a higher level of scrutiny. This new approach to technology can be labelled as a cautious scepticism, a residual attitude manifested by the downturn in the technology industry. The new stance on technology is largely due to two factors: the enormous effort expended on the Y2K problem, and the meltdown of Internet companies, which symbolized the dawn of a new era in business.

More importantly, society's attitude towards the lack of delivery on the promises that heralded the last wave of new technologies has created a technological paradox for business. New information technologies have not delivered quantum returns, nevertheless they are now vital in the performance of business processes. It could be argued that companies today can no longer afford to view technology as a luxury. Technology must be engaged to achieve superior capabilities over rival firms. Companies engaged in a globally competitive market need technology simply to survive and maintain a level of parity in competitive performance. In Foster's words:

> Strategic errors, however, are not always to blame when a technology leader is overtaken by a competitor. Incorrect perceptions of technical limits, inability to measure technological progress, faulty interpretation of market signals, and unrealistic faith in understanding customer needs tend to mask the deterioration that sets in when an existing technology matures and the superior potential of an alternative begins to affect the competitive balance.[3]

The result of the dot-com meltdown and the reduced confidence in technology providers is a 'wait and see' attitude towards corporate investments in technology. This new attitude – less aggressive and risk averse – originated first with the technologies used as a connective mechanism (such as the Internet) and has quickly spread to eCommerce, and other information 'delivery technologies'. However, this cautious attitude may be premature, as Lynn White observes: 'As our understanding of the history of technology increases, it becomes clear that a new device merely opens a door; it does not compel one to enter.'[4] During the last few years of the twentieth century, businesses and individuals raced through the door of opportunity offered by technology, unfettered by the stark realities of capitalism and the need to operate profitably. The initial gold rush of the Internet may be over, but its use as a medium for business and cultural change has just begun. Companies no longer have a choice whether or not to use technology, but instead must weigh its impact on their value proposition. Each successive upgrade brought by each new generation of technology must also be assessed as to its relative value. It is now a matter of assessing at what time to make the investment in new technology, and whether it still adds the same or greater relative value. Organizations must develop the ability to evaluate a technology for its potential to add value and quickly understand how to absorb it into their current business offering and/or rank its applicability to a future value proposition.

The Challenges of Technology

The technological challenge faced by businesses operating in an interconnected global economy is to strike a balance between technology investments which are intended to improve a firm's market offering or those which aim to improve the efficiency and effectiveness of internal and external business processes. Innovation technologies are essential to growth-oriented market offerings, and they require regular investments to maintain a competitive edge. Firms frequently invest in technologies to innovate only as a short-term reaction to a change in the competitive landscape, and therefore play a continual game of follow the leader with their competition. One could make a case that following a market leader is not a detrimental strategy because it eliminates the cost associated with continuous research and development. This is true only if the organization has the ability to match the competition's offering rapidly. It can be surmised that technology investments are not simply a case of selecting a vendor and making a purchase, rather, it is a continuous process of assessing the capabilities offered by technology and determining their applicability to a firm's value proposition. The impact on value is either enhancing the offering to customers or increasing the performance of the firm for shareholders. To complicate matters, the continual onslaught of competition coupled with the ever-changing level of customer expectations make investments in technology an integral part of the firm's profitability equation. Overinvesting in technology can be detrimental to short-term profitability and longer term viability, as experienced by dot-com firms such as the US grocery home delivery service Webvan. Webvan's technological sophistication was superior to its competitors, but its cost structure – burdened with large capital expenditure in technology – thwarted the returns on investment expectations of short-term investors. Conversely, organizations such as the United Kingdom's Tesco employed the same basic operating model for home delivery, using the Internet as an order processing system and not pursuing complex inventory sorting technologies, simply using lower cost manual labour to pick the products directly off the shelves. Tesco realized that with wafer-thin margins on grocery products, the additional cost of electronic warehousing, cross-docking and automated picking could not be justified until the number of people using the Internet to place orders increased the volume of transactions to offset the cost. The lesson learned is that the underlying business model is sound, as demonstrated by Tesco; however, the investment in technology is directly proportional to the revenues and profits generated by the volume of the transactions. Therefore, one could surmise that when more consumers adopt the Internet as a primary mechanism for grocery purchases, the volume will rise to a point at which a firm like Tesco will have to make a technology investment decision.

The relationship of profit per transaction to volume of transactions processed is often used as a method of justification. However, organizations need to measure and understand this relationship in order to anticipate efficiently and proactively the rise and fall of transaction volumes due to changes in the competitive environment. During the closing years of the twentieth century many firms made substantial investments in eCommerce technologies, justified by the exuberance of the Internet's potential to open new markets. In fact, during the course of several lectures, when participating senior technologists were asked which method was used to justify their website projects, they almost invariably responded that they had a website because 'everyone else has one'. Unfortunately for dot-coms, such as Webvan, Peapod and Streamline, the technology to process the considerable forecast in transaction volume was significantly ahead of consumer demand. Consumers in high-profile niche segments demonstrated their interest in transacting business using the new medium, but the switch to using the Internet for everyday purchases by the majority of consumers did not occur at the same rate. Seemingly, this pseudo overcapacity has left numerous firms with a new capability that is often misunderstood and rarely capitalized on. This capability, which can enable 'business agility', will be discussed in Chapter 2.

Regardless of the intent of technology investments, firms are tasked with the additional burden of sometimes purchasing technology solely to maintain technological parity with suppliers, distributors and customers. For example, when adapting to the world of eCommerce, a firm's business processes may demand a higher level of automation to integrate with the methods of a supply or distribution chain. Moreover, technology should be assessed within a framework of operational obsolescence to determine their applicability to the business processes they serve. All technologies are temporary, and the duration of their operational usefulness is proportional to the cost of maintenance and their ability to interoperate with other technologies. A small stand-alone computer directing a plasma cutter in a steel mill has a much longer operational life because it does not require the additional functionality of the next generation of hardware and software. The plasma cutter's computer enjoys this longevity of purpose because it is an isolated technology application only requiring data from other systems to complete its assignments. This condition is commonly referred to as an 'island of automation', in which the system either completely stands alone or is integrated by data transfer only. The simplicity of its interface and its non-dependence on additional functionality insulates the plasma cutter's computer from the continual process of hardware and software upgrades. This is why one can observe these isolated technologies running outdated operating systems and requiring little software maintenance. Unfortunately, this technological state is only true if no additional functionality is required by the plasma cutter or the operating computer. In this scenario, when change does occur, it is usually a major refitting or total replacement of the mechanical device (that is, plasma cutter) and/or the controlling computer.

Another challenging aspect facing technology organizations and technology users is the set of decisions governing the application of technology as a consequence of a merger or acquisition. Any instance of two firms coming together triggers a review of the various technologies employed by both firms to determine if consolidating and standardizing to a common technology offers any additional economy to the organization. These sets of decisions typically occur within the technology organization, but are increasingly becoming part of the management decision process prior to a merger or acquisition. The ramifications of these activities and the role that technology plays will be discussed in section 2.8.

The final set of challenges which organizations face with regard to technology is assessing the value of adopting a new business model as a result of the introduction of a new technology. Many firms, seduced by the Internet's siren song, learned that adopting a new business model must be tempered by the firm's ability to maintain a viable and sustainable margin of profit. Technologies such as the Internet create a catalyst for business to readdress the value added to products, the structure of the organization needed to provide support services, and the entire process that the organization uses in order to add value.

Technology's Value Proposition

Each new technology should be assessed on its potential business value or, more importantly, its ability to facilitate improvement along one of the three dimensions of business adaptation, as illustrated in Figure 1.1. The three dimensions can be categorized into discrete activities that the organization can embrace to realign the firm's resources and adapt to changes in the business environment.

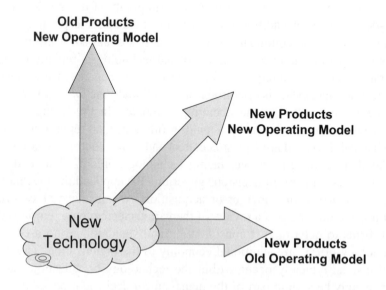

Figure 1.1 Technology's value proposition to business

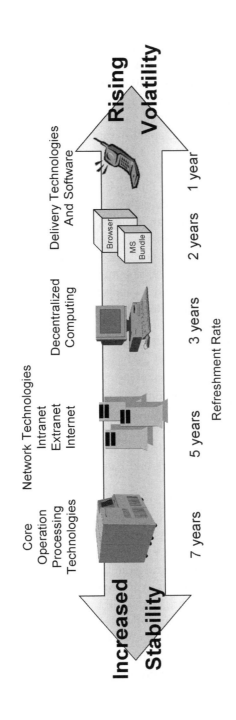

Figure 1.2 Stability and the technology spectrum

For example, a company can introduce a new product using the existing operating model, thus performing what is called 'product leadership'; changing the fundamental process used to deliver existing products (performing 'business transformation'); and/or bringing new products to the market by abandoning traditional methods previously used in the firm (what the industry calls 'reengineering'). In each case, the role of technology is to advance or facilitate a change in direction. However, in all cases, technology is a temporary state of capability and its ability to be used as a bridging mechanism between old and new must be an integral part of corporate strategy.

Fortunately, the application of technology to generate value within a firm follows a somewhat predictable pattern which is recognizable when viewed in the context of society's relationship with technology. Figure 1.2 depicts technologies employed by a firm as components of a spectrum that corresponds to the maturity, turnover or replacement upgrade rate of each type of individual technology category. The rate of refreshment obviously varies from company to company and by individual technology components. The rates in Figure 1.2 are based on approximated averages from industry sources such as *Computerworld*, *Beyond Technology* and various market sources. Technologies on the far left of the spectrum mature and reach stability at a slower rate, and are replaced over longer periods when compared to the technologies on the far right. Not surprisingly, they typically require greater capital investment, being more corporate oriented and least affected by changes in consumer sentiment, fashion or adoption. Conversely, specialized modules of core processing software that have direct links to customers or allow customers access to data (such as online brokerages, consumer goods shopping and banking) will change at a rate faster than the core system itself.

The volatility and rapid change in the lower priced consumer technologies, such as personal computers (PCs), mobile phones and personal digital assistants (PDAs), is largely due to the commercialization of the products to the mass market. For example if one examines television commercials for PDA technology during the two-year period from 2000 to 2002, one realizes that the focus switched from function to form as the technology shifted to appeal to a broader – and in some cases less sophisticated – group of consumers. The early PDA television commercials centred on the functions of the technology, speed in megahertz, storage capacity and memory. Later commercials imply that these functions are irrelevant, announcing rather that the product is now available in six different designer colours, and emphasizing the capabilities of the technology, such as eMail, in-room wireless messages and video/music reception, shifting the consumer's focus away from the device itself towards how to use it in everyday life.

The same social shift in attitude towards technology can also be observed within business, as exemplified by the proliferation of PCs. Originally the purchase and installation of PCs was the sole responsibility of the data processing department. Nevertheless, over time users have become extremely computer literate and now the purchase of a PC and instalation of software require assistance from technology organizations only for the interoperation with the corporate infrastructure. From a business perspective, technology is mostly associated with the reduction of cost, and can be viewed and broken down across the four-part spectrum consisting of hardware and software combinations that perform core operational functions, devices to interconnect business processes, and mechanisms to interact with external entities, amongst others. Each band of the spectrum reflects not only a social shift in attitudes, but also a different rate of technological maturity.

Examining the technological implementation within firms across all industries during the last two decades of the twentieth century, it can be observed that different technologies mature and change at different rates. The rate of maturity can be understood by examining the technologies associated with core business activities, which change less often and remain relatively stable for long time periods, whereas end-user technologies tend to experience a higher degree of volatility and change due to the influence of employees (or users) and consumers (customers). Technologies associated with external linkages such as customers and suppliers can be labelled as delivery technologies. These technologies will continue to change at a faster rate due primarily to competitive pressures faced by hardware vendors. The number of firms that raced to experiment with the Internet during the late 1990s is evidence supporting this phenomenon.

The continued introduction of delivery technologies understates the requirement of greater integration with existing infrastructures. Implementation of consumer-driven delivery technologies will also require a value proposition focusing on the needs and desires of the end consumer. At the other end of the spectrum, the value proposition for core operations technology and, more importantly, infrastructure technology is shareholder value, the ability to reduce cost. Strategically, a robust infrastructure provides a stable connection to the core operations and anticipates continual changes in the delivery end of the spectrum.

It can be argued that within each category of the technology spectrum there are transactions that originate with one group of technologies and flow through to any and all other technologies. Within each type of transaction, a variety of partnerships or relationships will be required, unless a firm is prepared to invest in all the technologies necessary to perform all internal and external information functions. One alternative is to outsource each technology function to third parties that can deliver discrete components within a linked architecture. In the last five years, application service providers (ASPs) have introduced services that facilitate many discrete corporate information functions such as Web-servers, eMail services and eCommerce engines, thus reducing the need for firms to acquire the capabilities in-house.

One can observe that technologies performing core operation functions and inter-networking are reaching a greater level of stability due to the overall maturity of the underlying infrastructure technologies. The higher level of maturity can be measured by the lower amount of intrusion on systems surrounding the core technology when the core is replaced or drastically changed. This degree of stability can be clearly observed in the core processing systems of banks which have undergone a silent revolution from traditional batch processing to continuous real-time processing without a major redevelopment of associated systems.[5] In fact, the relative stability of core operational systems allows organizations to refocus resources on new delivery mechanisms and concentrate on integrating new technologies. Nevertheless, devices on the far right of the spectrum – those providing conductivity for end-user computing such as PCs, PDAs, mobile phones and other consumer-driven technologies – will continue to be volatile, having ever-decreasing lifespans and therefore increasing the complexity of delivery systems.

Technology's Applied Value

A value proposition, not a cost justification, should be developed for each part of the technology spectrum to assess each technology's overall applicability to the process of the business. Business processes often decompose into a collection of tightly coupled and yet distinct activities without clear lines of demarcation such as brand, staff ability, customer demand, partnerships, rates and customer satisfaction. Each distinct business process step is typically facilitated by some facet of technology, and it needs to be viewed as having a defined contribution to the fulfilment of the process. Technologies that cannot be directly attributed to the performance of the value propositions should be questioned, and companies should seek to understand why the incremental cost is associated with the process. However, sometimes a value proposition is enhanced by the indirect contribution of a technology, such as infrastructure technologies, in which the technology performs a service or function that merely enables other processes to be executed. Infrastructure tchnologies cannot always be justified by quantitative measures such as return on investment, or earned value. Technologies applied for the greater good of the firm must be justified holistically and measured by their impact on productivity and customer service levels. In many cases, the indirect effects are difficult to measure and, if not obvious, must be attributed to intuition. Regardless of which approach is used, technology decisions are no longer the sole responsibility of the firm's technology group. Technology is integral to the business and must be justified by assessing its potential to the organization's value proposition. It is important to remember that the acquisition of technology is not just a one-time capital expense, but a continual process in which each successive generation of technology must be assessed on its ability to add to a value proposition. Therefore, it can be said that corporations should minimize the process of justifying the capital expense of technology in order to focus on the timing and application of the technology to the basic value equation (Figure 1.3).

In a private interview on project management, Martin Dolan of Misys International observed that:

> Often corporate management makes the technology decision and passes the responsibility of implementation to a project team. In many cases, the knowledge gained in the evaluation and selection process is inadvertently lost.

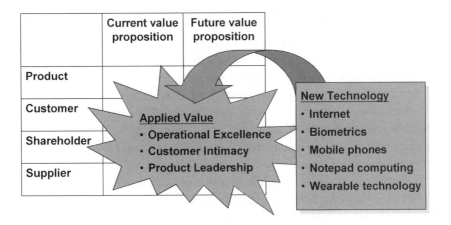

Figure 1.3 The applied value of technology

The achilles heel in many technology projects is the lack of continuity in the knowledge and vision of how technology must be applied to a business process. It is typically not a product design flaw, but the failure of an organization to adapt it to the value proposition and adopt it into the mainstream of operations. Projects which are for the most part labelled as 'technology projects' should be stopped by management teams. *Projects must be focused on business process creation or optimization.* Technology is merely a mechanism for realization. Technology projects come complete with a preconceived prejudice as if they were to replace the old technology and labour to meet the users' demands to emulate the old system. The question that should be raised is if the funcionality of the old system is enough to support the business process, why change it? Reminiscent of Don Quixote chasing windmills, the longing for the old system must be stopped. Technology should change and optimize business processes. Changing the process invariably means changing the way in which the work is done to achieve the goals of the firm. Therefore, a greater return on investment is gained when users develop understandings of the new system and spend energy in its application. Little return is achieved in replicating the old way, which was already deemed inadequate by the decision/selection process.

Lines of business organizations and technology groups should be looking at technology as a mechanism to optimize one or all of three areas: increasing market share by introducing new products; improving customer satisfaction; and reducing the cost of operations by streamlining processes and service offerings. These three areas can be correlated into the value disciplines framework to assess readily the relative value that a technology brings. Technology's relativity to a firm's value proposition will be discussed in detail in section 1.5.

That said, corporations today are starting to realize that although technology has been perceived as the mechanism to differentiate oneself in the marketplace, it is in reality only half the value equation. Unfortunately, while technology is rapidly becoming easier to obtain, it is also turning out to be more complex in construction and integration costs, although its acquisition cost is gravitating towards commodity pricing. As a result, one can observe that because any firm can acquire and apply technology equally, technology is no longer a market differentiator. How individuals in a company apply a technology generates the market differentiation. Market differentiation based on technology alone is rare and in many cases does not exist. The next generation of market differentiators will be developed by considering the ways in which an organization applies the technology for product delivery or to achieve higher levels of customer service. In this new business paradigm, technological innovation shifts its focus from the *creation* of new technologies to the *application* of technology to a company's value proposition. How a firm uses existing and new technologies to enhance its product offerings, customer service levels or operating efficiencies is the market differentiator.

This chapter will endeavour to examine the traditional ways in which technology has been applied to business, and how its adoption by society is influencing the formation of new social classes, driving the behaviours of customers and altering the nature of work. Additionally, reviewing the migratory trends of technology's ever-increasing complexity will illustrate that the original intention of technology is often not its long-term use, but that during the process of continual improvement it transforms society and – perhaps more importantly – customers' expectations. Finally, we will discuss the use of technology in a broader context in order to provide an overview of how to use technology to compete in a global marketplace.

1.1   Technology Invention from Medieval Agriculture to Computer Chip

Roger Bacon's thirteenth-century view of the applied use of technology demonstrates how individuals are able to imagine the ways technologies can be put to use long before the actual technology reaches the maturity in which it can be put to use. Bacon predicted:

> Machines may be made by which the largest ships, with only one man steering them, will be moved faster than if they were filled with rowers; wagons may be built which will move with incredible speed and without the aid of beasts; flying machines can be constructed in which a man ... may beat the air with wings like a bird ... machines will make it possible to go to the bottom of seas and rivers.[6]

The acceptance of an invention or the extent to which, once accepted, its implications are realized by the majority of a population depends on many factors. Influencing elements, such as the economic condition of society, the imagination of its leaders (businesses and government) and the attitudes of the people towards the invention, all lead to the acceptance of technology more than the application of the technology itself. As demonstrated by many cultures across the globe, the past is littered with philosophers, scientists and inventors whose ideas were such a departure from the popular belief that, in order to suppress a challenge to an old belief, the innovator and early adopters were often imprisoned or killed. Pre-modern scientists such as Johannes Kepler and Giordano Bruno were persecuted because they believed that the dogmas of the Catholic Church were wrong. In 1616, in order to prove his theories regarding the non-stationary position of the earth, which he claimed to revolve around the sun, Galileo developed optical technology – the telescope – which offered proof to corroborate and substantiate his claim. Chastised by the Inquisition, to save himself from being burnt at the stake Galileo was forced to recant, and that the earth was, as expressed in Christian theology, stationary in the centre of the universe.[7]

Galileo's example illustrates the fact that, for a very long time, society has met technology with some resistance. In our twenty-first-century western culture we do not value the importance of religion and the church so much as in the fifteenth to seventeenth centuries. The resistance to Galileo did not derive solely from a fear of loss of power from the church. The very basis of human life and existence as it was then was being questioned, merely due to a technological invention. Technology was seen as disruptive of livestyles. This was as true then as in the late nineteenth century. Thomas Edison was also persecuted when society started adopting electricity with more enthusiasm, as Israel documents: 'Edison was "continuously being annoyed by letters from cranks and lunatics from all over the world", several of whom made threats against him for perceived wrongs.'[8] The application of technology is not always obvious, and foreseeing its impact on business and society is often regarded as 'wishful thinking'. Traditionally, prognosticators have been met with scepticism, not because of a lack of comprehension by the rest of society, but due primarily to two factors: the slow communication of a technology's benefits to the majority and fear when it appears to undermine a pre-existing value or belief. This condition is evident in today's society; one could argue that it is even amplified by the very technology that has been labelled as the problem. For example, anti-capitalist and anti-globalization groups using the Internet to communicate their protest are enough to show how ironic is the position of anti-technology groups. Of course the issues which concern anti-globalization groups are mostly noble (environmental issues, exploitation of labour, amongst others), but the focus of their criticism is not always the root cause of the problems, only the instruments used in the process, such as technology itself.

Early adopters of the Internet recognized the potential use of the technology for commerce and formed companies to capitalize on the technology's ability to revolutionize business. Many of these firms, the so-called dot-coms, met an untimely demise, not due to the functions of the technology but the rapid decline of the industry in which they were operating, accelerated by investors' changing attitudes. Unfortunately, these early pioneers were swept up in the ensuing euphoria, exacerbated by the media hype on the potential returns of technology. Many of these start-up firms (today called 'dot-bombs', with reference to their failure) developed technology-based business models that – to their surprise – were not viable when applied to either a traditional low-margin business (such as the afore-mentioned grocery delivery firms), or were dependent on achieving an unrealistic number of paying subscribers. Other firms, suddenly deluged with operating capital, lost sight of the fundamentals of running a rapidly growing business and adopted poor management practices, seemingly for-getting the basics of cash management. Tragically, after a relatively short time in historical business terms, the promise of continued double-digit returns was met with the realities of competition. Investor expectations rapidly eroded, and the market reacted by reducing the amount of available new investment capital rather quickly. Thus, at a time when many of these firms needed additional investment capital to grow, the change in investors' attitudes towards the technology industry reduced their ability to secure funding to develop to the next level of business maturity. Oddly, the original value propositions of the technologies used in conjunction with the Internet have not changed; it is merely the perception of benefits that has been reduced. Reminding us of the California gold rush of 1849, the majority of start-up firms did not strike a vein of gold and establish busi-ness activity that would sustain them as viable long-term entities. Nineteenth-century firms providing the infrastructure for the migration to California – such as the railways and the merchants supplying picks and shovels – made the lion's share of the revenues from the gold-miners.

The Advance of Technology

The need to advance technology as a mechanism to improve the human condition appears to be a universal constant in society in all geographies throughout history. The only variables that separate one generation from another – and one culture from another – are the rate of technological change and the acceptance by society. The boom and bust cycles of eco-nomic activity are of course linked to the introduction of new technologies and their adoption by large segments of the population. This cyclical pat-tern of adaptation is expressed by Jean Gimpel's observations on the technological breakthroughs of the Middle Ages:

Between the tenth and thirteenth centuries, western Europe experienced a technological boom. Both that boom and the subsequent decline can now be seen to offer striking parallels to Western industrial society since 1750, and to the present situation in the United States in particular.[9]

However, our popular notion is that during the past 200 years, the speed at which technology is advancing has been moving at an ever-advancing rate. Not surprisingly, the rate of technological acceptance by society appears to be moving at a faster rate. However, this rate of acceptance follows just slightly behind the rate of technology innovation. The increased rate of acceptance is attributed to the steady increase in the education levels of society. Thomas Stewart observed:

In a report issued in 1995, which controlled for factors like age of equipment, industry, and establishment size, EQW [educational quality of the workforce] showed that, on average, a 10 percent increase in workforce education level led to an 8.6 percent gain in total factor productivity. By comparison, a 10 percent rise in capital stock – that is, the value of equipment – increased productivity just 3.4 percent. Put another way: the marginal value of investing in human capital is about three times greater that the value of investing in machinery.[10]

As society in general becomes more computer-savvy or technology literate, the net effect is an increase in overall productivity. In other words, the next generation of graduating students will come equipped with the knowledge of fundamental business tools such as eMail, word processing and spreadsheets, therefore reducing the need for this type of training expense. Consequently, the next generation of workers will need to learn a new class of technologies and will require even greater amounts of additional training in order to take advantage of the new advances in technology.

Therefore, one may surmise that the rate of technological acceptance by society is directly proportional to the educational level of the individuals in society. Investing in education appears to have a high long-term payoff, yet training budgets are often cut at the first inkling of spending reduction. Conversely, part of this increase in computer literacy can be attributed to the effectiveness of mass media marketing in generating peer pressure within society to acquire the latest technology, hence shifting training for these basic skills to the individual on his/her own time. Regardless of which factor has the greatest influence, the adoption of technology by society cannot be generalized, but must be analysed on a case-by-case basis. In addition, the attributes of a technology must be viewed in the context of its overall value to the segments of population it intends to serve. Developing an understanding of the features of a technology and the rate of adoption in each segment of society is necessary for businesses using technology in the delivery of their products and services to determine which technologies have the greatest effectiveness within population segments.

Statistics illustrating the accelerated adoption rate of new technology showed that while it took 38 years for 50 million people to listen to the radio, 13 years for TV, and 10 years for cable TV, it has taken only five years for people to use the Internet. Richard Buckminster Fuller observed in 1980 that there is a time lag between a technology's invention and its practical social adoption. In his words:

> My half-century experience also discovered the natural, unacceleratable lags that existed between inventions and industrial uses in various technical categories, which occur as follows: in electronics – two years; aerodynamics – five years; automobiles – ten years; railroading – fifteen years; big-city buildings – twenty-five years; single family dwellings – fifty years.[11]

The time lag he observed represents the time required to educate the population on a technology's benefits, convince society of the technology's improvements, and allow the business economies of scale to reach a point of production where the acquisition of the technology becomes affordable and desirable. As I discussed elsewhere, architects incorporate practical advantages of new technology into structures shaping our behaviour, while architecture involves employing a more complex process of changing social taste. The matter of adoption of any sort of technology by individuals is an exercise in shaping the behaviour of consumers as new technological marvels emerge.[12] Traditionally, the factors propelling the advancement of technology have been centred on three basic themes: to reduce the amount of labour required for a specific or general task; the direct application for military use; and/or to facilitate commerce. These objectives have not been mutually exclusive, in many cases they enjoy a product/by-product relationship.

The Reduction of Labour

During the Middle Ages and subsequently until the late eighteenth century, the majority of the population was engaged in agriculture and the production of foodstuffs. The segments of society such as the ruling

class, gentry, merchants, clergy, scholars and artisans were the minority
and the gap between the haves and have-nots was much wider than in
today's society.

In medieval society, the socio-economic conditions were amplified by
changes in climate and the development of technology that directly reduced
the need for labour in agricultural production. The effects of natural changes
in the environment (that is, droughts, floods, plague, amongst others)
significantly affected the availability and productivity of the labour force.
Like the ebbs and flows in the information-based eBusiness society, the
shortfalls in revenues, compensation packages, working conditions and living environment make the labour force of today extremely mobile. Unlike
their medieval counterparts, contemporary labourers can adapt and seek out
work more akin to how they want to work and in the type of organization
which suits their work style.

The 400 years between the eleventh and the fifteenth centuries brought
a period of deliberate development in technologies that would harness the
power of nature to serve man. Simply converting the forces of wind, water
and fire to reduce the amount of labour needed to produce foodstuffs was
the most desired goal. At that time, approximately 90 per cent of the population was engaged in agricultural production; foodstuffs were priced
based on seasonality. Nowadays, however, the bulk of the population is no
longer engaged in food production. Foodstuffs are now tied to commodity
pricing with very low margins. It is interesting that, like our medieval
counterparts, one of the first uses of the Internet and eCommerce technologies is the distribution of foodstuffs in home grocery delivery. More
surprising is the fact that Internet business models centring on complex
technology-intensive solutions were not sustainable under the low volume
of transactions generated by early adopting households. As seen above,
organizations such as Webvan demonstrated that the technology-intensive
solutions could facilitate an interaction with a customer to order goods, but
that delivery of groceries and other products was only cost effective under
business conditions of high volume, due to the nature of the low-margin
grocery business. Conversely, the hybrid approach used by Tesco exploits
the Internet to streamline the order-taking process, while the fulfilment of
each order is done by low-cost labour. In this hybrid model, when the volume of business increases to a point when it is no longer efficient to use
the existing labour resources, technology will be added at key points
within the order fulfilment process, justified by the aggregated savings of
labour cost. Clearly, a manual process facilitating a low-margin product
must reach a substantially larger volume before a large capital investment
in technology can be justified. This seemingly simple axiom has been true

since technological implementations began and can be witnessed in grain milling during the Middle Ages as well as in harvesting wheat in the early twentieth century. Surprisingly, it was a lesson that many dot-com firms and investors learned (again!) at great expense.

The underlying reason for technological change in medieval times was to improve the utilization of peasant labour, thereby creating additional resources in order to increase the amount of land that could be cultivated. The by-product of the increase in food production was population growth. The advance of mechanical technology during the twentieth century changed the output of society from agrarian to industrial. At the dawn of the twenty-first century, very few farmers actually exist. Now, the lion's share of agricultural output is produced by large conglomerates such as ADM and Cargill, who use a vast array of technologies such as geo-positioning satellites (GPSs) and soil fertility monitoring systems to maximize crop yields. Very different from the simple three-field rotational crop farming that was the technological breakthrough in the Middle Ages.[13]

In modern terms, technology was employed to replace certain aspects of the workforce and redirect it to new activities, or even increase the capacity of agricultural production. Medieval people did not see these improvements as a threat to the workforce, but rather as a means to channel more energy towards the improvement of living conditions. Unfortunately, an alarming number of segments in our modern-day workforce view technology and the globalization of the labour market as a threat to their ability to earn a living. Ironically, the attitude of contemporary societies toward employing technology as labour-saving devices is rooted deeply in the medieval mindset. In some ways, the adaptability and ingenuity of the medieval workforce was more advanced in its approach to disseminating technology within specialized labour groups as a product of the guild system, as will be explored insection 2.4.

The Rate of Adoption

Twenty-first-century technologists and technology marketing professionals often cite the accelerated rate of technology adoption by society as a product of the sophisticated modern world. However, when a technology has a clear value proposition to a specific market segment, it is invariably adopted at an accelerated rate. This higher rate of adoption can be seen in a variety of technologies from today's sophisticated mobile phones to medieval windmills during the twelfth century. Taking a retrospective look at the adoption of windmill technology by northern European countries during the Middle Ages indicates that the rate of adoption was so rapid that, if charted, it would resemble a chart of potential sales growth used in a dot-com company investment prospectus. Although the exact date is not known, approximately between 1170 and 1179 the windmill became a standard feature of the medieval countryside. In fact the 'charter of St. Mary's at Swinshead in Lincolnshire, England in 1179 mentions the windmill as if it had been in use there for quite some time'.[14] Within a generation, the windmill was no longer considered a novelty in Britain or Europe, but a recognizable technological improvement which enhanced agricultural output.

Furthermore, it can be argued that the adoption of a technology by society is made complete when governments begin to tax its use. Taxation indicates that a technology has reached a level of saturation within society that its everyday use can generate enough revenues to make its regulation worthwhile. If indeed taxation validates the adoption of a technology by a culture, the integration of windmills into medieval society was complete when Pope Celestine III (1191–1198) ruled that windmills should pay tithes.[15] This rapid acceptance of technology reminds us of the proliferation of PC technology in contemporary society and the rapid demand to be connected to the Internet. Furthermore, as soon as the Internet and associated transaction technologies became a legitimate mechanism for conducting business, then world governments and local authorities started to introduce legislation to levy taxes on eCommerce. Fortunately for business and individuals, governments have not yet imposed widespread Internet taxation. This is due to the long-term uncertainty of how eCommerce will facilitate global commerce and affect trade relations. At the present time, governments do not wish to stifle its growth, as businesses have only started to define the value proposition for the new technology. However, once these technologies reach a sustainable and substantial level of business transaction volume, national and local governments will impose taxable regulation.

The rapid dissemination of technologies such as the PC into corporate operations is also similar to the spread of windmills in the thirteenth century, in their ability to adapt to environmental conditions, or, in the case of the PC, changing business conditions. Like the windmill, the primary distinction of the PC was that it could be used when the computer mainframe was down due to failure of maintenance. The windmill offered a competitive advantage over the water wheel, which could be thwarted by simply going up stream and interrupting the water supply, or downstream and damming the river to raise the level of water to a height where the wheel no longer turned efficiently. The PC, although more expensive than a computer terminal, did not become useless during interruptions in the connection to a mainframe computer. In some cases, transactions were simply stockpiled locally on the PC and transmitted to the mainframe later. The important differentiator of windmill technology was its superiority over the water wheel, which froze in the winter months. PCs offered limited 'detached capabilities', and allowed orders, inventory movements and other production transactions to be recorded for processing when the mainframe was restored.

There is another parallel between PCs and windmills: the spread of windmills in the Mediterranean area was slower because the environmental conditions (such as freezing) were less prevalent. Likewise, the spread of PCs occurred at different rates in firms due to corporate cultures and progressed at even slower rates across industry sectors such as manufacturing, banking and retail goods. Organizations that were knowledge worker intensive rapidly adopted PCs, while the adoption by manufacturing operations occurred slowly over a longer period of time.

The adoption of the PC can be attributed to its availability to basic business functions and its adaptation to industry-specific tasks. Contrary to the medieval windmills' adaptability to a large variety of tasks, the PC's diversified abilities were often retarded by a technology organization's desire to exert control over the PC by reducing cost, by standardizing on single hardware and software platforms. Technology organizations moved to limit the number of vendors that could supply a firm by discouraging the purchase of PCs by business units. Technology organizations faced with rising costs moved to adopt technological standards, originally focusing on merely buying equipment and software from a single vendor. This purchasing philosophy was challenged by business users as PC technology offered a wide variety of solutions, often from many sources. Organizations then developed hardware or software policies that shifted their specific vendors to interconductivity standards of operations. This shift resulted in the acquisition of suites of products that were specific business solutions and limited their ability to integrate into a comprehensive business framework. These loosely coupled software packages presented a new challenge, that of integrating dissimilar hardware and software components in which data and information became the commodity of exchange between business units and other parts of the organizational hierarchy. In this commoditization of information, technology groups once again strived for standardization of information in the form of data models and focused on providing a stable and dependable infrastructure to facilitate widespread data exchange. However, while these centralized efforts of standardization were taking place, PCs ushered in a change in popular culture, stressing individualism (that is, personal) and offering higher degrees of personalization. These two contrasting computing philosophies resulted in heated tensions between users in the business units and the technology organizations that provided centralized computer support services. This same type of conflict in operating philosophies can be witnessed today as firms providing products and services in global mass markets strive to commoditize their offerings into a 'one size fits all' solution for customers, regardless of culture.

Cultural Adaptation

Twentieth-century business often disregarded the diverse needs of individuals from varying geographies and attempted to provide a generic technology solution to all problems for all people. The idiosyncratic factors that are indigenous to a geographic region, cultural preferences or religious doctrines are often overlooked in many of today's eCommerce, banking and retail product strategies. For example, few western banking software companies offer comprehensive Islamic banking applications. The opportunity for twenty-first-century businesses is to develop value propositions that leverage the cultural and behavioural differences in the world's regions. This is done by assessing the relationship between technology and the people it serves. Organizations need to think global when planning and implementing technology infrastructures in order to achieve their goal, such as economies of scale. However, they must act local when applying technology directly at the point of interaction between the firm's business processes and their customers in order to become flexible to market conditions. That said, technology's true value proposition gives a firm the ability to use a common infrastructure, allowing the recasting of technology as a behavioural choice to become an essential component of the mass customization to a market of one. Especially at the local level, when dealing with a wide variety of disparate cultures, a technology's value proposition must be clear and concise, not abstract. The relationship between culture and technology's value proposition is explored on Chapter 4.

In cases when a technology has a clear and desirable value proposition, the rate of adoption is primarily driven by the communication of the benefits. Communicating how a technology is used, and the subsequent benefits to be gained, is closely linked to the language associated with its components. It is harder to disseminate the benefits of a technology until the general population understands the words used to describe it. Prior to the nineteenth century, communications were governed by time and distance. Technologies such as the telegraph and, later, the telephone, revolutionized communications which resulted in the elimination of time and distance as people could learn of world events as they were unfolding. However, when these technologies were first introduced, disseminating the benefits of technology was a dramatically slower process than today.

Looking back once again at the medieval world, communication was a slow process when compared to modern standards. Considering the rapid adoption of windmill technology in the late twelfth century, communicating its benefits and its resulting use was much faster than its incorporation into the popular lexicon. However, Lynn White observes that: 'By 1319 at latest the windmill was familiar enough in Italy to permit Dante to use it as a metaphor in describing Satan threshing his arms "come un molin che il vento gira [like a windmill that the wind spins]".'[16] In contrast, computer jargon and Internet terminology have become part of the mainstream language within a generation, and incorporated into languages in all corners of the world.

Reaching all corners of the globe, terms such as Internet, ASP, WAP (wireless application protocol), mobile banking, dot-com and broadband are crossing linguistic and national boundaries and are being absorbed into local languages by technology-based knowledge workers and consumers influenced by the media, such as television and the Internet. In parallel, when it comes to communicating the benefits of technology, the process of adaptation is closely linked to the application of the technology to a wide variety of uses.

Technological Adaptation

Similar to the transformation experienced by contemporary technologies such as the Internet, during the course of the thirteenth century we see the evolution of windmill technology and its adaptation to a broader range of uses. The windmill's original focus was to grind grain. Over a short period its applicability to other manual tasks was realized and it was adapted to a wide range of activities, such as fulling of cloth, tanning, laundering, sawing, crushing ore and olives, operating furnace bellows, manipulating forge hammers, rotating grindstones, reducing pigments for paint, pulp for paper and mash for beer.[17] Likewise, the Internet is being adapted to the needs of a global society through a rapid evolutionary process. The Internet was originally designed for simple communication between military and academic communities, and it has now been embraced by business as a valid medium for conducting the transactions that enable commerce. With business activities such as selling directly to customers through the integration of complete supply chains, the technologies that plug into the Internet are rapidly defining how society will adopt the new capabilities that the new technologies present.

The Internet evolution will continue beyond the simple application as a means of conducting business. It will transform the very nature of what it means to be in business. Ultimately, the Internet will be embraced by the average citizen who will use it as a mechanism for saving time. The value proposition for Internet technologies is convenience, timeliness and cost savings. Even though the average person has now embraced the concept of the Internet and greater numbers of people are using it, few people have assessed the impact of the Internet on their everyday lives. Merely having a large percentage of a population using the Internet does not constitute adoption or adaptation of a technology to everyday life. When the technology instils in the population a sense of trust stemming from a sustained level of reliability, security and availability, people will alter their lifestyles and integrate the Internet into the activities of living. Citizens of the United States have reached a mature state of adoption with the automobile where the activities of society are now structured around automotive technology. For example, a non-driving suburban citizen is limited – almost thwarted – in any attempts to participate in social activities because of immobility. This is due to the fact that the automotive technology shaped the construction of communities and the distances between them; in Europe, on the other hand, the transportation infrastructure enables people to travel even to smaller towns via trains and buses. One could argue that Europe's comprehensive transportation infrastructure provides its citizens with more freedom and mobility by offering a convenient alternative to air transportation or automobiles.

The next evolution of Internet technology will not be one of awareness, it will be one of applicability. In time, Internet technology will be assimilated into such activities as voting, bringing about a host of government transactions allowing the average citizen more direct participation in national, state and local government. Moreover, the Internet's ability to facilitate communication will be used as a mechanism to bring parents and children closer together in a disconnected social world. The Internet offers parents a new opportunity to participate actively in the education of their children by creating a three-way communication between teacher, student and parent. Most teachers will agree that the use of technology generally stimulates a positive learning environment. However, the use of the

Internet should be considered as a component or tool to use in the larger educational context, defined by sound instructional theory. Parents can coordinate their efforts with teachers to ensure that the focus of computer learning is not simply to learn how to use hardware and software, but also to develop critical thinking skills to solve problems. Unquestionably, technology can facilitate students in unearthing answers, being an important tool in the education process.

Parents often struggle with how to get involved with children and technology other than by acting as a shield against pornography and other unsuitable subjects. Simply creating a dialogue with teachers provides a realm of opportunities for parents to engage technologies and supplement the relationship with their children. For example, your knowledge of the Internet and a subject such as medieval history surpasses your 12-year-old child's level of knowledge. It would be easy, although time consuming, to spend a few moments organizing an Internet-based treasure hunt in which your child has to find specific things on a list of websites that you have pre-selected, or to help him or her do the research for their homework. This type of proactiveness may take an hour or two of your time, but you now know which websites your child is looking at and you are providing a structure that will help a child to learn responsible navigation through the Internet. A simple axiom might be that *technology is not a stand-alone substitute for basic parenting*; however, it can become a convenient excuse for bad parenting. A more distinct view is expressed by Neil Postman, who goes right to the heart of the issues:

> In introducing the personal computer to the classroom, we shall be breaking a four-hundred year-old truce between the gregariousness and openness fostered by orality and the introspection and isolation fostered by the printed word. Orality stresses group learning, cooperation, and a sense of social responsibility ... Print stresses individualized learning, competition, and personal autonomy. Over four centuries, teachers, while emphasizing print, have allowed orality its place in the classroom, and have therefore achieved a kind of pedagogical peace between these two forms of learning, so that what is valuable in each can be maximized. Now comes the computer, carrying anew the banner of private learning and individual problem-solving. Will the widespread use of computers in the classroom defeat once and for all the claims of communal speech? Will the computer raise egocentrism to the status of a virtue?[18]

Individuals who have experienced 'the work at home' syndrome may agree with Postman in the one criticism echoed by many people who perform distance work using technology to telecommute: isolation. Telecommuters who experience this feeling of isolation are indeed maintaining the same or greater volume of communications using technologies such as eMail, video conferencing and collaboration software; however, they still desire physical human interaction. The interchange that occurs between colleagues before, during and after a meeting and the conversations conducted at lunch or non-meeting times act as a fertile ground for the exchange of ideas and the refinement of an organization's culture. In this perception of detachment from the social aspects of work felt by adults engaged in distance work, one could argue that children who spend increasing amounts of time on the Internet as a substitute for playing outside run the risk of not developing the necessary social and interpersonal skills required later in life for a career. One of the dangers for the new generation is the rising number of children being taught at home. Fearing violence at school and negative interaction with other children, parents believe that they have the necessary skills to educate their children in arts, languages and maths, relying on the Internet to supply the missing elements of the children's education. The problem with this could hardly be more obvious: not only does home teaching lead to isolation and the underdevelopment of children's social skills, but also to the use of unreliable sources. Anyone who has done research on the Internet lately has realized that there is an immense amount of nonsense available to everyone, sometimes with encouraging icons and a very professional look. The relationship between technology and parenting and its role in elevating moral and social values are discussed in greater detail in section 5.4.

The Military Advancement of Technology

As in today's society, the advancement of military technology had an impact on the direction of technological development during the Middle Ages. Military technological progress was very slow in influencing the average peasant, if there was any influence at all. However, advances in military technology that resulted from travel to distant lands did influence architecture, weaponry, political relationships of feudal lords and the upper levels of the social structure. Military technology is often the product of applying technology under adverse conditions to produce a breakthrough in how and for what a technology can be used. Military technology often finds its ultimate use in everyday society long after its primary military application to gain a strategic or tactical advantage over an enemy.

One of the earliest medieval technologies to present these attributes was the simple stirrup, and it can be used to show a parallel with modern start-up companies such as the dot-com. Originating in China many centuries before its appearance in Europe, the stirrup was a technology that revolutionized warfare. Used by Muslims in the Holy Land and later in the seventh century by Eastern Germanic tribes, the stirrup changed the very nature of how warfare was conducted. By the eleventh century, the stirrup in one form or another was in use by most of Europe and England. However, the military advantage of stirrup technology was not understood equally by all armies of the day. The principal advantage of the stirrup in combat was that it allowed the mounted rider to transfer both the energy found in his thrust of a weapon with the velocity created by the movement of the horse. This combined thrust was converted into a devastating blow against an opponent. This mechanical advantage made possible by the stirrup was not fully understood by the Anglo-Saxons' leader Harold, when he fought William the Conqueror at the Battle of Hastings. Although both armies were equipped with stirrup technology, Harold's army dismounted to conduct the battle in the traditional manner (on foot), thus creating a Germanic overlapping shield wall which resulted in their defeat.[19] Although Harold's army had the stirrup technology, they did not apply it to a new battle strategy, that is, they did not adopt it into their strategic thinking. Although both medieval armies were equipped with the same technology, the advantage was to the one who rapidly incorporated technology into a strategic advantage by its tactical application. Similarly, many businesses are using the Internet as a mechanism for facilitating sales, but have yet to embrace it in their strategic business thinking. This behaviour is still exhibited by large venerable corporations and contributed to the development of new market entrants, such as Amazon.com with its ability to redefine the way in which people look for and acquire books.

Typically, organizations often purchase technology to engage the competition on a level playing field, and then use it in the same way as previous technologies. For example, look at the number of times a firm implements a new order entry system over a 20-year period without redesigning the fundamental order-taking process. Like Harold at Hastings – using the new stirrup technology with seventh-century tactics – many long-established Fortune 500 businesses have been engaged in a similar battle with the Internet and its integrated suite of technologies. At first, the industry scoffed at the Internet as an unproven and unsafe medium which lacked security and was not suitable for interactions with technology-illiterate consumers. However, businesses soon became painfully aware of the application of the technology as new competitors appeared literally overnight. These competitors were not fettered with bureaucratic business processes and 'slow to change' legacy systems. The nimble start-up companies captured significant numbers of customers while the big corporations first went into a denial phase, dismissing the start-ups as unprofitable. When start-ups did not disappear, big business moved into a 'hurry and catch up' mode which continues today.

It is clear that, over time, many technologies have been driven by military applications first, later finding use in everyday society. From the military campaigns of the Crusades to the Cold War, products such as ARPAnet, which was the beginning of the Internet, will continue to be assimilated by society. The military objective of technology is to anticipate scenarios and extreme conditions in order to develop countermeasures which will thwart or subdue an opposing force. The commercialization of military ingenuity is becoming a goal of governments eager to discover new sources of revenue without compromising national security. One such example by a European government involves adapting battlefield software that assesses and prioritizes incoming missiles to act as a predictive indicator assessing the daily changes in equities on the stock market. Fund managers, like battlefield commanders, would be able to analyse the rates at which stocks rise and fall and speculate based on projected movements. Businesses operating in the global economy must regard technology in the same light, and use it to anticipate future scenarios of competition and proactively engage technology to retain a competitive advantage. The role of new technology is to provide capabilities enabling an organization to expect changes in the business environment and rapidly deploy new capabilities.

Facilitating Commerce

Building and construction technology is another example of the continuous improvement in both technology and its application. In the Middle Ages, the construction of a cathedral progressed over a long period, often accelerating and slowing with the availability or lack of funding. Some churches started their construction in the western end of the church, and worked towards the east (altar end). Other builders started at the eastern end and worked towards a great window in the west wall. Whether medieval builders consciously or subconsciously knew that the technology for windows would improve over the years, permitting larger windows and thinner walls to allow the maximum amount of light into the structure, is not readily documented. Medieval builders employed a method of trial and error,[20] but all with the same expressed value proposition to pilgrims and the congregation, that is, to create a space that would be expansive in appearance, filled with light to produce the presence of God. The grandeur of the structure, its iconography and imagery acted as the brand identity, advertising and guaranteeing future revenues from pilgrims and acting as a central hub for medieval commerce.

Over the past 20 years, the evolution of computer software application development, more specifically graphical user interfaces (GUIs), such as Microsoft Windows, has been similar to the evolution of a medieval cathedral's window technology. Like the windows in a cathedral, the end-user interface has been a primary focus of the Internet's adoption, because it enjoys the most visible connective point between people and machines. Software developers know that all aspects of technology will continue to advance at an ever-increasing rate. Windows technology, the most visual element seen by end-users, has been the easiest component of a technological solution because it can be demonstrated visually. Back-office systems and infrastructure – which may have a series of blinking lights on a control panel – do not offer the same visual stimulation as observing a software application which can plot the latest stock price movements. Both components are required to achieve the end result. However, the end-user mechanism is often the easiest to justify with sources of funding within the business simply because it is often used exclusively in the business unit. Oddly, the less visible component has the higher effective value because it can be applied to many tasks and in most cases outlives the initial application program on the end-user delivery technology.

1.2 Technology Acceptance and the Establishment of the Technoclass

In March 2001, John Manley, the Canadian Foreign Affairs Minister, noted:

> Right now, half the world have yet to make even their first telephone call, while the other half are conducting Internet stock trades through their cell phones. There are more telephones in New York City than on the entire continent of Africa. And while e-commerce amounts to a C$200-billion-plus industry in the West, less than one percent of the developing world's population has access to the Internet.[21]

World leaders are growing increasingly concerned with the ever-widening digital divide between the wired and the non-wired nations of the world, moving this issue onto national agendas.

Surprisingly, the state of being connected to the Internet has risen to become an issue of international importance, spawning organizations such as the non-profit group Digital Divide Network (sponsored by the Benton Foundation) which provides a network of information and resources to narrow the gap.[22] It is interesting to note that world leaders are evaluating the potential of the Internet as a means to distribute education without placing the use of the technology into the larger context of applied use. The inequality of nation states and more specifically people within those states is growing seemingly larger due to three distinct factors: the availability of technology; the overall affordability of technological components; and the rate at which technology can be adopted by each social group. Obviously, members of the upper third of the economic spectrum in all countries have the opportunity to acquire and utilize technology in both business and personal pursuits. Politicians and anti-globalization advocates have expressed concerns over the role of technology in widening the gap between rich and poor. This gap is now being expressed in technological terms as the increasing digital divide between nations and cultural subgroups within each nation. Ingrid Burkett argues that the awareness of the impact of technology is merely being used as a distraction from more pragmatic underlying global issues, such as economic, social and cultural inequalities.[23] The deeper understanding of the issues under the surface of a broader social agenda are also reflected in Micklethwait and Wooldridge's *A Future Perfect*, in which the authors brilliantly dispel the five myths of globalization (see section 3.3 for more on this).[24]

The last two decades of the twentieth century witnessed the dawn of the information society, in which data and the technologies associated with its dissemination have become a highly valued commodity. In some cases, the value of information is greater than the physical asset which it represents or describes. For example, the up-to-the-minute information regarding the price and direction of an individual financial instrument – such as an equity trading on the stock market – is sometimes more valuable than owning the shares themselves. Day traders demonstrate the overall value of this information by using market trend information to buy and sell shares, irrespective of the underlying value of the individual company. In effect, these traders assess the value of pricing trend, develop a sense of direction and speculate on the momentum of the trading activity. In this case, the trend data and movement information are a product of analysis of the stock's trading data, and have achieved a relative value greater than the data about the equity it represents. Taking the basic trading data and assessing an upward or downward trend and subsequently executing trading orders to anticipate predicted movements elevates the value (or relative worth) of the data in many cases beyond the value of investing in the equity itself. Therefore, one could accept the axiom that technology's real value is directly proportional to the information or capability it provides and the application of the user employing it. This relativity is at the heart of the issue surrounding the proliferation of technology across the globe and the backlash towards it by special interest groups under the general category of anti-technology or anti-globalization.

In a global context, technologies such as the Internet – and the information that it distributes – do not have an expressed intent of creating a homogeneous global culture. They merely amplify the pre-existing socio-economic inequality between rich and poor (inside the same country), and between more developed and less developed countries. Technology did not create the gap between the social classes; it brought it to our attention due to the pervasiveness of our mass media culture. Plainly, technology in and of itself does not keep the social classes in place or act as a mechanism to sustain the gap; it simply makes us more acutely aware of the growing disparity and its increasing rate. Conversely, one could argue that technology presents a compelling opportunity for individuals to bridge that gap and use it as a vehicle for movement between social classes. To address this issue from a technologically neutral perspective, one can postulate that two groups of people within a social class or from disparate classes, if given exactly the same technology and associated infrastructure, will use technology in different ways to the exclusive ends of their varying individual agendas. Therefore, just shipping technology to the less wired peoples of the world does not resolve the economic gap; it only masks the underlying problems. Technology does not expand or contract the economic gap between the wired and non-wired peoples of the world; it does however highlight the pre-existing issues surrounding the distribution of wealth. As Stanovnik put it:

> The major global problems of the present age have emerged as a consequence of the socio-economic, political and power relationships within which science and technology have developed. The advanced stage our civilization has reached has often been called 'technotronic', 'post-industrial', 'technological' or even 'scientific'. But science has never been just a factor of its own, obeying autonomous laws of dynamics. Just as the emergence of global problems is not simply the result of the application of science and technology, so the solution of world problems cannot be achieved by the simple application of science and technology as the 'problem solvers'.[25]

Technology does not accentuate the gap, and access to technology by itself cannot narrow the gap. Society must not rely on the application of technology alone as a means to improve life quality and change existing socio-economic circumstances. However, once there is a clear project to deal with the existing problems, technology can and should be employed as part of the solution. With regard to developing countries, the problem of the adoption of technology brings up another problem, that of technological dependence. As Stanovnik put it:

> Science and technology cannot be just 'transferred' from the more developed into the developing countries. There is, indeed, an inherent contradiction in placing too great insistence on the 'transfer' of technology. To realize their objectives of greater economic independence and equality the developing countries must strive also towards greater technological independence.[26]

From a business perspective, the continued decrease in the cost of technology is closing the two other gaps: firstly, the insulated commerce gap between multinational corporations and traditionally domestic companies operating as global trading organizations; and secondly, the competitive gap between large corporations and the small and medium-sized enterprises (SMEs). The common element in each of these gaps is an organization's ability to establish a channel to global markets. For example, traditional domestic firms can now use the Internet to fulfil orders from customers in any geography due to the greater reliability of logistic services and the individuals' increased propensity to absorb shipping costs. Additionally, smaller firms can use the combination of the Internet, outsourcing and white labelling to compete head-to-head with their larger rivals within a domestic marketplace and in the international trading arena. In both cases, firms are leveraging technology to create value by exploiting opportunities that are a direct result of new technology and the inability of larger, more established firms to move quickly to fulfil the new expectations of customers.

Here again one could debate that firms of equal size armed with the same technologies will yield dissimilar results, due to each organization's ability to apply technology to a basic value proposition. The wide variability in results can be attributed to the company's understanding of how to apply the technology, its ability to innovate, the skills of the employees, the receptivity of technology by their customers and the availability of funding. The funding of technology projects has risen steadily over the past 20 years as a percentage of the total operating cost. Organizations using technology as their primary market differentiator must rethink the way in which technology is justified, by taking into account two diametrically opposed factors: a total dependency on technology and a questioning of technology's effectivness. Firstly, technology is now so integral to business that firms can no longer function manually and should view the acquisition of technology as a continual process, not a periodic capital expense. Secondly, the laissez-faire approach towards purchasing technology during the dot-com boom has left many top management teams and investors with a new-found scepticism on spending additional resources without short-term results. This paradox between the need to acquire additional technology to remain competitive and the new requirement of hyper-justification artificially creates the same set of conditions commonly found in social hierarchies, reflected by the haves and have-nots.

Increasingly, the cost of technology is creating a line of demarcation between companies which can afford large investments in technology and those struggling to justify the continual demands for additional technological interoperability. Technology – regardless of the purpose – must generate a measurable payback to the process of business, considering that the relationship between the payback to the investment made is relative to the firm's overall aspirations and goals. For example, investments in technological infrastructure are often difficult to justify because they cannot be attributed to the delivery of a single product line or operating department. Infrastructure which is shared by all, providing a platform of capability, should be the easiest set of technologies to justify because it provides a mechanism that enables all products and departments to participate in the overall process of the firm's business.

The Latency of Technology

Technology must be continually incorporated into the fabric of firms' business processes so that they remain competitive and drive down long-term operating cost. Business units that develop a wait and see attitude towards technology spending are placing themselves at risk and creating a condition which could be labelled the 'dos' and 'do-nots'. The post-dot-com retreat on technology spending in many corporations is artificially amplifying the tendency of firms to hesitate when making technology decisions and can be called 'organizational latency'. Typically expressed as managed risk, this latency is often representative of an organization's inability to take rapid action because of an overarching bureaucratic structure. One could argue that business has reached a temporary technology saturation point, where, although it is desirable to continually apply technology to the process of business, rising scepticism is retarding their drive to continue at the pace dictated by the previous generation of technological innovation. Moreover, consideration of the applied value of technology may not have the same sense of urgency as the dot-com fervour of the 1990s, but permeates a sense of a qualitative approach to the application of technology to business. It is premature to predict if businesses are moving from a quantitative approach to technology, where the more technology one purchases the more successful one will become, to a qualitative approach, which asks 'what are the right technologies to add value?' However, organizations must be aware that in a shift of this kind any increase in organizational latency presents new opportunities for competitors to rapidly service niche demands from customers.

Technology latency can also be attributed to the behaviours of the technoclass within the organization. The technoclass is categorized by technology literacy combined with an individual's behavioural approach to technology. People within a firm have varying degrees of technology literacy; the familiarity with individual technological components influences their approach to applying technology to add value to the business processes and, more importantly, to the value proposition presented to the customers. Regardless of their level of technology literacy, individuals develop strong attitudes towards the technological components of hardware devices of software programs. This can be seen in the relationship between Apple MacIntosh users and Microsoft Windows advocates. Firms dominated by a single class or a majority within two closely associated classes take on the collective behaviour of the dominant group. Often, the behavioural traits permeate from the leadership of the firm to every level in the organizational structure.

Interestingly, the composition of the techno-social classes is reminiscent of the social classes that existed in the Middle Ages. A more whimsical perspective would be to associate the new form of technoclasses with their medieval counterparts in the social hierarchy (see Table 1.1).

One might assume that the technology elite are merely the captains of the technology-producing companies, such as Bill Gates and Larry Ellison. They are, however, a more pragmatic group of individuals who embraced technology in the 1980s and 90s. Most of this group, seduced by the siren song of Internet start-ups, enjoy not only an in-depth knowledge of information technology, but also possess a familiarity with the national application of technology. More precisely, the generation of technologists and people closely associated with technology have developed a relationship with technological advancement that will allow them to see how to apply technology to a firm's value proposition.

Traditionally, the external consultant was the bridge between technology and its applied value. These individuals provide a valuable perspective on how to integrate technology into a value proposition because they have incorporated the use of technology into their own everyday lives.

Table 1.1 Comparison of medieval social classes
and modern technology classes

Medieval classes	Contemporary classes
Royals: responsible for shaping the direction of the nation state.	Technodeterminists: shaping the output of the industry.
Nobility: warriors who guard the kingdom against its enemies.	Technoelitists: members of the technology bureaucracy, guardians of the legacy of technology.
Clergy: keepers of the faith, the practitioners in the bureaucracy of central administrative functions.	Technologists: practitioners of the craft of technology, the humanistic oil on the cog of mechanized advancement.
Merchants: responsible for the trade of goods.	Technocrats: businesspeople who have mastered the use of technology to facilitate commerce.
High nobility: warriors who exhibit fancy weaponry rather than defend the kingdom.	Technophiles: individuals who acquire technology simply for the joy of ownership; they revel in gadgetry.
Peasantry: those who fear losing their jobs in agriculture.	Technophobes: individuals who are slow to adopt technology and fear its repercussions.
	Luddites: individuals who loath technology and reject its adoption.
Foreigners: those who did not quite manage to incorporate themselves into the social group.	Techless: people in disparate geographies who do not plan to participate in the technology society.
	Anti-techiles: individuals who take action against the continued spread of technology and its influence on the spread of capitalism.

Nonetheless, consultants now play a more comprehensive role in the aggregation of cross-company functions to internal and external sources. This change in role can be attributed to the broader range of experiences that consultants bring to a firm, often cross-pollinating industry knowledge and best practices.

That said, there is a small percentage of this group who are, as Micklethwait and Wooldridge put it, 'technodeterminists', those 'who think that it is merely enough to be universal'.[27] These individuals are shaping the technology industry as a whole, and although they have an agenda to sell more technology, they provide the catalyst for technology innovation by investing in research and the development of new ideas.

In short, similar to customer segmentation, organizational categorization between technology literacy and attitude can be associated qualitatively to a firm's technology latency. Although it would be difficult to measure quantitatively, nonetheless its influence is demonstrable in the speed of reaction to changes in business conditions. The behavioural aspect of the workforce is often discounted by management groups as trivial; however, its effects on productivity are measurable. For example, organizations implementing Microsoft Windows PCs whose computing base originally was Apple MacIntosh, experienced significant short-term reductions in productivity not just because of the unfamiliarity of the software, but, more surprisingly, a perceived sense of loss by the users. In most cases, the underlying application software was the same suite of Microsoft Office automation applications, such as Word, PowerPoint and Excel, which represented the bulk of the time spent using the computer. Nevertheless, users were dismayed by management's decision to switch, irrespective of their individual feelings. Users' attachment to one or the other dominant variations of PC technology can almost be likened to that of a religious preference. In any case, the attitude of users reflected the paradox of PCs in the business environment, the struggle between corporations applying the PC to specific, discrete functions which depersonalized the device, and the users' regard for the machine, specifically the choice of applications to run and the available space on the disk drive as personalized for their productivity.

1.3   Migration from Mainframe to Personal Computer

It can be argued that technology changes the method of work, but the nature of work remains constant. Previously, technology's traditional application was to automate or mechanize predefined activities increasing the productivity of workers and their associated output. Unlike previous generations of technologies, the PC, combined with the Internet, has changed the definition of work in three distinct ways. Firstly, PCs changed the *method* or approach of the work being performed, coupling technological tools together for greater productivity, for example the techniques used in activities such as voice dictation (when it functions properly!) and response systems. Secondly, the *time* when work is performed, and thirdly, the *manner* or behaviour in which work is done, meaning that it is becoming more difficult to separate work and personal activities. For example, one may write a memo at the weekend when the idea is fresh and then during the working day, access the Internet and order home office supplies to be collected on the way home. This alteration in the basic premise of what constitutes work places technological capability slightly ahead of the ability of many organizations to apply it to business processes. It is premature to assess the long-term impact of connective technologies on the value propositions of organizations. Regardless of geographic location, companies will recast their organization to accommodate the innovative work activities made possible by new technology and the most recent role that individuals play in the workplace.

Business, people and social structures in the Middle Ages are often viewed through a lens of romantic fondness in which kings and knights wooed beautiful ladies on their way to win a battle against the unfaithful ones. In reality, the Middle Ages were a brutal and harsh period in world history. Now, at the turn of the millennium, one looks back at the working society of the last half of the twentieth century with growing nostalgia. As time passes, individuals often reminisce about the conditions that existed before the latest implementation of technology, thus forgetting the inherent frustrations of the previous technological generation. During the implementation of a new manufacturing system, it is quite common to hear individuals refer to the 'simpler times' when the KARDEX system was used, conveniently forgetting its limitations. One by-product of technological advancement is how technology is rewriting the social contract between employers and employees. In just one generation, we have gone from having a sense of belonging to an organization with lifetime employment to a sense of disconnection from the workplace as a result of downsizing, rightsizing and other corporate cost-cutting activities. In many US organizations, workers have developed a rightly deserved attitude that 'corporate loyalty and a dollar will buy you a cup of coffee', which is not far from the truth. White and blue-collar workers are developing a feeling of detachment from their employers because of a rising attitude projecting labour as a commodity made disposable by the application of technology. Seemingly, this new feeling of disorientation in the workforce is perceived as a modern phenomenon brought about by the rising use of technology as a substitute for human labour. However, in the past, one condition of disruptive technologies is that they reach a level of maturity and a subsequent saturation point within society.

A stark contrast to today's social structure is the medieval period, when everyone was keenly, sometimes painfully aware of their place in society. Whether serf, noble, cleric or tradesman, a person's lifetime employment was traditionally within a narrow band of preconceived activities, typically following in the footsteps of one's parents. In medieval society, the ability to read and write was restricted to a few social classes. The technology for communicating the written word was stagnant for several centuries, only to undergo a gigantic transformation to mass communication with the introduction of the printing press. Similar to medieval society, in the early days of the Internet, a select, elite group of academic researchers working on military projects developed a network of interconnection that allowed the interchange of ideas and research materials. As the collaboration technology matured, the ability to connect increased for many individuals and other groups. This early collection of academic and military collaborators found that the robustness and complexity of the infrastructure was less important than the value of the communications it facilitated. Thus the Internet was born, promising to provide what other technologies had failed to provide, namely two-way communications independent of time, accompanied by a written record of the interaction.

The Internet fits the classic description of what Christensen calls a 'disruptive technology', – 'technologies which are considered a threat to incumbent technologies are simply applied to improve upon or present a radical alternative to something that you are already doing'.[28] However, disruptive technologies typically generate value to customers who rarely understand the value proposition of the new technology during its introduction. Christensen illustrates that traditional sources develop a relationship with customers that becomes familiar over time. When a new product or a change in the structure of acquiring that product is radically altered, the receptivity of customers to the new way becomes less than enthusiastic. If a product has an intrinsic value apart from the price of the item, customers are inclined to stay with the product, using the traditional structure. When the potential of a disruptive technology is significant enough to change the structure of an entire industry, this type of institutional thinking is not limited to customers, as demonstrated by Norman's observation of industry leaders:

> Thomas Edison turned down the radio because it had no commercial value; Western Union turned down the telephone because management thought 'it will never be more than a toy'; Thomas J. Watson Sr., founder and head of IBM, turned down the computer; and Kodak turned down the Xerox copier.[29]

Like other disruptive technologies, the Internet is the latest in a series of technologies that alter and advance the communicative behaviours of people and business activities. People using Internet technology have undergone a change to a new state of interoperability with the new mass media delivery technologies.

The fundamental shift made possible by the Internet is the movement from a broadcast medium to an interactive or transaction-based set of activities. Previous communications technologies were single direction transmissions that informed a passive user. The progression of technology as seen in Figure 1.4 depicts four generations of technology which have pro-

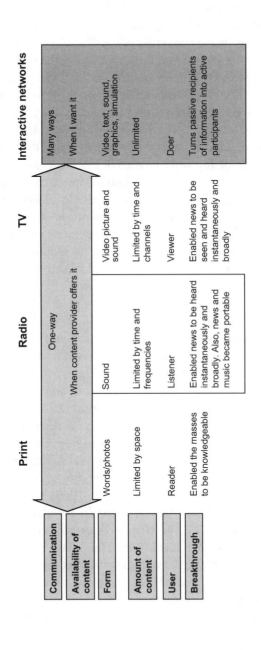

Figure 1.4 The evolution of interaction

gressively altered the behaviour of individuals, changing them from readers to listeners, to viewers, and finally to doers. Each successive technology generation facilitated a short-term effect which altered business activities such as advertising, marketing and customer services, and cultivated a longer term change in the behaviour of society, reaching beyond simple consumerism. For example, the radio's short-term effect was that it provided news and information to a mass audience a short time after the actual event had taken place. The longer term effect was to move music from a localized event such as a concert, recital or performance to a national offering of music to ever-increasing categories of specialized tastes. The radio generated a widespread demand for music which elevated the sales of recordings as a consequence of reaching larger audiences. It can be postulated that before the radio, music could be categorized into two broad classifications: an elite classical music culture and a popular or local folk music culture. The radio acted as a catalyst to mass produce music which eventually drove down the overall production cost, enabling more and more artists to be recorded. Advances in technology continued to reduce costs making it possible to produce music across an ever-widening range of classifications, such as reggae, blues, pop, country and techno.

In the early days of radio, it would have been difficult to imagine the broad selection of music and the higher fidelity of the product that we enjoy today. It would be even more difficult to picture the complexity and idiosyncrasies of today's music industry, based on the behaviour of first-generation radio sales. In the 1990s, the average person's ability to be connected to an electronic society blossomed, and the demand for this interconnectivity overwhelmed even the most seasoned technology-trend visionary. Newspapers and magazines were littered with many techno-futuristic dreams that have fallen by the wayside. This phenomenon is not surprising since it is a repeated pattern throughout the history of technology. For example, the videophone, first on the scene in the sci-fi movies of the 1930s, appearing later on TV in the 1960s and popularized in the 1969 movie *2001 A Space Odyssey*, has had a chequered track record. Companies such as AT&T and British Telecom have both had pilot programmes that had less than promising results. Two principal problems can be identified. Firstly, the technological infrastructure needed to implement videophones was not available at a price affordable to consumers. Secondly, the existing infrastructure did not have the bandwidth capacity to produce a stream of pictures (30 frames per second) and audio acceptable to consumers used to seeing television quality images. Now the technology needed to transmit this high capacity data has caught up with the technology that can produce videophones. These two conditions still existed when ViaTV, Connectix and others reintroduced videophone technology using both regular phone lines and the Internet in the late 1990s. A third problem for people who subscribed to the videophone was that unless people they knew also subscribed they had no one to talk to. The radio, the videophone and the Internet have had a profound influence on the behaviour of society. Business is now starting to understand the fundamental elements of the Internet and how the Internet affects the behaviour of individuals, consumers and organizations. More importantly, corporations can employ the Internet and its related technologies to develop new ways of ordering, distributing and utilizing their products. The disruptiveness of the Internet gives companies the opportunity to think about *how to conduct business.*

Originally, the Internet was thought of simply as a communications medium for data and information exchange. The second generation of the Internet proved to be the age of the marketer; marketing mavens flooded Internet newsgroups, eMail boxes and bulletin boards with junk mail and a flood of product literature. Now, in the third generation of the Internet, users are discovering a new use for the Internet, that is, the establishment of materials and ideas that can be explored collaboratively in a dialogue within a linked digital community, which is discussed in Chapter 5.

Collaboration

Businesses have yet to realize the potential value of third-generation collaborative technologies and their effect on the organizational structures of corporations. The underlying potential of collaborative technologies is to alter drastically the roles and responsibilities of workers. Consulting companies are learning that the cost of maintaining a relationship is less than the cost of acquiring a new customer relationship. Client familiarity reduces cost because it minimizes the need to orient the consultant to the idiosyncrasies of the client's business culture. Technology is the lever that will propel the communications between consultants and customers to reduce the amount of time needed to sell the next project by demonstrating the success of the last project. Consequently, the poor performance of the project is also clear to the client and consulting companies will realize that quality of service is the essential driver rather than price. Unfortunately, collaboration and the use of consultants does complicate the issue of intellectual property rights, work for hire and other legal and technical aspects of the new work environment. These issues, although not addressed in this text at length, are growing concerns, as organizations now span international borders and are testing the limits of laws and regulations.

The technologies enabling this new era of communications and collaboration between parties create the need to develop a new set of skills in order for workers to remain competitive. The combination of technologies used to communicate these transactions (that is, confirmations of meetings, agendas, receipts of materials) with intelligent agent technology creates an initial flood of messages, data and information which is overwhelming. The key to this new wave of communications is to develop an agent that does messaging arbitrage, looks for confirmations and other generated correspondence, and reports only the anomalies. Messages that did not receive the anticipated response are passed to the user as priority items. This type of interaction by exception is often counterintuitive to individuals who grew up using computer mainframe eMail systems, whose fidelity was in the completeness of each transaction. The migration from legacy mainframe to personal computing was a generational experience that does not prepare us for the next shift to an even higher degree of personalization in the next generation of technology. The next wave of more intrapersonal technology comes with the express intent of permeating the actions of everyday life and will foster a new set of issues centring on individuality, security, privacy and disclosure.

One thing is clear: Internet-based technology became popular because it allowed individuals to serve themselves and perform functions at a convenient time. Businesses eager to reduce customer service labour costs quickly engaged the new medium as a direct method of eliminating customer support staff and other typical middle income jobs, without addressing the root cause of why customers wanted to serve themselves. In many cases, the answer is simple dissatisfaction with the firm's performance, or to avoid the inconvenience of changing suppliers, and consumers welcomed the opportunity to take control of the situation. However, as interactions mature and the next wave of interconnective technologies allow for greater self-service, one could argue that customers will eventually develop a sense of the value of their time and reach a point where they are performing so many self-service functions that it is no longer economical to do so.

Individuals and corporations may realize that all this self-service activity (such as tracking your own packages, booking flights, banking and so on) simply shifts those imperceptible costs to you and/or your organization. Few companies have analysed the impact on productivity after they eliminated travel agents and allowed individuals to book their own business travel. The savings received from no longer paying travel agents' commission is not compared to the internal cost of personnel (mostly personal assistants and secretaries) now performing the same basic functions. On the other hand, it might be faster to spend 5–10 minutes online shopping for a ticket rather than spending maybe 10 minutes on hold on the phone plus the actual time to define the date, time and availability with the travel agent. The point is that until companies start researching the impact of eCommerce to their business, all arguments will remain inconclusive.

Technology's next migration will be towards personalization, in which case ever smaller individual components of technology will be integrated into the average person's everyday life. Technologies such as biometric devices, avatars and wearable computers will produce volumes of information about an individual and, more importantly, their behaviour. Whether people will gravitate to the new, more intrusive generation of technology remains to be seen. However, as history demonstrates, it is highly possible that individuals will accept intrusive technologies and will, one day, wonder how they ever lived without them. The driver of these types of technology may lay in the intention of the technology and the value proposition it presents to society.

1.4 The Intent of Technology

How society adopts and uses technology is frequently not as the technology inventors had intended. Contemporary futurists and other technology prognosticators ponder on the Internet's ultimate influence on business. Their predictions will, in many cases, be wrong or in some cases half right. Nicholas Negroponte of the MIT Media Lab predicted that by the year 2000 more people would be entertaining themselves on the Internet than watching programming broadcast on network television. In some niche demographic market segments, he may be right, but the majority of the population has not yet moved toward the new medium.[30] However, Negroponte brilliantly surmised that due to the capabilities inherent in the Internet, changing customer behaviour towards self-service and a reassessment of personal time management, individuals would begin to regard television differently. Negroponte stated the 'the key to the future of television is to stop thinking about television as television. TV benefits most from thinking of it in terms of bits.'[31] This observation does reveal that our behaviour adapts to the new technological capabilities, as witnessed by users of TiVo[32] who overwhelmingly choose to download television programmes and watch them at times which are convenient to them, jettisoning the television network programming schedule altogether.

Another historical example is the original express intention behind the use of television, which was showcased at the 1929 World's Fair. Television was presented as the technology that would bring a college education to everyone in the privacy of their own home. Early adopters rapidly embraced television as an entertainment medium, and television programming has matured over the years from pure enlightenment to sheer enjoyment. A quick channel surf through today's hundred-plus cable offerings finds that television's most recent role is that of the continuous merchandizing of products, now incorporated within the programmes themselves in addition to the commercials. In fact, educational programme channels are in the minority, very different from the original intention.

Neil Postman describes this transitional intention of technology as the passing of a baton between one generation of technologies and another:

> We can imagine that Thamus would also have pointed out to Gutenberg, as he did to Theuth, that the new invention would create a vast population of readers who 'will receive a quantity of information without proper instruction … [who will be filled] with the conceit of wisdom instead of real wisdom'; that reading, in other words, will compete with older forms of learning. This is yet another principle of technological change we may infer from the judgment of Thamus: new technologies compete with old ones – for time, for attention, for money, for prestige, but mostly for dominance of their world-view. This competition is implicit once we acknowledge that the medium contains an ideological bias and it is a fierce competition, as only ideological competitions can be. It is not merely a matter of tool against tool – the alphabet attacking ideographic writing, the printing press attacking the illuminated manuscript, the photograph attacking the art of painting, television attacking the printed word.[33]

One could argue that each successive technological leap does not simply replace the previous technology, but also offers an alternative to a pre-existing coordinal use of technology. For example, television has not replaced the written word because reading a book is a different experience altogether. In many cases, the solitary aspect of reading combined with the seemingly personalized dialogue between the reader and the author is, to some individuals, a more intimate experience when compared to that of the television. Needless to say, television, movies and books present individuals with no more than portals into experiences, values, beliefs, adventures and knowledge of people of other cultures, crossing social barriers of age, race, religion and political persuasion, geography and time itself. The value in the intent of technologies that offer new avenues of communication such as the Internet, television, radio and books is not found in the mechanism used or the method of delivering the communication. The true value of these technologies is that they facilitate a dialogue and enable individuals to acquire knowledge in a medium that is most conducive to their personal learning style. That said, Internet learning, CD-ROM and other technologies are not conducive to all types of learning. It could be argued that there is very little corroborating evidence to validate these technologies as an effective and value-adding way of learning.

The transitional nature of technology, especially information systems and end-user interaction devices such as PDAs, laptops and mobile phones, reinforces the statement that technology is temporary and its half-life of use is proportional to its perceived value by the individual or organization using it. Therefore, any given technology used by business must be viewed in the same light as a liability, not an asset. I have argued elsewhere that technology provides organizations with the opportunity to rethink the products or services that they offer, how they are delivered and, more importantly, why a product or service offering is valuable to a customer. In the case of organizations embracing new technology and applying it wisely, their value propositions are presented with a dilemma, as devices are perceived to have a decreasingly effective lifespan. The longer term implication of the application of technology is to consider putting aside our view of technology as an asset and begin to manage it as a *liability*. The management of technology should be as if its value declined over time, which it does. In order to put this concept into perspective, the legacy of information technology is rooted in the high capital equipment cost of an investment with a useful lifespan, requiring maintenance and support personnel. Thus the typical classification of technology should be 'an asset which depreciates over time and provides a mechanism for improved information flow'. However, technology is advancing at an accelerated rate, making older technology not only less valuable, but costly to maintain. Despite the rapid decay of technological value, technology is still regarded as an essential asset of the organization, without which it cannot function. The idea of treating technology as a liability is not an oversimplification of the balance between technology investment and technology deployment; it is merely to say that now technology should be viewed and managed in ways different from those in the past.[34]

If one takes personal computing as an example of technological transitional value, it can be observed that two distinct social behaviours have developed with regard to hardware and software. A technology user's attitude follows a pattern in which the underlying number of months is controlled either by personal preference or corporate policy. In information-intense organizations where computational speed and data retrieval time command a premium, it can be observed that the effective lifespan is shorter on the left side of Figure 1.5. Typically, the initial purchase is for the primary user, who will justify passing the technology to the next user in the corporate 'food chain' based on a justifiable requirement. The process continues throughout the corporation until the hot personal computer – without which the original user could not live – finds its home with the car parking attendant tracking parking permits, or is subsequently discarded due to higher maintenance cost. US corporations are finding it increasingly harder to give away old PCs to schools and charities because it raises the level of complexity and cost to integrate many makes and models of equipment into existing infrastructures.

However, the behaviour of software companies is strikingly different from that of hardware companies, as seen in Figure 1.6. The initial motivation in acquisition is the same, but as individuals invest their time in learning the application, they develop one of three attitudes towards the product. It becomes indispensable, occasional or disposable. Firstly, indispensable applications typically exhibit characteristics that facilitate one's lifestyle (such as Microsoft Money and Quicken, which allow people to control their finances). The amount of time invested coupled with the transactional data accumulated over time makes switching to a package offered by another vendor undesirable simply on cost. Electronic mail is another example of software in which the relearning is hard, but the incompatibility between filing cabinets and address books makes it impossible to switch.

On a historical note concerning eMail, one of the tools used to develop a picture of a historical period is correspondence via private letters, personal papers and other tangible evidence of communications. In their electronic form, eMail that is sent and received today will be irretrievable ten years from now. This raises concerns when we consider that future generations may not be able to retrieve any record of conversations which happened last month, this week or today. It may be prudent to print out some eMails and paste them in a scrapbook just to preserve some evidence of your personal contacts at one point in your life. At the same time, eMail makes communication a lot easier, and people tend to be very clear and 'to the point', whereas private correspondence invariably requires more time to write and thus presents more detail. One way or another, what we can observe is a generation of individuals who do not communicate by letter, and whose writing skills are getting less and less powerful due to spellcheckers – which sometimes do not even allow you to err, correcting your grammar errors as you type. If there is a positive side to using computers as text-editors, the loss of writing ability is certainly to be seen as a negative side.

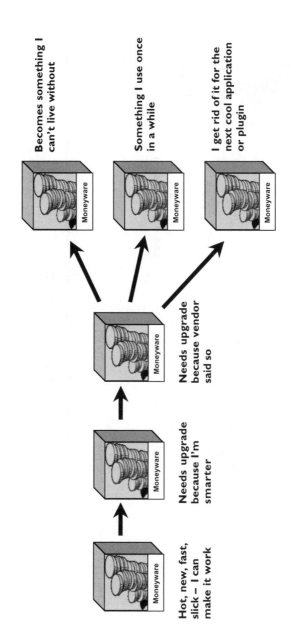

Figure 1.5 Software life cycle (PC)

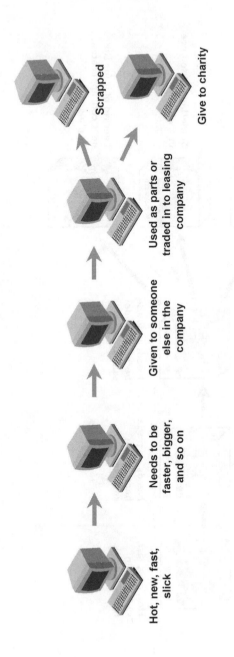

Hot, new, fast, slick

Needs to be faster, bigger, and so on

Given to someone else in the company

Used as parts or traded in to leasing company

Scrapped

Give to charity

Number of months

Figure 1.6 Hardware life cycle (PC)

Secondly, occasional software comprises those applications with a highly specialized function which an individual needs only occasionally or which were acquired because of a temporary need. Many of us could not wait to get software that would allow us to make and edit our own videos until we realized what a time-consuming process it is. Today, some people will only use the software package when they have a large amount of leisure time. The third category of software is that of disposable or temporary applications, which in many cases were acquired either as a whim or for a specific purpose. These applications are often 'lead ins' to more advanced software capabilities. For example, one can purchase a low price architectural drawing application and, once one has learned it, one realizes the need for a professional version, so abandoning the original program. All these behavioural factors lead to the temporary nature of technologies that are closely associated with the end-user. In this case, the similarities of the technology to a liability are magnified by the volatility of the refreshment rate.

Technology as a Liability

The character of technology as a liability can be seen in the following example: there is a fundamental difference between the strategies of an *equities fund* manager and those of a *bond portfolio* manager. Both specialists are managing assets; however, their strategies were born from two very different philosophies on investing. Taking these conditions into account, the management of the technology liability will be different from core back-office systems to end-user or consumer devices. If one considers that consumer retail delivery devices (such as PDAs, PCs, WAP phones and many others) will continue to undergo a high turnover due to the nature of the innovation of devices and consumers' demand for new technologies, it can be concluded that the delivery of retail banking products using these technologies will have a much shorter half-life than a core processing system. Simply, the rate of the half-life of technology is proportional to the distance to the end-user. Core systems are replaced at a rate of five to ten years, whereas retail end-user technologies range from six months to four years.

The key issue to consider when a company manages technology as a liability is that each technology should be handled based on its application to the business process that it serves and linked to a realistic expectation of a phased retirement. Again, the closer a technology is to a consumer, the faster the rate of decay and the greater the tendency to 'overmanage' the asset. For example, a consultant was engaged to review the operating cost of the technology group within a large bank in New York City, and found an ongoing cost of warehousing a stockpile of outdated PCs because they were a depreciated asset. The cost of warehousing these non-functioning computers added to the cost of the labour associated with inventorying and tracking these assets was greater than the new replacement value. Therefore, not only was money being spent on keeping these unusable PCs, they were also purchasing new ones.

So, what is the end state of the Internet and how will it add value as a medium for commerce? In 1975, it would have been next to impossible to foresee the interconnected technologies of today. It is just as impossible today to predict the next generation of technologies. However, reviewing the history of our relationship with technology over the last 70 years, it is clear that the trend in our use and expectations with regard to technology remains consistent:

- people will adopt and use technology

- technological adoption occurs at rates often governed by dissociated factors

- people want to be connected or linked to others

- people will be mobile

- convenience carries a premium

- people need to feel in control.

That said, these observations are general and very broad, but they do provide a window into technology's basic value proposition and the ways in which it alters the creator's original intentions over time. Individuals find value in technology when it fulfils a primary need such as mobility, convenience or timeliness in the pursuit of both business activities and actions associated with customers' lifestyles.

1.5 Contemporary Technology Transformation

A few inventions have had a profound impact on the social structure of man and the operation of businesses and government, such as the windmill and the stirrup in medieval times, the printing press of the late Middle Ages/early Renaissance, and PCs, the Internet and the mechanisms for

electronic currency in modern times. The requirements of the new technological state make it possible for contemporary society to question the
very underpinnings of how business, government and social structures
are organized and – more importantly – how they function. In business,
the quest is for a continual addition of value in the exchanges between
trading partners. In government, the objective is to provide a suite of
bureaucratic functions that provide services to the broadest number of the
population. In a capitalistic society, the goal of an individual is to accu-
mulate as much wealth as one's abilities will allow. The aspirations of
business, government and society are predicated on the continued evolution of technology and its ability to enrich the world population's standard
of living by adding value in our everyday lives. The rate at which technology in general affects society was observed by Buckminster Fuller, as
discussed in Section 1.1, and by Gordon Moore, of the Intel Corporation,
who unravelled the rate at which microprocessing technology advanced in
1965. Moore observed that each new generation of computer chip contained approximately twice as much capacity as the previous generation.
Considering that each new generation was being introduced into the
marketplace every 18–24 months, Moore concluded that the rate of
computing power would increase exponentially over time. This rule which
still holds true today is known as 'Moore's Law'. The implication of
Moore's observation is not that computer technology would simply
produce faster machines, but that the size and cost would decline as a by-
product of the production process. Since the advent of the computer, technology has been faithfully applied to every aspect of business activity in
an effort to increase profit continuously.

Organizations have recently learned from the dot-com experience that
simply investing in technology does not ensure profitability if it does not
convey a distinct increase in value added in the eye of the customer. The
value proposition must centre on several elements, such as unique product
offerings, cost efficiencies, regular returns on investment, optimization of
a business process to increase productivity, top line growth and benefit to
the customer relationship.

Section 1.4 argued that technology is a temporary state following an
evolutionary pattern. The temporality of technology is due to two factors:
firstly, that of science, resulting in a seemingly endless display of new
capabilities and the ceaseless thirst for continuous improvement. Secondly,
from a business perspective and, more importantly, from the perspective of
generating value, the temporary nature of technology must be factored into
any product offering. For example, it is rare to see a retirement plan for an
existing computer system or any indication of how and when a software

application will be phased out when the original cost benefit analysis is developed. In fact, many firms during the acquisition of a new technology treat the purchase as something that will continue to add value indefinitely, despite the historical evidence to the contrary. Inherently, technologists know that a system or, more specifically, a collection of hardware and software components, has an expected lifespan but rarely is that lifespan considered at any length beyond that of simple financial depreciation.

In contrast, technology historians offer a large body of discourse on how the advancement of technology does not follow a linear path, but rather a chaotic sequence of events and actions. Figure 1.7 depicts a simplified view of technology trends that should be considered in the development of a firm's value proposition and internal technology strategy. In a business context, technology trends fall into four broad categories: networks, hardware, software and user behaviour. Network technology links similar and dissimilar technologies through a common mechanism for the exchange of information. The basic trends in network technology are its increasing ability to connect greater numbers of associated processes or transaction sources used to continue to drive down the cost of an individual transaction. Hardware, and all its subcategories of types of device, continues to increase the speed of processing data while reducing the cost of acquiring traditional components. Software, on the other hand, is not only continually expanding the capabilities of corporate functions, but also creating new, previously unimagined functions to add value. However, the issues of licensing, intellectual property and privacy will challenge software development and, in some cases, inhibit businesses' ability to explore new avenues of value. This can be observed, for example, in firms such as Napster, whose technology changed the underlying value proposition in the music industry and became the recipient of the wrath of a well-entrenched institutional bureaucracy. Whilst users are seeking greater levels of sophistication to supplement the increasing complexities of their jobs and lifestyles, they are also demanding lower cost of ownership and reduced operating expense.

As Internet technology matures and the initial excitement of its creation and adoption begins to wane, users are shifting their focus, trading cutting-edge technology prestige for less glamorous profit improvement. This can be attributed to increased familiarity with the technology. Now that users are applying this familiar technology to a wider variety of uses, they are beginning to realize that the rising incremental cost of technology may limit its overall application. Table 1.2 provides a convenient framework in which to apply technology as part of the value equation.

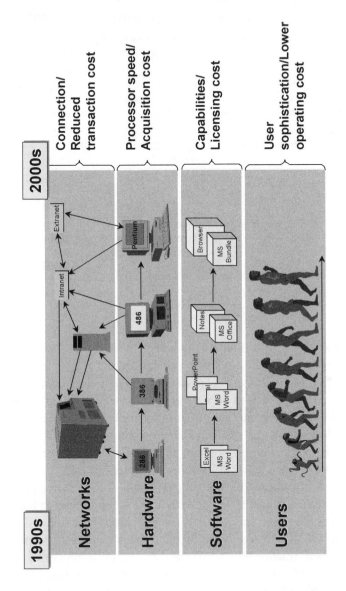

Figure 1.7 The evolution of technology

Table 1.2 Technology's value proposition			
	Operational excellence	**Product leadership**	**Customer intimate**
Consolidate overheads	Centralize services	Combine sales and marketing functions	Blend customer services
Pool resources and technology	Reduce variations to minimize maintenance cost	Combine research and development functions	Create standard interface for consistency
Optimize infrastructure	Common information transfer	Ability to plug in new features quickly	Common look and feel
Economies of scale	Better purchasing	Reduce product cost	Lower overall cost
Combine knowledge capital	Best practices	Incorporate customer needs into designs	Know more about the customer

Source: Adapted from Treacy and Wiersema (1995)

Determining a value proposition is sometimes not as straightforward as it may seem. Treacy and Wiersema define a value proposition as: 'the implicit promise a company makes to customers to deliver a particular combination of values – price, quality, performance, selection, convenience and so on.'[35] For example, the former consulting organization PricewaterhouseCoopers (PwC) has developed tools such as the value proposition calculator (VPC)[36] to assist clients who are engaged in maintaining and managing their physical assets. The VPC helps a firm in its initial search for value and, more importantly, the establishment of a quantitative side to the value equation. Although PwC's tool is illustrative not definitive, it permits individuals to begin to construct tangible measurements for an intangible subject, that of value to a customer. It educates an individual about the key performance indicators and their relationship to elementary business processes. The measurement of value is in many cases not a quantitative measure, but the product of combining quantitative and qualitative properties mixed with simple customer emotion.

Technology's value proposition is often elusive because it is a relative measure of a business need, want or desire that requires varying degrees of justification to an organization as a whole. One can equate the use of PCs to that of the value of diamonds. Diamonds are valuable because they are rare. 'Rare' typically means uncommon or unusual; yet almost every woman you meet has a diamond ring. Diamond exchanges and jewellers sell millions of diamonds each year, so when did millions of anything become rare? Diamonds were rarities in the Middle Ages, thought to have curative powers; later they became a symbol of love. Today they are no longer rare. In fact, diamonds are a commodity, just like the evolution of the PC's value proposition; it is relative to how the item is applied by society. The relativity of value as it applies to technology with global customers is discussed in Chapter 4.

Therefore, determining a value proposition is a process of orchestrating a complex combination of qualitative and quantitative characteristics into an offering that can be easily accepted and adopted by a customer group. In this process, technology often plays a dual role, as a physical component of the offering or as a mechanism to facilitate the business processes that result in a product. In either case, developing a value proposition for technology is no longer a task restricted to systems analysts in the technology department. Technology's value proposition must be derived by a collection of individuals within the business in partnership with the technology group. The collaborative process of determining technology's value proposition within the firm, to the products of the firm and as an extension of the firm with external entities becomes more complex when applied to doing business in a global commerce environment. It is to this environment that we now turn.

1.6   Technology's Global Challenge

The new frontier for technology in the twenty-first century will be that of global information proliferation. The impact of ubiquitous technology on societies with a slower rate of adoption is a growing concern for business leaders and is rapidly becoming a political issue. Governments are weighting the benefits of using technology as a lever for progress and economic viability over the stigma associated with technology's adverse effect on local cultures. The world's perception of new technology as a mechanism for cultural erosion, more specifically as a tool to propagate western ideals, influences the depth to which governments will employ technology as a part of the social infrastructure. The dichotomy between technology's benefit and adverse effects on culture makes the applied use of technology by local governments more a political decision than an economic one. Technology's direct application to the advance of education (as discussed in section 1.1), its ability to transform small businesses and its use as a medium for cultural exchange must have an express goal of increasing the quality of life and an implied goal of being used as a mechanism for economic growth. Society in general assumes that the continual evolution of technology and its effect on everyday life leads to an increase in our quality of life. Naturally, 'quality of life' is a relative expression, being open to a wide range of interpretations. On the whole, however, the quality of life is accepted as the contribution to a positive progression of society.

Technological progress is a process of replacement and renewal, which implies that for new technology to add value, it must make previously unknown things possible, or older technology obsolete. Put simply, the effect of technology is causal: for every winner there must be a loser. Unfortunately, in most cases the losers only become apparent when viewing the transition from a historical perspective, such as the agricultural technological process of shifting the agrarian workforce to an industrial production workforce in the twentieth-century United States. In this case, US farmers actually lost their vocation or career, although the productivity per acre improved, as well as the volume of production, which increased with technology. Farmers were thus what the industry calls 'tech-losers'. As Postman observed, as the ubiquity of technology spreads progress across the globe, it also creates these two categories of people: tech-winners and tech-losers:

> This was the question, by the way, that gave rise to the Luddite movement in England during the years 1811 to 1818. The people we call Luddites were skilled manual workers in the garment industry at the time when mechanization was taking command and the factory system was being put into place. They knew perfectly well what advantages mechanization would bring to most people, but they saw with equal clarity how it would bring ruin to their own way of life, especially to their children who were being employed as virtual slave laborers in factories. They resisted technological change by the simplistic and useless expedient of smashing to bits industrial machinery, which they continued to do until they were imprisoned or killed by the British army. 'Luddite' has thus come to mean a person who resists technological change in any way, and it is usually used as an insult.[37]

Technology thus creates tech-losers, people who cannot be integrated into the changing technological environment, or fear losing their lifestyle due to the progress of technology. By the same token, tech-winners are people like Bill Gates:

who is, of course, a winner, knows this, and because he is no fool, his propaganda continuously implies that computer technology can bring harm to no one. That is the way of winners: they want losers to be grateful and enthusiastic and, especially, to be unaware that they are losers.[38]

Postman also has strong views concerning schoolteachers and their constant enthusiasm for the idea that there should be more computers available in schools. In Postman's view, computers in classrooms do not add value to the education given to children. What would indeed add value is better wages and better training for teachers who are actually performing the difficult task of educating future citizens. However, schoolteachers, whom Postman clearly identifies as tech-losers, are the first ones to enthuse for an increased investment in computer technology. If there is no data supporting the idea that computers in classrooms do add value to the educational process, then why spend even more money on them? Postman uses as a case study the $100 million investment on computer technology in the state of Maryland in 1996. He wonders if the state of Maryland had decided instead to spend the same amount of money to increase the number of teachers and pay more to the existing ones in order to reduce teaching loads, how teachers would have reacted:

> One might think that most teachers would support such an investment, but we hear very little from them on the score. In fact, many teachers are thrilled by the thought of a $100 million investment in computer terminals. Bill Gates must love this sort of stupidity.[39]

Postman's caustic observations indicate that our perception of the 'goodness' of technology reduces our ability to place its application in a wider context. There is little supporting evidence to substantiate the perception that knowledge is increased by the use of computers in the classroom other than the fact that they enable students to gain access to additional sources of information, that is, Internet sites. The perception is based on the preconceived notion that information on the Internet has a qualitative value. Without a comprehensive study of the Internet's contents, the quality of information is only a myth, whereas the quantity is indeed a reality. That said, one could argue that giving schools access to a comprehensive university library would have the same or greater effect as that of the computer, as Rasmussen points out:

> Although information technology may undoubtedly be a good tool in education, it is at the same time evident that it may develop into a dangerous direction in

the case of exaggerated use. Collection and processing of data may be an end in itself or another excuse for not trying other forms of education.[40]

Conversely, one value proposition is clear: computers in a classroom do allow students to study independently of a teacher, effectively allowing teachers to spend more time with students with special needs. In either case, computers in a classroom offer students a glimpse of the skills and tools that they will need to develop and acquire later in life, such as word processing, spreadsheets, search engines and familiarity with source materials. The by-product of their computer experience will be an increased awareness of the world and a keen understanding of how to communicate via the Internet with other world citizens.

The emerging generation of students possess a greater understanding of how the nations of the world may turn to the Internet to influence their progress. Richard Meier postulates that information technologies such as the Internet can be used as a two-way bridge between the newly aware digital population and the technologically challenged nations.[41] His 'technological gap theory' seeks to explain changes in the pattern of international trade over time. It is based on a dynamic sequence of technological and product innovation and diffusion. Technologically advanced countries with a high propensity to innovate are able to achieve trade advantages by offering sophisticated new products, initially unobtainable from other sources, on to the world markets. Over time, however, the technology is diffused and adopted by other countries which are then able to supply the products themselves. As less digital populations acquire interaction community technologies, they can use them to facilitate the distribution of aid to highly targeted areas of need. Meier additionally identifies six distinct areas in which technology can be used to reduce the 'technology gap' and eventually the socio-economic gap:

■ *Eleemosynary exchanges:* Matching donors to needs in a coordinated global network consisting of governments, charities and other action groups, pinpointing populations which require assistance, thus reducing the time between need and relief.

■ *Micro-enterprise formation:* Providing access to micro-capital markets to stimulate investment and loan activity in small businesses.

■ *Interactive learning:* Supplementing education by connecting teachers, sharing research materials, providing remote lessons and access to hard-to-find source materials.

- *Famine prevention:* Prompt distribution of foodstuffs using expert systems and predictive weather satellite data to deliver emergency subsistence immediately.

- *Social justice and political stability:* Facilitating a higher degree of social communication, thus increasing the awareness of human rights.

- *High-level entrepreneurship:* Educated local entrepreneurs can readily assess opportunities and match talent to facilitate small business growth.

Freeman rightly points out that access to technology alone is not a viable solution; it must be part of a more complete solution. In his words:

> What the post-war experience demonstrates therefore is an extremely uneven process of catch-up by developing countries, depending upon their technical capability and on imports of technologies. But the import of technologies is very far from the costless diffusion of perfect information assumed in pure versions of neo-classical economic theory. Technologies cannot be taken 'off the shelf' and simply put into use anywhere. Without infrastructural investment in education, training, R&D, and other scientific and technical activities, very little can be accomplished by way of assimilation of imported technologies.[42]

It is clear that technology does not have a curative effect on social, economic and educational deficiencies. Technology must be used within a comprehensive social agenda, economic plan or educational curriculum. The application of technology to global problems is not limited to information or communications technologies. A host of new technological offerings that are not necessarily connected to information systems possesses the power to influence global social development (and business growth). They include: automatic replenishment, biometrics, compact long-lasting energy sources, digital high-definition TV, edutainment, hybrid fuels, pen-computing, personal security technologies, smart cards and eMoney, smart cash and cash registers, smart maps and tracking devices, the next generation of PCs, wearable technology and wireless technology.

However, as discussed in section 1.4, the intention of these technologies may not be the use which generates its long-term value propositions. Value propositions change with society, and many factors contribute to the successful renewal of a technology to influence socio-economic progress. Czerniawska and Potter identify two primary obstacles facing the application of technology:

The first is a lack of imagination. Look at the press today (1998); some 90 per cent of its reporting on the information revolution revolves around the Internet and the World Wide Web. Look at where today's talent is going. It is flooding like lemmings into the sexy subjects of multimedia, developing web browsers and so on. In short, it is moving into the technological plumbing as if this were the next gold rush. Changes to people's lives are not made by changes to technology but by the application and exploitation of that technology. We do not see the training, the university courses, the enthusiasm for understanding how this technology can be exploited.[43]

The shortfall in imagination with regard to the application of technology can be attributed to some extent to the high premium industry has placed on the creative aspect of technological innovation. Research laboratories such as IBM's Hawthorn lab in New York have in recent years turned their attention to the applied side of innovation, working closer with customers and users in their design research. This process in effect endeavours to build applicability into the innovation and design processes. Unfortunately, this marriage of applied and design sciences has not proliferated throughout the software industry, as also noted by Czerniawska and Potter:

The second [obstacle facing the application of technology] is the software industry. Whereas factories and machines are the building blocks of economic life in the physical world, the building blocks of the virtual world are software programs. And the problem with software is that its development is essentially an art: people redesign and reinvent with alarming regularity. The industry is new. It has yet to develop specialist roles such as architects, structural engineers and quantity surveyors; it has yet to develop the concept (although people are trying) of reusable parts.[44]

In this sense, one of the problems facing the industry's ability to create an inventory of reusable component parts is the lack of specificity on what the components will build when brought together. The lack of a final product coupled with the problem of keeping components technologically up to date is discussed by Pacey:

Most inventions have been made with a specific social purpose in mind, but many also have an influence which nobody had expected or intended. The reality is perhaps easier to comprehend by thinking about the concept of technology-practice with its integral socio-components. Innovation may then be seen as the outcome of a cycle of mutual adjustments between social, cultural and technical factors. The cycle may begin with a technical idea, or a radical change in organization, but either way, there will be interaction with the other factors as the innovation comes to fruition.[45]

From a business perspective, the new-found global character of technology presents a myriad of opportunities on which to capitalize, requiring a pragmatic approach to strategic initiatives. As businesses large and small operate globally as international commercial entities, the business processes which define firms' value propositions will become less defined as organizations outsource, affiliate, collaborate and engage in new forms of co-opetition. This level of business redefinition will cause organizations to examine the underlying business processes, from a value perspective, not in the classical sense of a benefit, but with a focus on total cumulative process value. When firms engage in this business realignment, individual processes will experience a *progressive assimilation* due to the new capabilities which technology brings to execution processes and, more importantly, subprocesses. Progressive assimilation is when a business process is modified by – or becomes so closely aligned to – the preceding or adjacent process that some of its functionality is replicated or engaged in a similar function. This state of process operation is often overlooked when processes are continually being revised to accommodate changes in the business environment. Organizations operating or anticipating operating in a global environment must not develop specific rules on how to conduct business in each geography, but adopt an operating philosophy in which individuals in the firm understand the express goals but are granted latitude in crafting solutions that conform to the idiosyncratic characteristics of their local business environment. When developing globalizing business plans, three interoperating factors must be considered:

Think global:

■ Economies of scale (reduce cost of service)

■ Brand strategy (reduce cost of sales)

■ Service aggregation (increase revenue)

Act regional:

■ Tailored services (increase customer satisfaction)

■ Co-opetition with partners (increase customers)

Look local:

■ Interoperation with partners (increase service)

■ Merge brand/products (commoditize, customize and optimize)

The key to developing comprehensive business strategies that leverage technology, people and resources is to shift the analysis of adding value within a firm to a global perspective. As Capra succinctly puts it:

> The great shock of twentieth-century science has been that systems cannot be understood by analysis. The properties of the parts are not intrinsic properties, but can be understood only within the context of the larger whole. Thus the relationship between the parts and the whole are reversed. In the systems approach, the properties of the parts can be understood only from the organizations of the whole. Accordingly, systems thinking is 'contextual', which is opposite of analytical thinking. Analysis means taking something apart in order to understand it; systems thinking means putting it into the context of the whole.[46]

Basically saying that Aristotle would have been a lousy businessman, Capra believes that the evolution of technology must be seen in the context of not only how much it can contribute to a business's profitability, but also in a global context, which is the way in which businesses derive value. As we shall be seeing in the next four chapters, in a global context businesses derive value from:

■ Structure, people's skills and other business activities

■ The changes occurring in the global business environment, such as disintermediation

■ The shifting attitudes of cross-cultural customers

■ The extent to which the convergence of the above factors will influence design.

Let us now proceed to an analysis of the structure of businesses, people's skills and management practices in an appraisal of modern corporate bureaucracies.

CHAPTER 2

The Timeless Behaviours of Corporate Bureaucracies

The business use of technology must undergo a significant change in how technology is ultimately applied to business processes in order to create a condition that enables a fundamental rethinking of how a business works. How organizations apply technology is a trait inherited from the firm's knowledge of the limits of the previous generations of technology. This inherited understanding of the use of technology within an organization is called 'the organization's technology culture'. The relationship between people and technology is sometimes counterintuitive to our perception of progress when viewed holistically in the context of an organizational culture steeped in bureaucracy, as observed by Sean Cooney. In his words:

> Bureaucracy, whether as an arm of government, or of big industry, became wedded to this paradigm of promoting the growth of the trading economy and the expansion of wealth. The revenues of government and industry which provide bureaucracy with its power and social relevance depend on the generation of more and more monetary 'value added'. Given a means of promoting such growth, which appeared to be available through new technology, bureaucracy promises much and encourages people to become dependent on it.[47]

Once established within an organization, any technology becomes part of the bureaucracy, and people become attached to it as the physical manifestation of the command and control structure of the social hierarchy. In the late 1990s, long-standing firms were surprised by the nimbleness of start-ups and their ability to bring products and services to market rapidly and efficiently. Not surprisingly, the start-up firms did not inherit a corporate culture; they were the recipients of many cultures that were brought to the organization by individuals determined to introduce new business models. In many cases, individuals who came from large, established firms simply employed the best traits of their previous employer and consciously jettisoned bureaucratic, corporate behaviour. This blending of the best traits from many companies created a dynamic culture within the new organization that was the catalyst for firms to become new market entrants. These start-up organizations gained additional momentum by using technology in new ways that would have been stifled in traditional organizations.

In contrast to the start-ups, traditional organizations continued – as many still do today – simply to apply technology to existing business processes and employ technology as the mechanism for ensuring a standard behaviour within the organization. As Doz et al. put it:

> To carry out complex, interrelated tasks, large firms develop formal structures which fragment these tasks into elements that can be performed by individuals, and integrate these elements through formal hierarchies and rules. The bureaucracy that results, the power plays that surround the rules, and the often fragile authority of key managers discourage innovation and risk-taking. This has been variously described as 'segmentalist' behaviour and bureaucratic 'resistance to change.'[48]

In many cases, this type of technology implementation effectively restricts the capability of the organization to the lowest common denominator within the firm. That is not to say that this stops innovation, process improvement or other corporate initiatives; it simply means that it reduces the speed at which the firm is able to mobilize resources when business conditions change. Metaphorically, it is easier to turn a powerboat than a battleship.

The Nature of Bureaucracies

Corporations as a living culture develop bureaucratic structures to control the process of business that in effect extends from the founders' original thinking on how the organization should function to the latest recruits, through rules, procedures and policies. This traditional command and control philosophy endorses the concept that an elite group within the firm contains all the knowledge needed to execute the production of the business processes. In theory, this method enables a small group of individuals to channel all the information about the activities of production to them for problem resolution. Likewise, this structure assumes that individuals within the organization need very little cognitive skills and merely follow directions to ensure the timely execution of the firm's business activity.

In order to legitimize this structural need to control and disseminate information, organizations develop business processes which often contain similarities, although they may be designed by different groups within the firm, as Bushe and Shani describe:

> All organizations, however designed, share certain attributes. All involve division and coordination of tasks; all transform inputs into outputs; all involve information processing; and all require an uneven distribution of legitimate authority. The essence of bureaucratic organization is the production of standardized, predictable, replicable performance by many different people and/or groups.[49]

In other words, we create bureaucracies to administer the activities that are expected to be executed by the business processes in a normative state. This often hierarchical alignment of resources is primarily designed to codify activities in order to achieve an economy of scale. Hammer describes the incongruity that business management faces when considering the structure and function of organizations:

> Modern organizations have learned that the notion of economy of scale has severe limits. With size come diseconomies of scale. As organizations grow, multiple layers of administrative bureaucracy inevitably appear and it becomes difficult for any individual to have an overall understanding of what's going on. Breaking a large organization into several smaller ones avoids this problem, but at the possible price of inconsistency.[50]

The concept of 'reengineering' coupled with the new array of information and telecommunications technologies increased the range of alternatives for business to rethink the relationship between organization and process. The matter in question is the overall proportional relationship between the complexity that an organization acquires over time due to changes in the competitive climate and the administrative control of information needed to govern the process.

In his examination of the nature of organizations and their relationship with technology as part of the evolution to a 'benevolent bureaucracy', Petrella identifies the principal elements of diffusion and distribution of information:

> On the one hand, since the degree of complexity depends on the number and nature of the interactions between the elements of the system, the access to power (that is,

to the capacity of mastering the complexity) will depend upon the control of the information flows between the elements, in the subsystems and between the subsystems. This means that a benevolent bureaucracy will depend upon the diffusion and the distribution of the control mechanisms of the information flows. Evidence suggests that the diffusion and the distribution are not the norm, today![51]

Therefore, simply adding technology to the existing bureaucratic structure as a method of increasing productivity, while processes become more and more complex, may actually hamper the organization's ability to cope with the additional levels of complexity. It is clear that organizations must deal with the new complexity of business *not by adding technology, but by redefining its application to a new structure*. This introduces another dilemma for organizations, the complexity of a 'nested bureaucracy', that is, the bureaucracy of the technology organizations operating within the larger corporate bureaucracy. Subdivisions of organizations develop policies and procedures that are used as mechanisms to control the business processes executed by the organization and to define the behaviour of individuals performing tasks to support processes during a variety of business conditions. However, in many cases organizations which provide supportive or administrative devices to a primary business process develop their own secondary process, one which over time often works as a retarding agent to the primary business process activity. These added layers of bureaucracy in many cases replicate the controls of the primary process and place a higher level of granularity to the parameters that control the process. This higher degree of specificity is the crux of the nested bureaucracy, and leads to an eventual need for business realignment of organizational goals and objectives. Here again Petrella indicates the dual problem of 'access to the knowledge of the system' as a desired goal, and the needs of specialization as a potential counterweight to any theoretical productivity gains that should be realized in reducing a corporate bureaucracy:

> On the other hand, the greater the complexity, the greater must be the access from people and the organization to the knowledge of the system. Now, since this knowledge is a resource limited (in normal situation) to a restricted circle of 'specialists' (the so-called technocrats), it is reasonable to infer that for the time being the 'explosion' of the complexity and the requirements for its mastering are not going in the direction of the enlargement of the basis for a benevolent bureaucracy but rather this enhances the foundations for a technocratic bureaucracy.[52]

Petrella realizes that technology can indeed minimize the inherent delays normally caused by bureaucracy in the process of business, and that the

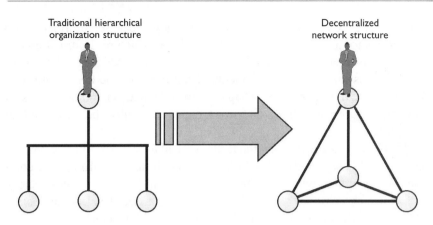

Traditional hierarchical
organization structure

Decentralized
network structure

Figure 2.1   Using technology to change bureaucracy

ultimate goal of technology would be to make a bureaucracy invisible or *benevolent* to any business process. However, in the establishment of a technology organization, another bureaucracy may form, thus annulling the gains associated with the reduction of the initial corporate bureaucracy. In order to combat this condition, the fundamental characteristic of structure should be examined relative to the relationships between process and technology. Lipnack and Stamps provide an oversimplification of these issues which provides a framework for thinking in which an organization can strike a balance between the inhibiting forces, as seen in Figure 2.1.

Organizations in transition require stability to neutralize the drain on resources that occurs when competitive forces place additional strain on the firm's resources, already expending energy on an internal realignment. Lipnack and Stamps point out that the two contributing factors which tend to create organizational stability are those of the command-and-control vertical hierarchy which is often without knowledgeable depth, and a bureaucratic process that is overlaid on to the struture. These two factors create a 3-dimensional view of the traditional organization and resemble a three-legged stool. However, in this example, three-legged stools are often overturned if a high velocity wind is applied across the top of the stool because the feet are not tied together, forming a stable base. By adding links between the lower nodes of the hierarchy-bureaucracy, stability is maintained by a structure symbolized as a tetrahedron, which Buckminster Fuller described as the universe's minimal closed structure. Lipnack and Stamps expertly put it into a simple axiom: 'To convert a hierarchy-bureaucracy to a network, just add links.'[53] One could argue that simply increasing the connectivity between people in the organization reduces the bureaucratic delays or 'organizational latency' because information no longer has to move up and down a hierarchical structure. Information can be broadcast to all individuals (network nodes) who need it in order to execute process functions. The elements of the bureaucratic conundrum will be explored throughout this chapter. The role that technology plays in changing our conception of bureaucracies will also be discussed in Chapter 5.

That said, if we strip away the technological aspect of corporate bureaucracies and how it adds value in business environments growing in complexity, we are left with the question of what is different in today's society, workforce and customer behaviour from previous decades. Berleur characterizes the problem in pondering the new information society:

> Underlying the link between bureaucracy and scientific and industrial society is an heuristic way of questioning the meaning of the so-called 'information society'. Is there any difference between an 'energy society', which could characterize the industrial age and an 'information society' of the post-industrial time?[54]

Almost half a century ago, Jay Forrester of MIT put forward an interesting question: society is bold in creating and adopting technology to test ideas which lead to major advances; however, why are societies timid when changes concern conventional social practices?[55] In the new information society, we have the opportunity to change the world, the structure of political, social and economic processes and practices. To do this, however, certain practices such as those of corporate bureaucracies must be modified. It is to the attitudes and potential elements of change in corporate bureaucracies that we now turn.

2.1 The Lost Art of Project Management

The topic of medieval masonry relates to corporate bureaucracies and, more specifically, to project management, because it illustrates a type of practice of project management which was extremely efficient but has been lost for centuries, only now being recovered by what the industry calls 'empowered teams'. Let us analyse how medieval construction technique relates to modern project management.

Throughout Europe and Britain, castles stand as a silent testament to the transitional state of knowledge and how the transference of knowledge must be nurtured and not assumed. Many people wonder at the scale, size and mass of medieval castles, often contemplating how the builders were able to engineer such structures with seemingly limited technology. One question is why the builders of castles, cathedrals, town walls and other medieval structures which were constructed during that period used stone and not concrete, as was previously used by Roman engineers in structures such as the Pantheon. A little investigative work reveals that in the fifth century the knowledge for constructing buildings using concrete was lost, as the social structure of the Roman Empire collapsed and Europe was plunged into what later became known as 'the Dark Ages'. The technology of concrete was rediscovered in 1824 by Joseph Aspdin, a bricklayer from Leeds in England.[56] The knowledge about concrete and its applied use was lost from the collective intelligence of builders for almost thirteen centuries.

No longer possessing the knowledge for concrete construction, medieval master builders developed a new set of skills based on the accumulation of empirical knowledge of the available construction technologies. Master builders and masons developed a comprehensive body of knowledge using centuries of trial and error to push the technology of the day to its design limits, making castles complex weapons and constructing cathedrals with ever-widening expanses of glass. Today, it is easy to look back and believe that the construction of these structures was simply a matter of gathering a large labour force and working for many years. In reality, medieval builders and their command of design, logistics and project management contain secrets that have been lost in the post-industrialized society. Contrary to common belief, many castles were built rather quickly; spurred on by invading armies making frequent visits. The master builder designed the structure without paper or computers, organized and managed labour (from several guilds, including masons, carpenters and so on), located the raw materials (supply chain, including feeding the workers) and acted as the intermediary between the building's sponsor, in most cases the feudal lord, a high clergy member or sovereign (top management) and the physical components of the structure. The intermediary role required interpreting the desires of the sponsor and assessing the feasibility of the design changes based on empirical knowledge of structural limitations. It is difficult to imagine how an individual performing all these complex and interconnected activities could direct several building projects simultaneously without the use of Microsoft Project or other contemporary tools. The secret is in the master builders' approach to building itself, simplification, innovation and high quality skills.

Firstly, builders reduced the complexity of design and construction by simplifying the way in which the structure was built. For example, calculating the thickness of a wall was not a complex mathematical exercise;

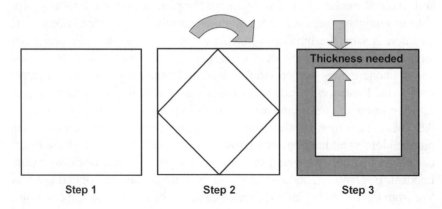

Figure 2.2 Calculating the thickness of a wall

masons and builders simply used a method that represented years of knowledge based on trial and error with regard to the relationship between the thickness of the wall and its ability to remain upright. Using a piece of string, they would stake out on the ground the overall dimensions of the structure, as shown in Figure 2.2.

The second step was to fold the string in half and mark the centre points on each wall, and then stretch the string between these centre points, forming a diamond inside the original square. The third step was to rotate the diamond inside the original square until the corners of the diamond were aligned with the corners of the square. The distance between the inner and outer squares is the desired thickness. Master builders and masons established simple rules that could be communicated and performed by any number of craftsmen who were engaged in the construction. Remembering that very few people were able to read or write in medieval times, their designs were converted into principles which did not require continual ammendments to specifications. Master builders resembled our contemporary ideal of a leader working with empowered teams. They did not micromanage the activities of individuals, as they did not have the time. The master builder defined the objective and provided a guiding hand in the specification of key details but delegated the execution of many aspects of the construction to the heads of the various guilds.

The second factor employed in the medieval builder's approach to project management was the incorporation of new ideas into the construction of a building as the structure was rising. The problem of continually changing design specifications sends chills down the spines of any modern project manager, considering the implications to cost and schedule. Countless technology project teams have witnessed the rate of introduction of new technological capabilities passing the rate at which they can implement technological change. This seemingly contemporary problem was also faced by our medieval counterparts; the desire to incorporate new capabilities into ongoing development projects. The ingenuity of the medieval builders is revealed in their approach which incorporates new technology with the acquisition of new skills. In medieval construction, master builders, masons and even journeymen often travelled and lived at each construction site. They simply followed the demand in construction, often moving from county to county, learning new designs as they went. It is easy to see evidence of this in the influence of Arab construction methods that were brought to England and France as a result of the Crusades to the Holy Land. Medieval builders were concerned with the quality of their work, not satisfied simply with mass producing or copying an old design. They readily incorporated the innovations into the building because, in case of a castle, it gave the structure a greater military advantage; they also taught all the masons, journeymen and apprentices the new technique. The continual methodological approach to innovation is recorded in the buildings which remain, allowing modern scholars to trace the technological improvements and map their migration from era to era across Europe.

The third factor in the masons' approach to project management was a higher degree of skills based on holistic knowledge, which was a product of the guild-apprentice method of learning, to be discussed in detail in section 2.4. This process, often taking seven years or more, provided a mason not just with the skill to lay stones, but also the knowledge of the entire process of masonry. Having a commanding knowledge of quarrying, shaping, carving and assembling, masons were interchangeable and needed lesser amounts of actual management, as noted by Andrews:

> the idea of design was already existent when the mason took up his tools, and he knew it and worked to it, carrying forward unconsciously the course of evolution. What was wanted and what was supplied was the man who would work earnestly and honourably and leave, so to speak, the designing to take care of itself.[57]

Because of this broad knowledge of the process of building, master builders could lay out a structure previously described and know with confidence that it could be done.

These three factors of simplification of method, continuous innovation and a highly developed set of skills reduced the amount of communication and intervention required to manage the project. This work environment is analogous to our contemporary empowered teams, in that if an organization adopts a process orientation to business, worker education is integral to achieving the desired levels of output. Considering the complex nature of managing a medieval building project, which included locating raw materials, coordinating logistical activities, managing large workforces consisting of professional guilds and common labourers and in many cases providing foodstuffs, the medieval master builder was faced with a daunting task. In the case of building a castle in unfamiliar land, his responsibilities were often expanded to include developing living quarters and sometimes building an entire town with infrastructure to ensure continuous progress on the structure. This ability to manage people, process and materials, often at breakneck speeds (castles were needed for immediate protection whereas cathedrals were longer term building projects), brings to mind one central question: What did medieval builders know about project management that we do not know today? Since medieval builders were unaided by a computer or calculator and rarely used paper, did they possess a knowledge of project management and logistical coordination that may have been lost when society shifted to the assembly-line compartmentalization approach to projects? One could argue that like the disappearance of the knowledge of concrete for thirteen centuries, master masons operating in the later medieval periods may have developed and possessed an in-depth knowledge of process-based project management that is no longer present in today's society.

Jeff Morgan, of the UK division of Computer Sciences Corporation (CSC), argued in the mid-1990s that project management needed to make a radical shift from a traditional, hierarchical model-tracking project activity towards a model focused on interpreting events and processes.[58] The simplicity of his argument is the genius of its design, stating that the management of a project is a set of processes connected by events in which each event characterizes a decision point in which the project manager must choose a course of action with regard to what is to be done to manage the consequence of the event. Similar to medieval building construction, Morgan describes projects as five processes running at the same time: preparation, production, improvement, acceptance and closure. Each of these is driven by events internal and external to the business and is directly part of an elementary process within the business. Projects are initiated to improve, alter or eliminate existing business processes or process components. These activities in and of themselves spawn the five processes typically called a project.

The Morgan event-process view of project management brings into focus the fact that organizations continuously spawn projects within themselves as a mechanism for improvement. These projects are often considered as one-time events and are not typically reviewed holistically as a process within a process of business. Morgan's argument is further reinforced by the fact that all organizations regardless of size have some form of project or projects occurring continuously. Few companies – if any – simply establish business processes and execute them without forming some type of project that brings together resources across the firm. Therefore, it can be demonstrated that a project concerning organizational improvement is an elementary business process in its own right, and it can be surmised that the process of project management is misnamed, because projects themselves viewed holistically represent the transformation of the business in direct response to changes in the competitive environment. The major criticism of technology projects today is that the majority of them never reach completion. This could be because business is not a static process but a continuous one. One could argue that the reason technology projects are never completed is because unless the business stops they cannot reach completion.

Morgan's point is that the traditional command and control structure of project management – which views scheduled activities as interdependent segments of discrete work – fails to incorporate the dynamic nature of organizational interruption and the root causes of the interruption event. The causality of events is often unrelated to the project until it interrupts the resources that have been allocated to it. Morgan's event-process view anticipates these events, and their execution is guided by the objectives of the underlying business processes, thereby giving the project a dynamic ability to adapt as internal and external events alter the balance of resources.

The dynamic nature of Morgan's event-process approach to project management requires a shift in thinking in the fundamentals of the dynamics in managing a project. Akin to the crux of Galileo's applied method of compounded motion, which as a means to express a compound phenomenon (such as a moving cannonball using a coordinate grid system) enlightens us to the fact that each plotted point does not represent any particular object itself, but a body's position at a given time. Morgan's point is simple; progress on a project is relative to the progression of the company towards reaching its objectives. Individual technology projects are in a state of motion that should be assessed along two dimensions: the progress towards the initial objective of the project and the value of the relative motion of the initial objective as it alters due to changes in the business environment. Hobart and Schiffman describe Galileo's cannonball motion as:

Unpacking the relational information contained in a point or equation will require, henceforth, devising the formula that captures the relations actually existing between phenomena.[59]

Therefore, the event-process view of project management assesses, monitors, measures and takes corrective action on the relative movement of the project, not the consumption of resources by individual tasks. This method anticipates the dynamic nature of change and reduces or eliminates the validity of traditional project-management methodologies such as percent complete. What Morgan has revealed is that corporate objectives change as market conditions influence customers, suppliers and other stakeholders within the company. Technology projects fall victim to changes in objectives that are not incorporated into projects once they commence. The changes in corporate objectives coupled with the continuous changes in technology create a condition of a 'project drifting off course', which in many cases is undetectable until it has already gained momentum. The traditional methods of project management measure these movements in a formalized structure that responds in a reactive sense, hampering a project manager's ability to take corrective action in a timely manner. The contemporary techniques of project monitoring and feedback are analogous to driving a car by looking in the rear view mirror and do not incorporate the dynamic nature of the motion between market-influenced corporate objectives and technological advancement. Taking an event-process approach to a project places the project manager at the heart of a problem which is the events that shape and reshape the project as it occurs dynamically. Therefore, the event-process method provides the project manager with a mechanism to control the project's relative rate using proactive and reactive actions. Clearly, the success of this method lies in the organization's design and the education of people on projects using this kind of thinking.

The event-process method may be the way in which cross-cultural, geographically dispersed projects can be effectively managed, since its notion of time as a relative event allows projects to be executed simultaneously and, by leveraging technology, across time zones. This method can be adapted to manage projects with a wide variety of talent pools such as found in new global partnerships because it focuses on the objective and not the organization. Cleland describes the environment in which the event-process method may eventually find its value proposition:

The formation of a joint borderless project team involves bringing people together who represent the different disciplines of the partners cooperating in the venture. A true intercompany and international project team is formed and organized. The intent of the project team, in accomplishing the objectives of the joint effort, tends to rise above the parochial interest of any of the members.[60]

New techniques such as event-process project management require organizations to unlearn the concepts and ideas that are considered fundamental building blocks of our corporate knowledge. Technology is changing our organizations, influencing our jobs and reshaping our business processes. Contemporary firms have traditionally compartmentalized job functions, effectively confining individuals into narrowly defined responsibilities requiring little knowledge beyond their own operating group. Concepts such as Hammer's process orientation and Morgan's event-process methodology demand that individuals develop a knowledge base that encompasses the entire process, similar to that of a medieval mason, who knew every facet of stonework. The goal is for people to develop an understanding of how their individual efforts contribute to the process as a whole. What is different today is the fact that 'No corporate father figure will take care of you' says Hammer. 'The feudal corporation – managers and workers in a lord-liege relationship – is gone forever. The person that the process-centred organization ultimately cares about is the customer.'[61] The transition that firms must make is to develop customer-centric processes, the trademark of early dot-com firms.

Hammer makes a key observation that in part explains the rapid rise of the entrepreneurial dot-com start-ups: 'Small companies can't afford the compartmentalization and specialization that cripple our holistic cognitive capabilities.'[62] The opportunity for large organizations with traditionally designed process is to rethink the application of technology as they redefine the process. Complicating the transition toward a process focus is the typical approach that organizations use to applying technology, which in many cases has the effect of 'dumbing down' the organization to the lowest common denominator in the firm. To summarize one of Hammer's lectures, an organization is typically composed of two kinds of people, in many cases a single founder or group of founders with an intensely specialized knowledge such as engineering, manufacturing or biotechnology, who then hire a group of administrative people with general skills. Wary of the quality of the second group, software designers (both in-house and professional software package designers) develop applications to ensure that the actions of controlling the process of the business are comprehensive enough so that no individual can accidentally create a transaction that will damage the entire production cycle. They basically strive to make the software system 'idiot-proof', designing the applications for the least capable individual in the firm, in essence lowering the capabilities of the entire organization to the lowest common denominator. Hammer argues, and rightly so, that computer software should be designed as if the founders were performing these tasks, thereby raising the effective knowledge of the firm to a higher level.

Unfortunately, when applying technology to communicate or educate large groups of people, the tendency is to continue this process of technological dumbing down as can be reconfirmed by watching television. This continual process, which could be called the misapplication of technology, and its effects on the corporate consciousness is at the centre of the conflict between the reinvention of bureaucratic structures and developing a process orientation.

In this chapter I do not intend to develop a definitive guide to fixing, eliminating or restructuring corporate bureaucracies; I will, however, discuss the many facets of bureaucratic thinking and the pitfalls of traditional organizational structure as it relates to the incorporation of technology into a firm's value proposition. In short, technology provides organizations with capabilities; the people in the organization make things possible. When applied to business processes such as customer services, technology gives way to new opportunities in process performance. When applied to bureaucracies, technology can make a small company appear large, 'teach an old dog new tricks' and, in many cases, upset the proverbial apple cart of corporate tranquillity.

2.2   Technology and the Control of Information

From the time of early books and manuscripts to the present day, the ever-increasing role of technology has been to engage in the control and distribution of information. Information in its many forms is an integral part of the process engaged by business to fulfil its mission. Data is the raw material of information, playing an ever-increasing role in the interoperation of business processes, especially in situations when processes become collaborative in their execution. Typically, data is required as an input to a process, is generated by the process and reported when the process reaches its desired end state. Information, on the other hand, is a product of manipulating data by summarization, aggregation, tabulation and other methods to report on a condition or trend that transcends a single piece of data. Put simply, data is the lifeblood of the business process, whereas information reports on the condition of the process during its execution life cycle.

The current generation of technology makes possible the realignment of data, information and process by assigning a relative value to each component and reassessing the relevance of one to another. Reengineering demonstrated that process is the key to how a business functions, and process is often influenced by technology – if not dictated by a technology's idiosyncrasies. For example, manufacturing companies often developed inventory part numbers comprising numbers and letters, each digit carrying a significant meaning. An inventory item such as a blue 5 watt 12 volt light bulb with screw connector might have a part number 'BB5W12VS-10-123'. Each number after the dash corresponds to its description, classification or location (for example aisle 10, bin 123.) In most cases, this is a legacy from the old KARDEX paper-based system or early computer file system, indexed by 8, 16 or 32 digit keys. These keys were mechanisms for the computer to retrieve quickly the entire record without having to read the contents of all the data associated with a single record. However, as technology improved the size of keys increased, databases became relational and any piece of data could be used as an index to retrieve itself. Ironically, when reviewing the business accounts in eras before computers, the reference to retrieve an item like a blue 5 watt 12 volt light bulb with screw connector was 'blue 5 watt 12 volt light bulb with screw connector'. Fifty years of data storage and retrieval technology development now makes it possible to retrieve the item in the same natural language as our grandfathers'. This progression of technological breakthroughs leads to the inevitable question: What is information and how does it affect the execution of a business process? Moreover, it gives us the ability to assess the relative value of the process itself and the steps within a process.

This reassessment of process and its relationship to data and information is the basic premise of reengineering. The challenge facing business in the twenty-first century is how to engage technology in a process of reengineering or, perhaps more drastically, to dismantle their functional structures to accommodate a process orientation. Unlike previous generations of technologies that manipulated information, the combination of PCs, the Internet, PDAs, robots, avatars and biometric devices enables a reworking of the fundamental processes established by post-industrialization or assembly-line processes in order to achieve greater efficiency. The basic intention is to reconstruct the relationship between the work or process steps of a business with the individuals within the organization. In many cases, altering both the process and organization to form a completely new approach to how a firm adds value often requires the rejection of the old process. Technology's legacy has influenced the way in which tasks are performed and the skills required to fulfil each step within a process. Now technology makes the total assessment and reconstitution of process and organizations possible. Warren Wilson observed that 'resistance to process management emerges from the realization that people are accustomed to working in vertical functions'.[63] The underlying concern of individuals who see technology as a threat is that when hierarchically organized business process functions are dismantled, circumvented or eliminated by technology, career paths are no longer viable in the traditional sense.

Business processes and their subsequent separation into discrete activities permit individuals greater degrees of specialization, leading to higher salaries and clearer career paths. Technology is now perceived as a threat to areas of specialization within certain industries and job categories. Very often, technology is met with resistance, typically delaying the implementation of technology components and resulting in a low or significantly reduced success rate. Business process redesign in general creates disquiet in the corporate bureaucracy and is magnified by technology in two ways: individuals suddenly realize they are seemingly redundant, and the traditional mechanisms used to control the business are less valuable.

Optimizing the process of business has been a continual quest for companies long before the economic conditions of the twenty-first century. Technology and, to a greater extent, reengineering are merely tools that have been applied to the old pursuit of operational efficiency. In Warren Wilson's words: 'It is not surprising, therefore, that massive uncertainty and resistance to change may be present in business transformation and specifically process reengineering and management.'[64] The result of streamlining processes and continually applying technology is clear: information about the business, such as production information, transaction data, customer data and the exchange of internal and external data, creates data which is commoditized. The resistance to technology in this sense stems from the decoupling of process from working in vertical functions. The redefinition of vertical organizations is discussed in greater detail in Chapter 5.

The world of the twenty-first century has been labelled 'the information society', but in the context of the need for information all previous generations had the same requirement. A more descriptive term may be the 'convenient information society', because the evolution of technology has simply made information easier to obtain or purchase. Conversely, the ability to produce mass information and disseminate it to ever-wider audiences brings into focus the need for quality and fidelity of information. To illustrate the problems regarding the mass distribution of information, one can use the so-called 'Wicked Bible' of 1631. In the English Barker Bible the word 'not' was erroneously omitted from the seventh commandment, thus resulting in 'thou shall commit adultery'.[65] This misprinting and rapid distribution of this Bible raised concerns over the control and standardization of content and, more importantly, increased the level of awareness in the importance of quality control. Not surprisingly, the same concern was raised with regard to the Internet in the wake of the 1995 Oklahoma City bombing, when it became evident that the formulas and procedures for bomb making were readily available to anyone who knew how to use a search engine. Nevertheless, the initial novelty of simply being able to find information on the Internet is waning, and now individuals and corporations are turning their attention to the quality and fidelity of the information as well as the integrity of the source. This concern regarding the control and distribution of information can be found in the life cycle of almost every technology used to deliver information.

Technology organizations today are experiencing a loss of control due to several factors such as the ubiquity of infrastructure, smarter technology users and easier software tools. The role of technology organizations is shifting from being a gatekeeper to becoming a guide to using technology and providing a technological capability. As McCarthy puts it: 'The command of information made possible by the computer should also make it possible to reverse the trends toward mass produced-uniformity started by the industrial revolution.'[66] Technology organizations and their business counterparts have a more fundamental challenge that is no longer associated with making the technologies interoperable. Now information must be gathered and assimilated by people within the business to determine its relativity to current business conditions and, more importantly, to the execution of the firm's value proposition. Postman puts aside the technological aspects of this challenge and draws our focus to the heart of the matter:

> The problem to be solved in the twenty-first century is not *how* to move information, not the engineering of information. We solved that long ago. The problem is how to transform information into knowledge, and how to transform knowledge into wisdom.[67]

This transformation is one not to be taken lightly; it requires organizations to have skills necessary to synthesize information into a cohesive tool that will direct business decisions and not simply supply fuel for reactionary management. Let us now identify and analyse the skills which will aid modern firms to transform knowledge into wisdom.

2.3 Modern People and Dated Skills

According to Davidow and Malone, the definition of a worker as someone 'without education' has permeated American history.[68] In the United States, the concept of manual labourers (blue-collar workers), or, more broadly, those not engaged in managerial roles or special professional careers such as lawyers, doctors and scientists (white-collar workers), was refined and reinforced by the education system during the latter half of the twentieth century. The reaffirmation of white-collar workers was inherent in the duality of an education system that pigeon-holed students destined for blue-collar jobs into less academically rigorous subjects, whilst providing students displaying potential for white-collar jobs with a curriculum that would prepare them for entrance into an institution of higher learning. In the post-Vietnam War era, a third option developed for students who were not considered 'college material': a career in the new voluntary armed forces.

Unfortunately, this educational dualism created the modern labour pool from which business must recruit workers, talented as well as educated. At the heart of a company's competitive advantage, especially those specialized in information technology or where technology labour constitutes an important part of their business, is the concept of 'human capital'. 'Human capital' is that knowledge, experience and know-how which individuals bring to the organization. It is a commodity owned by the individual; it can be accumulated by adding to it (for example by taking a course, reading a book, gaining experience). Likewise, it can be sold (by becoming an employee or contractor). Leveraging human capital is about maximizing the returns the company receives from its employees. As Conceição and Heitor put it:

> without skills, ideas may be irrelevant, and without ideas, there may be no need for new and better skills. The invention of writing (one important idea) required the development of writing skills. Similarly, the widespread diffusion of another important idea, the computer, requires increasing computer skills. New ideas spur the development of the skills required to use these new ideas. The bridge from production of ideas to the usage of ideas is established by producing new skills. Increased use of an idea, which requires its diffusion, will lead to a constellation of other ideas, aimed at improving and extending the initial idea, which will lead to the need for further skills and so on, in a self-reinforcing cycle that leads to the accumulation of knowledge.[69]

The accumulation of knowledge and, more importantly, its application to work activities, is the hallmark of the medieval craftsmen. Now, as then, the accumulation of knowledge can be attributed to higher levels of quality and business fidelity. Learning one's craft and its associated technologies, techniques, styles and innovation was a product of continuous learning within the guild. Accumulated knowledge was the prime reason that a master builder could participate in a project as both an administrator and a craftsman, as described by Andrews:

> Hence there was no architect to make a design – no superior or aloof person above and apart from the workers, save only where the magnitude of the work or the multiplicity of his undertakings made it impossible for the master-mason or master-carpenter to take actual tools in hand and labour with the rest of the workers. In the best periods he was always one of them – they were called his *socii* – his fellows, and he a fellow worker, but wiser – with a larger hope and a fuller vision.'[70]

The ability to achieve more complex designs – not simply the length of time in service – generated a professional respect for senior guild members.

As Naisbitt and Aburdene claimed, in the new information society there is no one education or skill that will last forever; the process of continual learning has to be developed in order to ensure that one's knowledge does not become obsolete.[71] For this reason, the 1990s were the age of adult education and re-education. This 'educational renaissance' is reshaping universities' curricula and increasing the number of courses in further education centres. The idea that a professional should go to college, get a diploma and never seek to be re-educated or recycle knowledge is gone.

Also, in Naisbitt and Aburdene's view, information alone does not make individuals 'competent thinkers'. Especially with today's Internet facilities, data and information are commonplace. To know what to do with that data and information, transforming them into knowledge and wisdom, requires talent and skills from employees. In information technology, 'thinking is now as basic as reading',[72] which means that employees are more and more challenged to be creative, to gather knowledge from different sources and combine it into wise, applicable solutions to business problems. The problem is not only that knowledge needs to be recycled; but also it runs the risk of becoming useless in a matter of years. In the 1990s, we believed that the Internet was about to usher us into an era of creativity, enabling everyone to use tools and be creative. Unfortunately, actual evidence has not supported this flowering of creativity because, like any skill, creativity requires a modicum of discipline and some level of stimulation. Stimulating creativity is the way to ensure that an individual's productivity is always compatible with changes in the industry and business environment. As David Sutherland of the Business Innovation Consortium[73] claims, all individuals possess the ability to be creative; creativity is not a gift. It is something that can be learned and developed over time. Corporations need to create an environment that nurtures the creative aspects of their employees in order to achieve true organizational innovation. Of course, not everyone will succeed in being more creative; however, this is no excuse for companies to stop stimulating and encouraging its employees to acquire the one basic skill that will allow them to be more useful and, sometimes, irreplaceable.

Sutherland advocates the use of a corporate innovation assessment to pinpoint those areas within a firm's business process that are most likely to harbour pools of innovation talent and, more importantly, identify organizational domains that need to develop environments for innovation and creativity to flourish. In this sense, the best way to treat one's employees and allow them to produce in a creative manner is to institute the practice of 'self-management'. According to this practice, management today cannot be conducted as it was in the industrial era. With regard to information technology, the use of computers, the increasing level of specialization of employees, the shift from hierarchies to networks and the new corporate structures (cross-disciplinary teams, partnerships, among others) lead to a working environment in which the position of 'manager' no longer adds value, being in some cases detrimental to the organization.[74] The shift from an authoritarian, hierarchical management style to a networking style of management is part of the 1980s trend of 'cooperative ethics' and 'healthy competition', by which individuals should get help from fellow workers in all divisions, instead of going to a manager who is supposed to represent one or another division.

Karl Erik Sveiby of Celemi's Tango Program claims that the shift from hierarchical management into a networked style coupled with the process of continuous learning gives business entities the opportunity to have recognizable 'organizational and individual talent' as 'intangible assets' on corporate balance sheets.[75] If indeed corporations profess that people are their greatest asset, it is baffling that these assets are often difficult to value. It could be argued that the non-disclosure of the quality and significance of these assets is misleading to investors. This is especially true when organizations are engaged in work that is directly dependent on intellectual output, such as research firms, consulting companies and universities.

Companies need to rethink how they hire staff. They should not be hired for specific jobs because this is too narrow and rigid in an ever-changing workplace. Instead, organizations must rethink the way they organize and accomplish work. The best method is to use behavioural interviews which identify their cognitive and associative skills, that is, their ability to think and apply knowledge gathered from experience. It is said that when Thomas Edison was recruiting new engineers, he presented them with an empty light bulb and asked them to compute the volume enclosed by the glass.

Engineers who laboriously grappled with mathematical solutions based on 3-dimensional geometric formulas were rejected in favour of those who simply filled the light bulb with water and then poured it into a graduated cylinder. P. Israel's words:

> Edison was always willing to hire ambitious young men who had practical experience, including several who had worked for the Lamp Company and Machine Works, and he often favoured those with practical experience when choosing someone to take charge of an important experimental campaign.[76]

Nevertheless, in this rapidly globalizing world, various countries face different labour and skill challenges as a by-product of technology's influence. Disturbing trends in early twenty-first-century nationalism and regressive immigration policies threaten to restrict the ability of businesses to attract and retain global workers who can cross-pollinate ideas, skills, experiences and, most of all, cross cultural barriers. Zachary notes that:

> Nations have long relied on mixing local and imported talent to stimulate activity. Movements of people are crucial to the diffusion of knowledge. People are the most effective culture-carriers, more effective than media or artefacts.[77]

The mixture of talent allows corporations to excel and remain viable during times of adversity and economic downturn. Equally, the same mixture of talent provides the catalyst for innovation and product development. The twenty-first century will see the rise of new cosmopolitan workers, or 'cosmocrats'. The new globally aware worker introduces new challenges to business and government, as identified by Zachary:

> The multinational corporations that promote a new cosmopolitanism may be the very force to undermine the social and cultural structures that are essential to holding together pluralistic nations. When merit is the master, performance obliterates distinctions between people based on colour, family background, religion, gender, place of birth and myriad other inherited or elected characteristics.[78]

Zachary rightly points out that how a company assesses merit and performance will have to be significantly different from the metrics of today. It is conceivable that in many digitally connected organizations in which work can be performed at any location, a worker will select an employer based on the firm's ability to provide a robust technological infrastructure in a location that best meets the employee's lifestyle.

The technologies promoting the business and social transformations of the workforce shift the focus of organizational productivity from that of utilization and output to that of applied knowledge and organizational dexterity. Organizational dexterity is measured by how a firm adapts to changes in business conditions, adjusts its production to new product preferences driven by changing consumer attitudes, exhibits mastery in aligning global resources to address new levels of production, and its proficiency in utilizing its resources within profitable operating parameters which translate into a return on investment. Manuel Castells cites the distinguishing characteristics of operating in the post-industrial world as a shift in perspective: societies will be informational, not because they fit into a particular model or social structure, but because they organize their production system around the principles of maximizing knowledge-based productivity through the development and diffusion of information technologies, and by fulfilling the prerequisites for their utilization (primarily human resources and communications infrastructure).[79]

In order to achieve this new global operating state, businesses will be required to streamline operations and reduce the amount of organizational resistance to change. The combination of a network structure, highly skilled self-organizing pools of talent, and a robust technological infrastructure presents a case for business entities to re-examine their structure and how they embrace organizational change. Corporations are learning that the human capital of the firm is a dynamically changing process that can be optimized by introducing a feedback loop, often enabled by technology. An individual's value proposition is not in the simple execution of predetermined business rules, but in their total contribution to the organization, manifested by the individual's leadership, interpersonal and technology skills. The value of people must be tracked on a leadership dimension and their contribution to the organization as well as their information technology expertise. Organizations today no longer comprise members of a single firm, but resources from a variety of organizations. In the construction of global pools of talent, information, knowledge and business wisdom are often lost as people transition between job functions, locations and organizations. In developing a globally connected organization, knowledge must be retained in such a way that it is useful to other knowledge workers. This retention is often difficult because many corporate cultures encourage knowledge hoarding under the old 'knowledge is power' model. In organizations exhibiting this symptom, the most effective method to curb undesirable organizational behaviour is by motivating individuals, not always in the form of salaries. The structure and behaviour of an organization reflect not only the attitudes, actions and attributes of the individuals within the firm; these collectively coalesce into what can be called 'business resistance to change'. Let us analyse how businesses are structured now and what they should do to change the way they work and the nature of their behaviour in order to stay competitive.

2.4   Business Processes: The New Medieval Guilds

The process of business comprises tasks that when combined with skilled people produce an added value to a product or service. The discrete tasks and the individuals performing them, do not add value when viewed as isolated components.[80] Rather, the entire process creates value by accumulating the value of each process step into a unit of value perceivable by the customer. Here again, today's organization needs to unlearn the command and control structure which is the legacy of assembly-line thinking and develop a process focus. However, adopting a process focus does come with a hidden price. Firstly, existing processes need to be examined and separated into their component parts, and the value of each assessed as to its relevance to the entire process. Secondly, people need to adopt a process orientation and jettison the traditional hierarchical organization structure in favour of a process focus. This includes the creation of process owners who are ultimately responsible for the performance of the processes and their component steps. Thirdly, during the transition to a process orientation and the subsequent establishment of a normative process, the issues of maintaining product quality and the introduction of product alterations such as engineering change orders must be addressed.

Strangely, the new process-oriented business imperative is once again evocative of medieval craftsmen who, during the creation of these goods, were process focused, because they themselves were the process. They possessed a uniquely proactive approach to maintaining a high degree of product quality. Marjorie Quennell describes the craftsmen of the Middle Ages:

> In the mediaeval period the arts and crafts were much more representative of the whole community than they are now. The craftsmen learnt not only the practical details of his trade, the way to use his tools, and to select materials, but was taught as well to design his work; and all his fellows did the same, working together on much the same lines – all interested in doing good work, and in trying to find better methods and designs. All this accumulated knowledge was handed down from generation to generation, and formed what we call tradition,

and it resulted in the work being extraordinarily truthful. The man in the four-teenth century was not content to copy the work done in the thirteenth, but with all his fellows was trying to improve on it; so if we have sufficient knowledge, we can recognize the details, and say this place must have been built at such a date.[81]

Medieval craftsmen employed a process of building in which quality and continual design improvement were integral parts of the normal course of work. This is evident in the numerous castles and churches still standing throughout Europe. Contemporary archaeologists, architects and histor-ians, using their knowledge of the medieval period, can look at a building and identify which parts were built when, based on the progression of tech-niques known to the masons of each era. An understanding of the medieval process thus provides a context for the problems that today's companies face in moving towards a process-oriented organization.

At the centre of the notion of 'medieval process' was the concept of 'guilds'. It is important to note that there were two distinct types of guilds in medieval society. 'Merchant guilds' were associations that brought together a town's tradesmen to exercise control over trade; 'craft guilds', on the other hand, were composed of master craftsmen, journeymen and apprentices in various craft disciplines. As we can see, each type of guild has its modern equivalent. Merchant guilds are analogous to today's market-makers and product aggregators, such as eMarketplaces and Internet portal providers, where customers can buy goods that have been brought together into an electronic market space. Our modern guild coun-terparts act in their own self-interest, contrary to the intention of the medieval merchant guilds as described by Christine Wiener:

> A medieval guild can be seen as a sort of early mutual benefit society for it had a dual purpose: to obtain a fair deal for its members as well as to protect the public. The merchant guilds for instance were to ensure fair prices while the master of a craft guild had strict responsibilities towards his journeymen and apprentices.[82]

Today these responsibilities have been assumed, to some extent, by govern-ment agencies and other regulatory groups.

Craft guilds, on the other hand, resemble organizations within modern firms such as the emerging centres of excellence and core competency groups which now focus on products, processes and customers. Wiener describes the master of a craft guild: 'He acted as business manager, planning and costing, deploying skilled labour – the journeymen – and looking to the future, training young men – his apprentices – into the profession.'[83] Only a few words short of the job description of today's process owner or manager.

In stark contrast to today's business processes, quality was taken for granted in medieval times. This is not to say that there was less quality; it was simply built into the fabric of the craftsman's work. In the case of medieval masons, the finished product carried a mason's mark indicating which crafts-man had done the work while simultaneously acting as a mechanism for pay-ment. Only a minimal amount of specification was required while constructing a building because the master builder had intimate knowledge of the capabilities of each mason he employed. For example, in the medieval stonemason's guild, quality was not maintained by a separate group inspect-ing the work of individual masons. Each mason was responsible for the qual-ity of his own work as a matter of course. Yes, medieval structures did collapse on occasion, but not due to any lack of quality in any of the individ-ual components. If they fell down, it was because medieval master builders were stretching the limits of their designs in an effort to maximize the use of materials, such as making the walls of a cathedral thinner, higher and lighter to enable the maximum surface area to be used for stained glass.

Needless to say, the craft guilds of the Middle Ages were not without problems which would today be equivalent to price fixing and monopolistic behaviour. However, their approach to continuous, lifelong learning and experimentation within each craft and their ability to incorporate new tech-nological improvements into the course of construction without significant alterations to the work flow stands as a benchmark which modern society has yet to replicate. Roman concrete's disappearance and subsequent redis-covery demonstrates how knowledge, even simple knowledge, can be lost over time as a product of poor or non-existent paths of communication. Corporations today must ensure that, when adopting a process-centred approach, the communications infrastructure enables individuals within the firm to communicate both hierarchically and laterally to other individuals within a process and to colleagues engaged in other processes.

Future Business Processes

Oddly, the hierarchical command and control structure in today's corpor-ations is based on the same feudal lord–liege relationship, actually referred to as 'fiefdoms' in some organizations. However, unlike the Middle Ages, adopting a process orientation means focusing one's allegiance to the cus-tomer, who is at the heart of the process's value equation. To what we can only imagine would be the dismay of our medieval counterparts, technology has brought to the process-centred organization of today the ability to produce enormous quantities of goods and the ability to adapt to repetitive work. Unfortunately, the legacy of post-industrial structures has, in many instances, led technology to be applied to the compartmentalization of work, where one person is the designer, and the rest tend the machines, often with a slow erosion of quality. The current generation of technologies, including the Internet, collaborative systems and distance-bridging technologies, is quickly reshaping not only business processes, but the actions taken by individuals who perform the work.

The far-reaching effects of the convergence of computing, telecommunications and software technologies is instituting an unavoidable change, and has become a major factor in the competitiveness of organizations. Each year, corporations invest billions of dollars on employee development, often without a clear mechanism for measuring their return on investment. David Sutherland, of the Business Innovation Consortium, identified another value proposition, the 'employee value proposition' (EVP), according to which a company needs talent to exist, and therefore must rely on the existing employees and attract new employees to maintain the flow of ideas. Linked to the corporate value proposition, the EVP is the base for a business practice which focuses on the idea that employees always have another job waiting. A company must then identify which employees comprise its 'strategic talent pool' in order to ensure that employees are satisfied. Certified employee attraction, retention and satisfaction is what makes a company a good place to work, keeping high production levels and good customer services.[84] This seemingly new concept is in reality similar to that of medieval guilds, more evidence of how much knowledge about business processes has been lost over the centuries, only now to be regained.

Organizations are now discovering an accelerated approach to learning called a community of practice. The establishment of an informal community of practice that exchanges lessons learned, case studies, best-in-class knowledge is reminiscent of the more formalized structure of the medieval craftsman guilds. Today's corporations have the opportunity to combine the best of both periods of learning by adopting the process of medieval learning with the advantages of technology. A technology-enabled virtual community of practice enables a firm to capitalize on not only industry-specific knowledge, but also on the multicultural aspects of specific market or socio-economic conditions.

Contemporary firms must engage employee knowledge or intellectual capital in order to drive factors like innovation and employee development. This can be economically achieved by adapting the attributes of a medieval guild system to foster a greater propensity for self-generating informal learning communities. In an informal knowledge system, each person will require two key components in order to be an active participant: appropriate technology and a series of interwoven relationships.

Business processes combine technology (in most cases) with people who can execute actions that facilitate a customer's needs. The execution of a process centres on the activities performed by the individuals as they participate in an interwoven set of relationships which are all dependent on information and subsequently communicating the results of their actions. The first component, technology, is at the heart of this complex set of relationships, providing the mechanisms that will facilitate communications and monitor the inputs, outputs and performance of executions. Developing an inside-out view of process is essential because applications are evolving to represent the business processes and communications they serve. Therefore, just sending eMail is not a solution. Collaboration and communication are two separate, distinct concepts that organizations often get confused. Technologies that permit collaboration and the exchange of ideas – not simply of words – enable individuals engaged in the process to discover further improvements to process steps during the normal course of execution. These discoveries are not simply a by-product of the technology itself, but the product of enabling individuals to see the entirety of the process and their relative contribution to the total process. A collaborative infrastructure combined with a formal and informal network of communications reduces process inefficiencies. The establishment of formal and informal relationships is a vital component and organizations are now developing new structures that foster communications that transcend traditional hierarchical structures.

The second component is a series of relationships – labelled 'thought partner model' – where the individual is at the centre of three primary lines of communication: a mentor, an apprentice and a thought partner (Figure 2.3). At the heart of the relationship is the individual. It is a given that each individual has a unique skill which contributes to the organization's ability to add value. Understanding this therefore creates the necessity for each individual to mentor another person within the firm. The mentoring process has a twofold impact on an individual: firstly, the passing of a skill to another, thereby reducing the amount of communication required while performing a specific task; secondly, the fact that it increases an individual's feeling of self-worth by establishing a value or field in which he or she adds to the organization.

Since an individual does not necessarily know every aspect of every added value skill within the organization, there is also a need to be mentored. As an apprentice, the individual receives the same basic type of informal knowl-

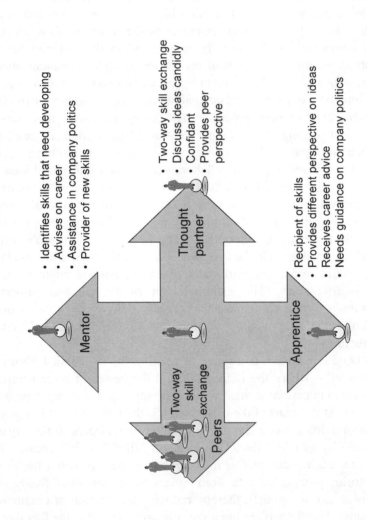

- Identifies skills that need developing
- Advises on career
- Assistance in company politics
- Provider of new skills

Mentor

Two-way skill exchange

Peers

- Two-way skill exchange
- Discuss ideas candidly
- Confidant
- Provides peer perspective

Thought partner

Apprentice

- Recipient of skills
- Provides different perspective on ideas
- Receives career advice
- Needs guidance on company politics

Figure 2.3 The thought partner model

edge sharing, and in many cases learns from the mentor how to be a better mentor to his or her apprentice. Finally, like the medieval guild structure, a thought partner is a peer within the firm. There is an ethical contract between two individuals in which the agreement is the free exchange of ideas, problems and information with the express condition that this is not to be shared with anyone else within the organization. A thought partner takes on the role of a devil's advocate, confidant, idea enabler and a host of other roles in which ideas are examined and refined before they are presented to other members of the firm. It is a mechanism for censorship, but in many organizations it provides a vehicle for flushing out an idea before it becomes an item for discussion within the community of practice.

However, unlike the medieval guild system, in contemporary organizations it is advantageous to rotate the members of the relationship on a regular basis, for example annually. This provides a greater variety of ideas and skills to be exchanged, also allowing the individual to develop an informal network of learning within the firm. The intention of the rotation is to foster new perspectives in the process of creativity and innovation while facilitating a systematic process of knowledge transfer.

Within this associate thought partner model, individuals can use the formal and informal network to form groups of special interest or those focused on developing a particular set of skills. Brown and Gray developed a similar idea, which they called 'communities of practice'. These consist of individuals who are connected via formal, informal and electronic networks, exchanging information and knowledge at regular intervals. These communities may be formed by individuals who work within the same company, or by individuals collaborating with others with similar job functions in external organizations. Like their medieval counterparts, individuals in a 'community of practice' are peers in the execution of tangible operating activities. These communities often emerge through a desire to learn what others know or in conjunction with a goal which is part of a business need.[85] The needs of the business are often translated into deficiencies of the process or changes in the business environment which were not anticipated by the limits of a business.

Michael Hammer identifies the reasoning behind developing a process focus. In his opinion, the metric in which business performance has been traditionally evaluated is rapidly losing its meaning. Likewise, process-oriented people can take proactive measures rather than reactive ones, as used to be the case in the traditional organizational hierarchy:

With a process focus, market share ceases to be the measure of success it once was. Among other reasons, economies of scale are no longer the key mechanism for achieving cost advantage and other forms of marketplace leadership. Although it may still be an important goal, market share is no longer a reliable indicator of current performance or a predictor of future success. A company with large market share today will retain it tomorrow only if the market doesn't change – an extremely unlikely occurrence.[86]

Measurements such as market share and economies of scale now have meanings that may no longer be a true representation of what is happening within the execution of a business process. It is clear that an increased level of information is required by people engaged in the process in order to function efficiently and make continuous improvements based on the feedback of information. By combining technology, a new philosophy about organizational structure and collaboration, corporations will develop a new level of business agility and increase their ability to react to changes in the business environment. The result of this combination will, by default, reduce organizational latency, which was discussed earlier. However, this new operating model is predicated on a quantum change in corporate policy on the treatment, utilization and relationship that a firm develops with knowledge workers. In many cases, a completely new relationship must be developed to ensure that the efficiency of the organization is maintained.

With regard to knowledge workers, one issue that is not clear in many organizations is the ownership or usage rights of the knowledge of an individual. This issue raises several interesting questions as cross-organizational communities form:

- Is the knowledge, experience and wisdom of employees a possession of the employer or is it rented, or perhaps licensed from the employee?

- To what degree is the total knowledge of the employee the property of the employer?

- To what extent can employers claim ownership of employee-generated knowledge that is only remotely connected with the employer's business?

- When knowledge workers provide their own office infrastructure (computers, backup systems, filing cabinets), to what extent do employers have access to search or claim ownership to the knowledge contained within the devices?

- What is the level of ownership between the consultant and the new knowledge he or she acquires while engaged in transient activities within a firm?

Few organizations have developed proactive polices to adequately address these issues. Opting for blanket legal contracts that claim ownership of intellectual property entirely in favour of the business holding sole ownership, many companies may be taking a premature stance on the issue. Legal issues aside, knowledge-sharing technologies used to form communities of practice have met with mixed results; in many cases it is an organizational lack of trust which is often attributed to failed implementations. Regardless of the technology selected, the essential element to leveraging knowledge successfully in any business is to establish an organizational culture that fosters and rewards the sharing of information and knowledge. Knowledge exchanges of this intensity must be encouraged formally and informally by all levels of the organization. This cultural commitment from management must extend into the formal aspects of knowledge exchange, such as providing time, space and opportunities for mentoring or facilitating sharing, and informal mechanisms such as electronic discussion groups, newsgroups and other technologies that enable interaction with colleagues during non-work times. The most important aspect of a community of practice is that each member of the community exhibits a mutual respect for one another and exudes a sense of trust, primarily to dispel any perception that this knowledge exchange is a threat to what they know.

Organizations are learning to address four key areas in developing an operating philosophy for human capital. They must adopt a process orientation, placing the customer at the centre of the process; create an environment of continuous education and mentoring to improve product quality; measure process performance to identify opportunities for improvement; and increase the level of communications to reduce the complexity of the business bureaucracy. At the crux of the application of human knowledge capital is technology, which plays a large part in the differentiation of corporate value propositions. The technology that presents some of the greatest areas of improvement is that of computer software, said to be the key to the information age. It is to this technology that we now turn.

2.5   The Golden Age of Software

If technology is at the heart of the new business agenda, then computer software must be the soul. Computer software is a collection of machine instructions programmed to execute actions of a preconceived design. The design and subsequent actions are primarily a direct utilization of a specific capability made possible by a subset of associated computer hardware. As the underlying capability of the hardware changes, software must be modified, altered or reprogrammed to take advantage of the new capability.

This continuous improvement process is often a function of the technology's maturity cycle, in which new capabilities are incorporated into the design as the application of technology to perform ever-increasing tasks becomes apparent. However, this seemingly modern phenomenon is found in the evolution of many technologies, presenting the same set of challenges in use and development. Let us follow the evolution of the castle as a weapon of warfare; as the technology to wage war on castles grew, the design of the castles to gain a military advantage increased. For example, a medieval castle was primarily a technology of war, a machine used to defend and protect its occupants. Examining the life cycle of English castle-building, the same process improvement development cycle can be observed. As castle design evolved, it incorporated both new military knowledge and empirical masonic knowledge to improve the tactical advantage of the defenders. In the later Middle Ages, castles reached a high level of efficiency and technological superiority, thus offering tremendous advantages incorporated into every facet of design. Inventions such as arrow-loops, murder holes and crenulations were continuously enhanced to keep pace with the ever-improving design of bow and arrow technology. Because these structures were made of stone and are still standing, they provide a record of the improvements over time. Visitors to a fourteenth-century castle can readily spot design improvements when compared to a twelfth-century castle. Similarly, a programmer reviewing source codes from a third-generation language like COBOL (Co(mmon)b(usiness)o(riented)l(anguage)) can read the intention of a subroutine and incorporate new functions into the design of a new program in a language like XML (extensible markup language). The development of the disruptive gunpowder cannon technology shifted the tactical advantage to the attacker, and warfare became increasing mobile, therefore reducing the importance of the castle as a military machine. Here again one can see that a disruptive technology radically alters the use and method of traditional technology. This could also be observed when computers suddenly embraced the shift from terminals to GUIs (graphical user interfaces), as in MacIntosh and Microsoft Windows.

Technology advancements that led the Industrial Revolution of the nineteenth century gave us the ability to produce enormous quantities of new technologies. Computer software, like manufacturing technologies, has for the most part been adapted to repetitive work. Manufacturing work, like software development, has evolved into one person designing, all others tending the machines or maintaining the code, with a slow and predictable erosion of quality.

Regardless of their scale, software development projects are intricate systems with dynamic interactions which interconnect them to both a supporting infrastructure and a process or initiation sequence, often represented by a human being. Traditional software development methodologies have inherited design and control mechanisms that were the product of legacy project management systems like GANNT, PERT and CPM, all with roots stemming from post-World War II military construction projects. These methodologies of project management focus on the control and time division of labour. In addition, they often break a project down into discrete tasks, matching them to resources and applying the result to a timeline.

There have been countless discussions on how technology is the enabler of business reengineering; yet, the processes of implementing technology, creating software and the integration with legacy systems are still burdened with ideas and methods left over from the information engineering concepts of the 1970s and 80s. During the 1990s, almost every technology project was marked as a reengineering project. In fact, very few were a radical definition of a process, most actually being process improvements or simple modifications of old systems. Reengineering became the management *trend de jour* because it was easy for most organizations to get funding by merely taking last year's project, giving it a new name and calling it a 'reengineering project'. Over three-quarters of the reengineering projects were process improvements at best, and numerous others simply repackaged old projects to get new funding. Many of the projects touted as reengineering were never completed, resulting in very little value added, or else they were a total failure. This was, in most cases, attributed not to the individuals involved or the technologies engaged to reshape the business, but to the lack of understanding of what it means to 'reengineer'. Michael Hammer and James Champy's definition of reengineering was clear and precise: it meant a fundamental rethinking and radical redesign. Rethinking a process is simple; unlearning all the years of process legacy derived from countless business changes is hard. Using technology as an enabler of an existing business process or a newly reengineered one is relatively straightforward. Nevertheless, can we say that it adds value? Many of the technology failures experienced in the 1990s might have been avoided if a simple test had been used when applying technology to reengineering projects: Is the proposed project a radical departure from what already exists, or have we re-examined the fundamental way the process works? This question seems simple, and yet it reveals a complex set of issues. To understand these issues we must first examine our information technology roots.

Most commercial technology implementation methodologies employed by today's technology organizations are overflowing with work product-based deliverables coupled with a complex method and process of creating, documenting and displaying the activities of a project. Looking briefly at where these methodologies came from and how they evolved provides a foundation for the reasons why and the ways in which these dated methods need to migrate to more dynamic processes.

The Art of Programming

In the 1960s, commercial information technology was just data processing, not much more than a fast adding machine with some extended printing capabilities. In addition, it also needed an entire support organization to keep it going. In the 1970s, corporations realized that information systems played an integral part in the day-to-day business of running the company. Great demands rose from the organizations using the technologies; consequently, the data processing department (sometimes called the 'IBM department') was inundated with requests for systems. Within a very short time, data processing organizations began to realize that the process of creating software was complex, tricky and ultimately similar to an art form, due to the variability in the quality of programming from one programmer to another. Complicating matters even further, programming was almost a method of self-expression for data processing personnel. Thus began the programmer's quest for efficiency, whose credo was 'if it took me this long to figure out, it should be twice as hard for the next person to work out'. Armed with good intentions, programmers worked to document their thinking while writing computer programs. However, they often jettisoned this additional task when deadlines loomed and the resulting program was desperately needed by the business, which was under the impression that program documentation could be written after the deadline was met. In the majority of cases, this rarely happened and orphan programs devoid of remarked instructions, that is, notes which programmers use to document their thinking, acted to hamper the data assessing department's performance over time. Most organizations tried to develop a consistent approach to software development; standards came along.

As the demand on information resources grew, information user groups put increasing pressure on management to squeeze data processing organizations to deliver functionality to business units and other end-user groups quickly. Typically, when these organizations received computer software solutions, they were significantly reduced versions of the original designs, falling short of the expectations envisaged in the design process. Users became discontented with the time taken to develop systems and the 'clash of the technology titans' was born. Data processing (DP) groups rose to the occasion by creating quality control mechanisms that resulted in tangible documentation to show corporate management that business users really did not understand how to specify what they wanted in a computer system. Armed with reams of technical specifications which only technologists understood, many data processing organizations used this as a shield with which to deflect the wrath of management and reset the expectations of the user community.

In the early 1980s, data processing organizations gained top management's attention (primarily due to the rising cost of capital equipment and personnel) and began to change their image from simple processors of data to management information systems (MIS) groups. It was about this time that technology groups began to be labelled 'professionals'. The newly labelled 'MIS organizations' took on the same type of appearance as the early federalists during the founding of the United States, emphasizing a strong centralized approach to hardware, data, applications and personnel. This centralized buying was justified by economies of scale and proved to be an effective short-term cost saver. One side effect of this process was that many IT organizations became locked into one particular technology manufacturer, regardless of whether the technology solved the business problem or not. Many users found themselves with a brand new terminal on their desk and a software application or two that automated only a small part of their job, while performing many functions and features that were alien to their business, but it was 'cheaper to do this way'.

In the late 1970s and early 1980s, in an effort to reduce costs organizations developed 'package mania', and purchased pre-built applications to drop in as a new solution. After experiencing a cultural backlash from user organizations, all claiming to have unique business processes, the next step was to try to modify these packages in order to fit the business. Most vendors disliked the idea of an organization wanting to modify their packages and discouraged purchasers by stating that warranties would be violated and the package would no longer be supported. Organizations which changed the packages they had purchased soon found that trying to unravel the logic of the vendor's programmers was a project in itself. Adding to these pressures, modifications to these packages became a maintenance nightmare, involving entire organizations to support one or two central packages.

Modifying software codes and developing new programs became of paramount importance to organizations, and then along came 'computer automated software engineering' (CASE) tools and information engineering. CASE tools allowed programmers to develop systems using generators, compilers, transform engines, that is, application programs that convert data, information or programming codes from a raw form to a refined one, and table-based functioning shells. These tools permitted the development of software applications in half the time of the labour-intensive task of writing COBOL code. Unfortunately, since then CASE has had mixed reviews by critics and practitioners. Many CASE tools were ahead of the technology and people that supported them. The early versions generated character-based screens, being well on the way to central repository functionality. Suddenly Microsoft Windows came along and few vendors were prepared to drop their current development plans. Several vendors tried to make the switch but the market was not ready for GUI-based tools. Vendors had to spend double the money maintaining the character-based version while diverting research and development money to GUI tools. To compound the issue, users had unreasonable expectations for the initial CASE tools. Data bigots wanted these tools to be data focused (if not centred) while the world actually was process oriented. Vendors, mistakenly interpreting the data bigot's power in the market, focused on the data tools instead of process tools. This was not sufficient to provide the cost savings that users thought they would get.

Disillusionment set in and many vendors paid a steep price – ultimately buried in the CASE software graveyard. Many vendors fell by the wayside while a few rose to the challenge and Upper CASE tools were the result. The use of CASE tools is still very much alive and vendors are rapidly evolving to an object-based repository. However, that would be the subject of another book.

Another phenomenon that many MIS organizations failed to realize – and thus did little to harness the potential – was the introduction of PCs. PCs took the user community by storm. They allowed users to acquire a certain level of freedom from the centralized, slow-moving machinery of the IT infrastructure, and permitted the execution of functions no longer bound to the central computer, with applications such as spreadsheets and word processing. Users could purchase a software package to perform basic office functions for several hundred US dollars and, since it resided on their computers, could bypass the slow-moving IT organization. The IT organization tried to get organizations to standardize on one package or one vendor. Similarly, every IT department felt the need to support these packages internally, duplicating the support effort of the vendor. Many organizations took over this responsibility and increased their workload, in many cases sidetracking their organizations' primary mission.

From Art to Science

In the mid to late 1980s, concepts such as information engineering (IE), joint application development (JAD) and rapid application development (RAD) sprouted from the ashes of major internal corporate battles as a new set of programming disciplines. In many cases, these techniques were presented as a way of involving the users, when in reality they were a means to perpetuate the centralized IT function. IE and its attendant books were, in most cases, fancy window-dressing on a dead group of principles which no one wanted to bury. After all, technology gurus, such as James Martin, (see Martin, 1986) charged people thousands of US dollars just to listen to them speak about it.

In the late 1980s and early 1990s, individuals began to realize the power of the PC. PC users started developing their own spreadsheets, notes files and databases to catalogue and retrieve data used in everyday processing. In the process, the islands of information were born. During this time, many IT organizations struggled for centralized control of resources, while the corporate user community opposed this trend by insisting on decentralization. Many IT organization executives were embroiled in a delicate balancing act between these two forces, thus failing to understand the users' primary motivation. Even today, in IT organizations, there is still a quest for 'writing new systems' versus creatively applying packages and minimalist programming. Most IT organizations had (and still have) a backlog of system requests; as a consequence, users flocked to spreadsheets and other PC programs in order to get a sense of progress. Business computer users often create their own information system using spreadsheets just to feel some sense of control over their own data destinies. IT groups have been distributing architectures that allow users to implement their own solution in a plug and play network. In turn, this network should allow users to connect into a composite navigational structure, one that allows the bulk of the computing to occur on the desktop, using the network as a data conduit supplying these applications with requested information.

During the latter part of the 1980s, users were told that they were empowered; however, they were just being patronized. Current applications were redefined as 'assets' by the organization in order to attach some value to a dying set of technologies and principles. In fact, during this period, centralized groups went through the process of decentralization and decentralized groups became centralized in an effort to retain control. They mistakenly thought that the IT organization and its products could be part of the 'solution'. In reality, they were a major 'roadblock' to progress. Without the huge problems they created, however, radical change might never have begun.

Organizations of the 1990s moved to 'empowered teams', cross-functional groups focused on solving business problems. IT organizations used this opportunity to establish close links with user communities providing them with the tools to define specifications. Teams developed aggressive technology solutions, only to face mounting obstacles in the bureaucracy of transition organizations. IT organizations started changing in the closing years of the twentieth century, and are now aspiring to a business process-focused set of activities. These organizations are rapidly learning that business processes are as important as 'data' in the corporate asset treasure chest. Companies combining business process and the data supporting the processes will soon realize that an object-oriented approach to systems design will help them to satisfy organizational requests for systems. This will be a major shift for them, both culturally and technologically.

The effects of downsizing the organization led to the piecemeal approach to systems integration and a rush to client/server-based systems which promised cost savings. A great number of technology organizations quickly moved to implement client/server technology, only to realize that integration between the new technology and the legacy systems became increasingly difficult and consumed more resources than estimated. Unfortunately, a number of chief information officers (CIOs) and IT managers failed to produce short-term benefits during the migration towards interconnective technologies which could only yield long-term benefits. A number of CIOs learned a new definition of CIO ('career is over') as they became some of the first casualties of the information age. Individuals in technology organizations discovered that when management decides to measure technology projects on very short-term deliveries of value, the term 'pioneer' was also redefined as 'people leading the charge of business change with a large number of arrows in their backs'. Many technology leaders realized that their technical infrastructure and organizations were not up to the challenge, being ill-prepared to meet the tremendous learning curve required to developing business solutions in the new environment. This situation was exacerbated by senior technical managers' failure to identify the users as the problem because of their inability to develop specifications that could be accomplished within budgetary limits.

Blame for early failures in client/server experiments can be placed at the feet of technology organizations which behaved like slow-moving dinosaurs. Fortunately, this organizational latency, which could be compared to the decline and demise of dinosaurs and their eventual transformation into crude oil, provided an environment of frustration which propelled management to initiate changes and provided a seedbed for the business process of 'reengineering'. Consequently, if things had run smoothly within technology organizations, and business units had not been frustrated by the efforts of the technology group, there would not have been such a burning desire to 'reengineer'.

In many organizations, teaching people the fundamentals of new systems design is a major flaw in organizational planning and career development. Many technology organizations find large gaps in the fundamental knowledge of how to use new technology to transform business, not simply imitate it. A classic example can be made by comparing the information contained within an old text-based computer screen and its contemporary counterpart crafted in the latest Windows display technology. In the majority of cases, the only substantial difference is in the greater amount of information now able to fit onto the screen. What is needed is a fundamental rethinking of the information required, not simply more information. Here again it appears that we are using technology to 'pour old wine into new bottles' as Hammer and Champy noted:

> The fundamental error that most companies commit when they look at technology is to view it through the lens of their existing processes. They ask, 'How can we use these new technological capabilities to enhance or streamline or improve what we are already doing?' Instead, they should be asking, 'How can we use technology to allow us to do things that we are not already doing?'[87]

IT groups should be focused on how to integrate these technologies to provide information services to these groups and create an Internet-like surfing capability for corporate users to obtain business process-based information. These technology organizations need to make a fundamental shift from 'pushing' information to allowing the user to 'pull' only what he or she needs to support the business. The change needed to provoke this shift is based on altering the mindset within bureaucracies and the behaviour of the workforce associated with the delivery of technological solutions, as we shall see below.

2.6   The Labour Shortages from the Black Death to High-tech Skills

Labour shortages occur when the demand for people possessing specific skills exceeds the supply of individuals who are qualified, not committed to other activities and prepared to do the job. In the seemingly fast-paced, high-tech world, shortages in talent appear from time to time with the introduction of new technologies, tools and software. This begs the question: Is there really a skill shortage of high-tech talent in today's business world, or are individuals simply located in the wrong places at the wrong time?

Perceived labour shortages are not new. However, their effects are often felt by businesses eager to capitalize on new opportunities and yet unable to take strategic action because of a shortage of talent. Labour shortages are a direct result of either a lack of people possessing a specific, desired talent or a lack of access to a talent pool which can provide the necessary skill. It is important to review briefly the fundamental aspects of traditional labour markets and their relationships with business in order to develop an understanding of the dynamic nature of talent, its subsequent availability and, more importantly, how talent will affect companies operating in a global marketplace.

The Black Death of the mid-fourteenth century resulted in a dramatic alteration in the relationship between a labourer's worth and his/her role in society. Europe experienced a drastic reduction in population across all demographic sectors of society. Some social pockets were devastated to a greater degree than others, but overall the death toll was catastrophic. The demand for foodstuffs, goods and materials was reduced owing to the reduced population, but the needs of the surviving population remained similar to pre-plague economic times. One could argue that segments of the surviving population were the recipients of the largest transference of inherited wealth between two generations in history. Reviewing the spending habits of the second half of the fourteenth century, one notes an upsurge in the purchase of luxury goods, attributable to the increased purchasing power of the surviving population.[88] This demand created an identifiable labour shortage and a realization by craftsmen that their services were now much more valuable than before. This change in attitude was also reflected in sudden changes in the cost of labour, moving governments to set limits on wages. Even with this intervention, the change in attitude was irreversible and eventually led to the capitalistic behaviour we have today.

The medieval change in attitude was rapid, brought on by the sudden change to the socio-economic structure because of the massive loss of population. Today, concepts such as 'virtual organization', 'free agent nation' and 'collaborative co-opetition' which use technology and have the potential to alter drastically how organizations view labour are moving at a much slower pace. This is because they lack the same level of societal stimulation. In the current business climate, when a labour market tightens and the number of individuals decreases, business must make concessions on the quality of the labour it requires, find a new source of labour or else invest in individuals within the corporation to retool them with the necessary skill sets. The underlying problem in any dash for talent is firstly related to the way corporations view labour; secondly, to their inability to redefine the social contract between an individual and the value he/she brings to the organization; and thirdly, the way in which firms apply labour. These three factors are exacerbated when coupled with the concept of 'collaborative partnership', in which the lines between what is part of the firm and what is not are no longer discernable.

The first talent-related problem is that organizations with aspirations of global operations whose mindset is to treat labour in a traditional manner and simply link operations, products and services together with technology will be disappointed with the results. Davis and Meyer recognize that the fundamental corporate attitude must be unlearned:

> The industrial company operated as if labor were another factory part. Men were interchangeable; they turned a wrench every seventeen seconds. This interchangeability made the labor market a buyers' market: Here's the job take it or leave it. Even when organized labor helped to balance power, union members were a commodity differentiated by seniority, not capability.[89]

Talented labour now has options regarding where and when it can add value to an organization. Investors are beginning to realize that talent is an asset that needs to be managed like other assets, with periodic investments and measured performance. This means that retention is as important as recruiting new talent, and that talent requires regular continuous investment in order to work at maximum productive levels. It is possible that in the not so distant future, prospective employees may factor into their job selection process the kind of technology the company has to offer. This may not be as outlandish as it first appears. In the 1960s to 80s, technology professionals considered what type of technology the company had to offer and whether it resulted in providing a set of skills that would keep them marketable.

The second aspect of the talent equation is a firm's ability or inability to redefine the social contract between an individual and the organization. Individuals should be valued by their direct and indirect influence on contributions to the bottom line. The value added to the business processes which they serve or the administrative process that supports the business should be considered in the overall relationship between the firm and the individual. Traditionally, business was viewed as: divisions of labour; functional organizations; hierarchy; standardization; these four items influenced the working conditions, relationships and organizational behaviour reflected in the contract between the individual and the company. Today, organizations must consider the changes in the working environment which encourage sharing knowledge in a network of work teams; a focus on core competencies; and a process of continuous learning and innovation which are sometimes not reflected in the often one-sided employment contracts. Building corporate loyalty and *esprit de corps* is paramount in retaining talented individuals and pivotal in promoting concepts like mentoring and thought partnering, as noted by Micklethwait and A. Wooldridge:

> Focusing on core competencies might mean outsourcing peripheral employees, but it also means creating a core group of long-term loyalists who are committed enough to the firm to transmit its ethos to new employees. Firms may not be able to offer people jobs for life, but most companies go out of their way to offer people *employability*.[90] [emphasis added]

The new relationship with labour should treat each employee with the same basic understanding as that of entering a partnership, affiliation or association contact with another firm. In fact, one could argue that since companies will be entering into more and more associative agreements with external firms in the new connected economy, treating employees as if they were an equal source of talent would simplify the total number of agreements and contracts administered. Employees would simply have miniature versions of the larger agreements and the depth at which they are linked to the firm would then be relative to the value they add to a process. Plainly, individuals who have the highest contribution are linked to the firm in the same way as a partner; people who add value to specific process areas may be affiliates and highly skilled individuals who are only needed for specific tasks and can serve several organizations may be considered associates. These relationships are all predicated on an organization addressing the third facet of the labour equation – the application of labour.

The third issue of the talent equation also resides in the area in which many organizations can make substantial gains without having to embrace the aforementioned issues in any depth, simply changing the way in which labour is applied. To illustrate this point, we will single out the technology organization, not because it is the greatest problem area but because technology plays a larger part in the corporate value proposition and it is an organization worth studying as a bureaucracy on its own.

Many corporations that took the business reengineering journey assumed that the IT organization would just go along for the ride. Business process reengineering teams expended a great deal of effort learning to 'think out of the box', 'bust paradigms', and 'question the traditional process'. This process of business discovery assumed that technology organizations were already functioning at an optimum level of performance, since technology was part of every recommended solution. Technology organizations needed to re-examine their fundamental beliefs and question how they were developing systems to support the business community. IT organizations were needlessly hampered with a legacy of dated software development life cycles (processes, methods, work products and deliverables). Reengineering advocated that a new business process is the key, not the IT documentation. The new working models – which in many cases were simply high-level process designs lacking any significant details – often created a conflict within technology organizations in that the reengineering process did not allow enough time for *proper analysis*. This was a point of contention for many technology groups in the early years of reengineering. However, some entrepreneurial technology organizations jettisoned the traditional waterfall development methodologies of the 1970s and eventually embraced the concepts of prototyping and later laboratory simulation.

The Dupont Information Engineering Associates

One of the early adopters of this concept in the mid-1980s was a group composed of Scott Shultz, Adrian Merryman, Deborah Pulak, Kitsie Holcumb and a select group of managers, software professionals and process experts formed within the E.I. du Pont de Nemours Corporation, later called Dupont Information Engineering Associates (Dupont IEA). Bringing business unit personnel together with technologists to rethink the process of software development, they created a methodology to speed up software creation called 'rapid iterative product prototyping' (RIPP). What was revolutionary about their methodology was that it created a new way to solve the software development problem by rethinking the composition of a project and calling it a *timebox*. It was similar to medieval holistic thinking; the beauty of their method is in its simplicity. It rejects the typical project management mentality of a team governed by a project leader who maintains a balance between four variables (people, time, cost and scope of the project) and changes the dynamics of the project by fixing three of the four variables. The timebox states that a project has a limited number of full-time people assigned to it and a fixed amount of funds culminating in an immovable deadline. In this model, the only aspect of the project that has to be managed is the scope of the work which is now the responsibility of the entire team. Therefore, instead of the single project leader managing four variables, three of the four are fixed and the entire team manages the remaining one. Dupont leveraged this new variation of the software development life cycle by embracing the embryonic CASE tools. CASE tools, although plagued with early development problems in their own right, made possible the ability to develop rapidly basic structures of software applications and test their designs with business users in a matter of days as opposed to months. This process eventually led to the development of prototyping laboratories, simulation laboratories and ultimately reengineering laboratories.

While reengineering was transforming the process of business, the business of technology organizations was experiencing a revolution in ever-increasing hardware speeds, continuously upgraded operating systems, new versions of applications software, and a quantum change in the methodology of systems development.

What the Dupont and other software development experiences have identified is that the process of software development has evolved over the last 25 years into a complex method of engineering information and designing features and functions for business users to do their job. Through successive generations of technology, tools have advanced the early process of translating that information into a series of procedural instructions which the computer can understand to a more complex process that looks remarkably similar to the new tools and even more complex tasks. As the art of software development aged, the variables that controlled it became more complex; technologies changed, skills required changed and how we used the computer changed. Consequently, the software development process changed for the worst. As the tools for software development became more efficient in automating the design and construction aspects of developments, IT organizations used this opportunity to erect a monolithic organizational structure to compartmentalize the functions, creating more and more areas of specialization. As new hardware is introduced, new programming languages come and go, and a myriad of software components move in and out of favour, as do the skill sets of people within the technology group and in fact in all parts of the organization. This state of waxing and waning skill sets is exacerbated throughout organizations as more and more jobs become inseparably linked with technology. Eventually, this leads to a mismatch of skills to tasks and labour shortages occur, creating an oversupply of non-vital skills and making previously desired people redundant, as we shall see next.

2.7   Bloodletting the Bad Humours and Corporate Downsizing

During the Middle Ages, the common idea of body and health was based on the principle that a human's body was a microcosm, that is, a minature representation of everything that happened in the universe. This notion, derived from the Greeks, led medieval people – and medieval doctors – to believe that as the universe was made of four basic elements – fire (hot and dry), water (cool and wet), earth (cold and dry) and air (hot and wet) – the body was composed of four humours which corresponded to these elements. These were choler or yellow bile; phlegm or mucus; black bile; and blood. Health could be maintained by keeping a constant balance between these humours, but sometimes one would become stronger than the others. Individuals whose blood humour tended to overcome the others were called 'sanguine', and their behaviour and health was thought to be related to changes in the air. Likewise, when an individual's yellow bile was more prominent than other humours, he was said to be choleric, and influenced by fire. The same was true for the other two humours and the influences they suffered from universal elements.[91]

Medieval people were very much like people today. When they were sick, they sought the advice of other members of the community who had a specialized knowledge of illness to find a cure so they could feel better. One of the most common methods to make individuals feel better was bloodletting. Since the Greeks, bloodletting had been seen as a beneficial curative method. Doctors equated bloodletting with the monthly changes that happened in women's body, thus claiming that it was natural for the body to need to release blood. During the Middle Ages, bloodletting was seen as a very efficient way of combating diseases, regulating health and the humours and relieving the spirit from carnal temptations. Weak as the patient became after a long bloodletting session in which a few litres of blood were let out, they were, however, sure that their health and spiritual problems would abate.

In today's business world, bloodletting is paralleled with the practice of downsizing. Let us analyse how downsizing became the new effective way to cure a company's problems. The economic downturn of the early 1990s brought forth four key factors that would in turn lead to the eight-year economic recovery that followed – and is still in progress. Reengineering, downsizing, outsourcing and the marriage of GUI with the Internet have, each in their own particular way, contributed to reshaping how business is conducted. These key factors are also redefining the social contract between employer and employee. Throughout the book, we have analysed the significance of the Internet and its influence on corporate value propositions. Let us now analyse the implications of reengineering, downsizing and outsourcing to organizational behaviour.

If one subscribes to Hammer and Champy's formal definition of 'reengineering' as 'the fundamental rethinking and radical redesign of business processes to achieve dramatic improvements in critical, contemporary measures of performance, such as cost, quality, service and speed',[92] it is obvious that reengineering involves hard work. An oversimplification of reengineering is basically to unlearn the legacy of traditional business processes and rethink how a new process, given changes in people, society, technology and economic conditions, can be best designed to leverage these factors with the resources available to the company. This is not to say that the previous generation of business knowledge is no longer valuable. On the contrary, previous business knowledge presents an opportunity to leverage existing knowledge by applying the advances of science and technology.

Unlike previous manifestations of technological advances, the reengineering phenomenon was led by businesspeople who developed a growing familiarity with the capabilities of technology, and not by technologists themselves. 'Fundamental rethinking and radical redesign' are not simple concepts which can be implemented without altering the fabric of the corporation and its basic beliefs regarding compensation and the behaviour of people engaged in the process of business. Any change that challenges traditional thinking will have its champions, detractors and, more importantly, the wariness of the majority.

Today's situation is similar to the shift of the later Middle Ages, in which the venerable Church witnessed changes along religious and technological fronts. During that time, segments of society began to question not the existence of God, but the dogmas of the Church. More specifically, they questioned the authority and bureaucratic infrastructure of Church doctrine which specified how one should live, worship and believe. Similar to the legacy of incumbent contemporary business rules and corporate policies, challenges to these institutionalized mechanisms met with resistance. In the case of the medieval Church structure, the consequence was the division of the Church into the Roman Catholic and Protestant doctrines (such as Anglicanism, Lutheranism, Calvinism and Presbyterianism), and counter measures such as the Catholic Reformation and the Inquisition. Today, the repercussion of the changes to institutionalized mechanisms and behaviours is *downsizing*, which has, for a decade, been mislabelled as 'reengineering'.

Reengineering is indeed about the reduction, redefinition and transformation of process steps or activities which do not add or increase value to the product, service or process as a whole. Unfortunately, the reduction of steps was translated into the reduction of labour. Throughout the 1990s, many organizations saw this management trend as an opportunity to shed middle managers and other personnel, thus institutionalizing the concepts of downsizing and rightsizing. This workforce reduction is, as said above, analogous to the medieval practice of bloodletting. It is also related to the part of medieval medicine that associated one's illness to the imbalance of good and bad humours in one's body. Humours controlled not only bodily functions, but also attitude, behaviour and manner. Medieval doctors' solution was simplistic: one could bring the body back to balance by adjusting the level of fluids in the body, or by bloodletting. In many cases, people were resilient enough to survive these ordeals which, as we now know, merely depleted their strength at a time when the patient was sick and strength was most needed. In some cases, the patient would die. The medieval notion of balance is not without merit, and businesses today make every effort to measure performance to goals and maintain equilibrium between corporate priorities.

Einstein noted that 'Our theories determine what we measure'. Corporations have always conceived business processes within the context of the industrial age metaphor of the machine. Now we realize that the interconnective nature of the process of business coupled with technology is more analogous to a living system. Similar to the ways in which a living system strives to balance its resources, management today strives to keep a balance between corporate resources which are applied to the process of business, evident in management practices such as the balanced scorecard introduced by Robert Kaplan and David Norton.

In the sense of keeping a balance in the living system of the corporation, it can be said that 'corporate bloodletting' had several negative effects in the 1990s, highlighted by Tampoe:

> Most organizations that have taken the downsizing route have done so to survive. They use the crisis to clean out the deadwood – people, stocks, assets and so on. This improves their financial situation and restores confidence in the short term. Sustaining these short-term improvements over a much longer time-frame is difficult. This is often because rapid downsizing destroys the infra-structures that sustain organizational performance. It demotivates. It creates uncertainty. It destroys informal communication channels. It saps the energy and enthusiasm of staff. It destroys trust and commitment. It destroys customer loyalty. None of this is inevitable, but it does happen.[93]

Indeed, downsizing tends to create an atmosphere of mistrust within companies, thus upsetting the firm's ability to produce and serve customers. However, one positive consequence of the 1990s' bloodletting can be identified: it provided the market with highly trained, educated and experienced white-collar workers, many armed with severance packages and substantial retirement savings. These individuals were the fuel to the dot-com phenomenon. Adrian Merryman of London's Interregnum put it to me succinctly: corporations periodically need to trim away a percentage of the workforce to remain healthy because, over time, organizations develop excess capacity during peak periods and, in the course of normal business, add personnel to improve processes by increasing the resources applied to process steps. Reducing the workforce at strategic intervals compels firms to increase productivity by reshuffling resources and, as a result, adjust their costs to be more in line with the competition. The result places talented people into the labour market who, in turn, start new firms or are engaged by other corporations needing specialized talent.

The longer term effect of downsizing and 'reengineering' as it has been understood by business has created a number of smaller, highly specialized firms offering clearly defined services and larger corporations whose operating division consists of talented groups able to perform discrete activities in internal and external business processes. These collectors of highly specialized labour pools are the lifeblood of outsourcing. Corporations today are realizing the operational benefits of engaging outsourcers and, to some degree, partners to perform activities traditionally accomplished by in-house staff. A prime example is technology services, which most firms are reluctant to outsource due to the perception of cost control in a vital resource. However, if we put this example into a historical context, almost one hundred years ago corporations discovered the indispensable use of electricity, as a technology that could reduce cost and revolutionize businesses. Many firms which took the electric plunge found that it required highly skilled individuals and created in-house electrical departments. Over time, the technology of electrical production, distribution and utilization matured, and the in-house departments were abandoned as external firms offered services which were competitive alternatives.

One could argue that as today's information systems technologies mature, in time technology departments will be outsourced to the same degree as their twentieth-century electrical counterparts. Organizations that have outsourced operations are learning that the key to using external resources effectively is to outsource business process activity that is defined, established and well known to the organization. This is counterintuitive because most firms try to outsource parts of the process in which they lack talent or resources. Outsourcing is based on establishing operational criteria and measuring the external firm's performance against operational benchmarks. Poorly designed or, to a greater extent, poorly executed process components are more difficult to outsource due to the lack of measured results. Put simply, outsourcers try hard to meet criteria typically not developed as an optimal process, and thereby never meet the firm's expectations. Combining outsourcers, partners and other sources of talents into a strategic operating plan is discussed in detail in Chapter 5.

2.8   Machiavelli and the Sport of Mergers and Acquisitions

The popular belief is that mergers and acquisitions create value. In some isolated cases, this concept may be true. However, in most instances, mergers and acquisitions fail to deliver significant shareholder value. The initial intention of a merger or acquisition is to create synergy, the speculation that two organizations are worth more together than they are apart, and the combined output is more than either could produce separately. The exceptions happen when the intention of the merger or acquisition is to combine and reutilize surplus cash, one firm is beneath market value and can be purchased, or to defend an existing product by acquiring a failing supplier, a new competitor, or investing in a complementary countercyclical company to offset resource demands. Although other authors have used Machiavelli in regards to business activity, we will now employ him only briefly to put the cultural aspects of mergers and acquisitions into the broad perspective of business value creation. Machiavelli talks about a prince and principalities, as we, in modern terms, talk about CEOs and corporations in the state of mergers or acquisitions. Machiavelli's observations of how a principality is formed, governed and ruled can be applied to modern merger and acquisition strategies with striking precision. Let us view how companies are acquired and/or merged using Machiavelli's principles.

Corporations either have an inherited organizational culture culminating from years of experience or they are new. In an existing corporation, a CEO of ordinary ability will be able to run and manage his/her organization with a management team of ordinary abilities unless or until some extraordinary business condition occurs which erodes the confidence of the investors represented by the board of directors. If the erosion of confidence is so great that a succession must take place, a successor from within the firm is often less disruptive to the organizational culture because the newly appointed CEO has risen from the ranks of the organization and is less likely to change the structure that brought him/her to power. In many cases, this internal policy of promotion is adequate to address the conditions that caused the succession because it refocuses the management team and allows the firm to continue to operate within acceptable expectations of the investors.

Yet, Machiavelli points out a potential area of concern which may adversely affect the firm's long-term value proposition: 'And in the antiquity and continuity of his rule, the records and causes of innovations die out, because one change always leaves space for the construction of another.'[94] This may explain why so many technology innovations have originated in smaller, less bureaucratic organizations in the last two decades of the twentieth century. If the corporation is new (such as a start-up) or nearly new (such as a spin-off) as in a merger or acquisition, two problems will arise. Firstly, workers, managers and investors will reluctantly pledge their allegiance to the new organization and give their support if they believe they can better themselves or achieve a greater return on investment. This was true at the time of Machiavelli's principalities and is even truer today, as allegiances are reviewed on a monthly or quarterly basis. When newly formed organizations have a clear vision of the firm's proposed structure and, more importantly, a value proposition that encourages cross-functional execution towards common goals, the traditional corporate politics is significantly reduced along with corporate latency. Organizational structures reflect, for good or bad, the attitudes, approaches and behaviours of the senior management team. For example, companies like G. O. Carlson, a specialty steel producer in Pennsylvania whose founders encouraged a sense of corporate community and family values, provide an organizational structure in which access to the senior management team is easy and commonplace for all levels of the organization. This is because of the senior team's desire to be a corporate family and play an integral part in the day-to-day operations of the firm. In contrast, larger organizations, such as Microsoft, General Motors, IBM and other multinational firms, emit a sense of hierarchal power that tends to isolate executives from lower levels of the organizational structure. Neither case is right nor wrong in their approach to organizational structure; they merely project the behaviour of the leadership down into the organization by means of formal and informal lines of communication. The subordinate levels of the organization develop traits reflecting the behaviour of the leadership as a means to support management's efforts to direct the organization.

That said, when larger, traditionally structured organizations for whatever reason (typically ego) decide to acquire or merge with smaller or newer organizations, the culture and technological infrastructure of the acquiring organization usually prevails, to the detriment of the acquired organization. A significant number of mergers and acquisitions in the 1990s failed to deliver any significant additional value to shareholders, customers or employees. One reason is that the cultures of the organizations failed to develop an operational synergy fast enough to reduce the cost of operations. This is often true when older, more established firms try to retain the management of the acquirer and acquired, keeping organizational structures in place and combining upper level management functions. This process in many cases results in a clash of organizational cultures, frequently attributed to each organization trying to retain the previously established patterns of corporate behaviour. However, firms which made the acquired management team redundant or selected members from both organizations to form a completely new management team often fared better at creating new value. The CEO who engineered the latter set of actions must have had Machiavelli in mind:

> And anyone who acquires these lands and wished to maintain them must bear two things in mind; first, that the family line of the old prince must be extinguished, second, that neither their laws nor their taxes be altered; as a result they will become in a very brief time one body with the old principality.[95]

Therefore, when merging, organizations should clearly sort out the management structure and quickly identify which individuals will play the key roles in the transitional organization. Organizations should also be hesitant in changing salary schemes and corporate policies at the same pace. Here Machiavelli gives good counsel in introducing potentially disruptive change to the organizations engaged in a merger or acquisition by clearly delineating the components of change into people (management), culture (behaviour and policies) and cost (salaries and expenses). However, organizations facing rising competitive pressures habitually cannot wait to introduce change over extended periods in order to minimize the disruptive aspects. Firms need to achieve organizational synergy quickly. This is principally true when companies also cast aside traditional hierarchies for a more networked approach to organizational structure. Here again Machiavelli provides insight that can be applied to modern business especially if a firm adopts the concept of a 'community of practice', as described in section 2.4:

> The other and better solution is to send colonies into one or two places that will act as supports for your own state ... , colonies do not cost much, and with little or no expense a prince can send and maintain them ....[96]

Machiavelli offers the conceptual formation of hybrid organizations in which new groups (or network nodes) can be formed by taking resources from both organizations to form highly specialized operating groups. These new enterprises require a robust technological infrastructure in order to facilitate the communications and collaboration needed to be a community of practice.

However, these organizational transitions are normally not the case when assessing a merger or acquisition from a technology perspective. Technology and, more importantly, technological infrastructure plays an ever-increasing role in assessing the value of a firm's ability to meet competitive pressures. Surprisingly, few organizations have embraced formal methodologies for technological assessment, and even fewer develop comprehensive technology strategies for the transition during the merger or acquisition. A technology battle that many organizations faced and, in some cases, are still facing is the product of bringing two technology cultures together. For example, many organizations experienced a cultural divide between MacIntosh users and Microsoft Windows advocates. This was especially true in production of graphics; office workers using MacIntoshes at home and other people engaged in visual media creation. Technology departments, eager to reduce the cost of maintaining computer hardware and software, strived for a standard corporate computing platform, often irrespective of the users' wishes, who, in many cases, were paying the bill. In their defence, the technology organization was acting in the overall best interest of the firm's long-term objectives, but in most cases could have used a few lessons in public relations.

2.9 Computer Viruses and The Black Plague

At the end of the tenth century, the population greeted the new millennium with anxiety. Religious cults with suicidal tendencies, nervous financial markets and the promise of an uncertain future created a mixed sense of wonderment and dread. This phenomenon is experienced to a greater extent or lesser degree at the turn of each century. In the Middle Ages, society at the turn of the fifteenth century did not experience this sensation. Rather, survivors of the Black Death were happy to be alive, and the change in social structure experienced by the elevation in value of the peasant class allowed the vast population of the late medieval period to embrace the new century with a feeling of self-worth and a sense of hope.

Today our technology-based civilization met the birth of the new millennium and the twenty-first century with a sense of trepidation. Technology organizations were unsure whether the change of the century and date-calculating routines might wreak havoc on financial and business transactions. To prevent the problem, they spent millions of dollars to correct the potential Y2K disaster. Fuelled by the initial media hype, consulting organizations capitalized on this opportunity by placing doubt in their client's minds that their computer systems might not work. Harvesting this bonanza of a once-in-a-lifetime revenue opportunity, and armed with an arsenal of tools, consulting organizations proclaimed that they could help most companies through this transition. With hindsight, business now wonders if it was all worth it. The same can be said of the new plague in our technological, global lives: computer viruses. Organizations are starting to look at ways of hedging their bets by going to insurance companies to underwrite the risk associated with systems not working when hackers breach corporate firewalls or users inadvertently introduce destructive computer viruses. The next predictable behaviour will be the legions of attorneys braced for the liability litigations that will ensue from corporations with problems because of poor programming and incomplete work. Consider for a moment the record of the quality of software applications and defects accomplished by the software industry. Considering the variability in software quality and the ever-increasing threat of Internet security breaches, it is surprising there have been no large-scale cyberspace bank robberies yet. There have been numerous individual cases of fraud, identified theft and errors that have been attributed to glitches in computer programming, but so far no emergence of web-based bank robbers to rival the folklore of the American Wild West. However, what is looming on the horizon is the new threat of cyberterrorism or eTerrorism, which to date has been linked to isolated cases of virus proliferation but is destined to become a widespread problem representative of the darker side of disintermediation. For more on cyber crimes, see section 4.5.

CHAPTER 3

Disintermediation

The value proposition of technology is often determined not by the capabilities it enables, but by the rate at which those new capabilities are accepted by society and can be incorporated into everyday life or, in the case of business, into the processes that add value to its production. The implications of technology are typically not reflected in its initial value proposition but realized after it has been adopted by society and put to good use, as discussed in section 1.4. The initial business/consumer value proposition of the Internet and eCommerce technologies was the ability to directly connect consumers to manufacturers, effectively bypassing several layers of seemingly non-value-added intermediaries resulting in purchase price savings for consumers and a reduction in distribution cost for the manufacturer. However, manufacturers, distributors and consumers are now realizing that this technological phenomenon brings both market compression and channel expansion whose effects on the marketplace are not completely understood.

The first effect of the Internet on the market was its original value proposition, that of compression, in which consumers could eliminate intermediaries and place orders directly with producers. However, customers soon realized that traditional manufacturers were not prepared for this new way of buying and were, in reality, uneasy with a process that would alienate their existing distribution partners. Additionally, manufacturers who did venture into a cyberspace relationship with customers were often unaccustomed to the demands of retail customers, and their customer services departments were unprepared for the volume and intensity of customer inquiries. The compressive capabilities offered by the Internet may be, as discussed in section 1.2, ahead of the rate of acceptance not by consumers, but by venerable manufacturing organizations, who are finding it difficult to adapt to the new channel to market. This effect of the Internet coupled with market resistance did not eliminate intermediaries. However, it did result in a reassessment of the relationships between intermediaries and manufacturers and a realignment of technology strategies. The market compression caused by Internet technology brings:

- A reduction of process steps within the firm and with external partners

- A transfer of various aspects of customer service to the customer along with the associated costs. Self-service now means that the customer is spending their own time

- An aggregation and consolidation of data which can be used to develop the associative characteristics of information to support knowledge work.

The second effect that the Internet had on the market is that of channel expansion. The shortfalls in manufacturers' ability to service vast numbers of retail customers and the inability of the existing distribution channels to adopt their systems quickly to the new medium brought about the introduction of new market entrants. These new entrants were small entrepreneurial organizations that did not have a legacy of business processes or pre-existing computer information systems. In effect, they were, to some extent, able to fill the niche opportunities caused by the shortfalls in the existing marketplace. These dot-com firms rose and fell rapidly not because of any quantum change in technology, but from a myriad of reasons discussed in numerous books and articles. The Internet's channel expansive effect:

- Created new opportunities for firms excelling in customer services

- Established new firms willing to become highly focused niche intermediaries

- Caused existing firms to reassess their value proposition to customers.

That said, technology has now advanced to the point where it can fundamentally change not only the role of the intermediary, but the social contract of trust in an exchange of value. Organizations in industries that were early adopters of Internet technologies are now in various stages of restructuring, which was, in many cases, caused by the effects of disintermediation. This restructuring was promoted by Internet technologies, transforming them into a value network in which cells of competencies (represented by either an entire firm or department within a firm) offer a product or service that fills a market niche or the needs of a market segment. These cells of competencies are manifesting themselves as new market entrants, previous functions within financial services firms in connection with a niche market, joint ventures with technology firms and retail merchants, and co-opetition agreements with competitors to service market segments. Internet service providers (ISPs) and application service providers (ASPs) are examples of new market entrants supporting niche market opportunities. Successful ASPs and ISPs offer a simple and distinct value proposition: providing a business with a technology capability that is readily available, simple to acquire and offered by many competitors. The ASP value proposition offers:

- The use of shared infrastructure which reduces a customer's operating cost

- Rapid time to market because the technology is already in place and is simply made available

- Flexible pricing based on fixed cost or transaction volume

- Little or no upfront capital investment in hardware and software

- A reduced number or no requirement for internal technology staff

- Comprehensive security resulting from combining the needs of multiple organizations into a cohesive framework.

What is new is that if the margins of providing the service fall below those of operating one of the types of businesses that are offered, the service providers now have the ability to become competitors in their own right with the underlying businesses to which they provide services. For example, Computer Sciences Corporation offers ASP services for property/casualty insurance, life insurance and annuities.[97] The only thing preventing them from entering the marketplace as a financial services provider is branding and a few licenses. To keep pace with the rapidly evolving competitive landscape, many firms will be challenged not only to redefine their value proposition to customers, but also to restructure their organizations.

The 'Death of Distance' Means that You are Now a Producer in a World Market

However, what technology has done to the consumer experience is usher in the concept of the 'compressive world geography', in which consumers now realize that any product in the world can be found and delivered to their door. The consumer finds the appropriate channel to acquire the product, specifies a method of delivery, assesses whether the cost of the product and shipping is a valuable combination, and authorizes the transaction. Producers of goods and services now realize that the rest of the world must be considered when developing competitive strategies. Many products can now be viewed in the same light as a commodity and their customer base is no longer insulated by a foreign producer's lack of access to a market. Hobson described the fluid nature of products that are considered commodities:

> Each kind of commodity, as it passes through the many processes from the earth to the consumer, may be looked upon as a stream whose channel is broader at some points and narrower at others. Different streams of commodities narrow at different places. Some are narrowest and in fewest hands at the transport stage, others in one of the processes of manufacturing, others in the hands of the export merchants.[98]

The description of a widening and narrowing channel identifies new market opportunities for a globally connected business. A widening channel is analogous to the demand for an ever-increasing selection of products, and the narrowing channel indicates shortages in supply or identifies the emergence of a demand for a new product. These ebbs and flows in demand reflect the changes in product value in the new interconnected world. Traditional product producers and their distribution partners need to view their customer base in new ways. Chapter 4 discusses the details of how demographic information is changing and what organizations must do to develop new market strategies.

Organizations formulating new competitive strategies must take into consideration not only market compression and channel expansion but the underlying capabilities that the technology introduces. The value proposition of the Internet to customers consists of four key attributes: convenience, savings, a broad selection, and trust. These key attributes can be translated into five distinct actions that are at the heart of the customer experience: search, price, compare, select and ship. Disintermediation occurs when an intermediary loses sight of these attributes and actions, failing to address each item with a change in technology and/or business process. As technology makes the dissemination of information easier, it presents the customer with an ever-increasing variety of products through an even larger number of new and existing distribution channels. The numerous ways in which a customer can acquire a product coupled with the technologies enabling its acquisition creates product transparency. This product transparency is a growing concern to manufacturers because of the possible loss of brand identity, which is discussed in section 4.5.

Throughout the world, product providers are witnessing a spread of the western ideology of 'anytime, anywhere, anyhow' consumerism, which demands better ways in which to fulfil the needs and wants of consumers. Organizations aspiring to transact business in the global markets of the future must resist the temptation to model all business transactions and products to western tastes and be mindful of the preferences for goods that are indigenous to diverse geographic locations. At the present time, the western digital nations are leading the adoption of Internet technologies and English is the most prevalent language but that is rapidly changing. As the Internet matures and becomes more a mechanism to facilitate the flow of commerce, culture, knowledge and communications between individuals will reflect greater international diversity. One could argue that the early domination of the Internet by the digital nations is in some way responsible for the rising aversion and restlessness with the proliferation of western products and lifestyles. The ubiquity of mass-marketed western products combined with the marketed perception of the lifestyle that accompanies their ownership can be perceived as an indirect cause for the erosion of local value systems and beliefs. This is not to say that the Internet can cause the erosion of local culture; but it can be *perceived* as being able to do so. This perception is giving rise to trends in nationalism, anti-globalization movements and isolationism which will slow down the adoption of the technology. *Conversations about the End of Time* (Eco et al., 2000) discusses the potential danger in following a compressive course:

> The globalisation of problems, however, will necessarily require solutions at a planetary level. And yet it is precisely at this time of globalisation that we feel the need to fence off our own sphere of action, the need to narrow our focus, the temptation to cut ourselves off.[99]

Technology can be used to combat the misunderstood side of the Internet's compressive disintermediation and be used to emphasize the expansive aspect.

As it matures, the Internet will undergo a transformation as a medium of exchange. It will not merely be a mechanism for facilitating commerce, but it will provide avenues to connect diverse people, ideologies and cultures. This is not to say that simply connecting the people of the world will solve global problems, political unrest and socio-economic inequalities, in fact it could conceivably raise the level of disagreement between world peoples.

However, regardless of the Internet's eventual value proposition and its effect on the people of the world, business must embrace the new medium as a mechanism to reach market segments which cannot be penetrated by traditional distribution channels. The opportunity for value creation is to facilitate customers seeking alternative access channels to products in a global marketplace. Firms will thus be more involved in eCommerce especially in market segments which cannot be penetrated by traditional distribution channels and with existing clients who are seeking alternative access channels.

3.1 Microsoft, the New Medici Merchants

Although disintermediation is often discussed as a modern phenomenon, using technology to eliminate intermediaries and bypass middlemen has been happening for a very long time. During the Middle Ages, rising levels of population fuelled agricultural growth, which was a prerequisite for a commercial revolution. For centuries, the amount of work required to generate sufficient quantities of food remained in a tight balance with the available labour. Technology slowly changed the amount of food that could be produced by a single agricultural worker. It would be difficult to tie the shift in agricultural productivity to any one technology during the medieval period. However, successive introductions of technology increased productivity gains until there was a shift in the balance between work hours and hours of rest. When food surpluses increased, effort was directed towards governmental, religious and cultural pursuits. Merchants and craftsmen discovered that there was a market for their goods beyond the aristocracy. As productivity increased, the workforce retooled and moved towards previously undefined opportunities.

In the 1990s, technology-based workers, who would later form the bedrock of the emerging knowledge society, began to consider the balance between work and recreation. As technology increases productivity – or at least gives the individual the ability to control when and how productive output is accomplished – knowledge workers (similar to their medieval counterparts) will find themselves with additional leisure time and the need to revise their skills. Unlike labourers in the Middle Ages, contemporary workers soon realized that more often than not, it was the skills relating to leisure time that needed improvement. Organizations such as CSC Index encouraged both employees and clients to develop balance contracts in which participants in a project would set quantitative and qualitative values to work and leisure. These balance contracts were set up at the onset of a project to identify the personal needs of each team member and the ideal environment in which he or she would be most productive. Ideally, the balance contract is a way for each team member to make other team members aware of the personal and business demands made on the individual's time to enable others to incorporate some sense of sameness between each team member. By looking for similar needs, goals, problems and commitments, the entire team could identify opportunities to collaborate on a solution to make the entire team more productive. The lesson learned was that knowledge workers have similar needs and requirements to maintain a high energy environment and these similarities create opportunities to fulfil an individual's need and raise the overall team productivity. Increasing the team's productivity can be attributed to three factors: an economy of schedule, an economy of task, and a higher working morale. Scheduling economies are the product of an increased awareness of each team member's commitment and through this heightened awareness team members often broker smaller meetings, often in coffee shops and other non-work areas, and teams seek out alternative forms of communication to avoid too many meetings. Economies of tasks in many cases are accomplished when team members realize that individual activities can be divided between team members. With a greater awareness of each individual's skill, a team soon realizes that many tasks can frequently be accomplished more efficiently by breaking up tasks into smaller, discrete activities, which an individual can accomplish unfettered by the physical constraints of the workplace or work time. A higher working morale is a by-product of each individual's greater awareness of personal demands and the formation of an *esprit de corps*. Put simply, a team of knowledge workers striving for a solution is more effective than an individual trying to solve multiple problems.

However, as knowledge workers move into the new millennium, there is a new examination of the nature of work itself. As individual knowledge workers reach new levels of economic security, there is a shift in thinking from having 'a job that one may need' in order to finance a lifestyle, to finding a job that 'one wants to have' to have more time to enjoy life. The important lesson is that today's knowledge worker is re-evaluating the role of work and leisure, discovering that an individual must strike a balance (with or without a balance contract) between the demands of work time and the needs of personal time. This reassessment is often attributed to reaching a desired level of financial security. One thing that becomes apparent is the need for a continual process of reskilling and re-education while pursuing a balance between work and leisure activities. The knowledge worker now realizes that knowledge needs to be continually refreshed, and that it comes from many sources, not just traditional higher education institutions. Possessing a greater knowledge of technology, process and key business functions not only adds to the individual's long-term wealth but also to increasing corporate profitability.

Our modern interpretation of business throughout history is that workers laboured merely to increase the profits of the enterprise. Businesses in previous centuries have been regarded as primitive, unsophisticated or even idyllic and the need to expand globally, increase profit margins, streamline distribution channels and negotiate labour relations are all complexities of modern business. The same basic problems of expansion, profitability, distribution and labour, which also existed in pre-modern times, without the luxury of mass communications technologies, are often overlooked. Imagine running a large multinational organization shipping thousands of tons of products to many countries, each transacting business in a local currency and negotiating trade with a plethora of indigenous peoples, without phones, computers or any of the technologies of the last century. The fundamental problems are there, but with a higher degree of complexity and uncertainty due to a lack of a communications infrastructure. It would be naive to say that business organizations of previous centuries operated with the same drive for short-term or next quarter profits in which later twentieth-century businesses have become accustomed. However, to claim that the idea of making a profit was alien to the feudal age is probably exaggerated. The instinct for acquiring material goods as an outward sign of prosperity is and has been typical in many societies throughout time. What has changed is contemporary society's attitude toward prosperity and social class, which has become voracious in the accumulation of goods and disparate in the distribution of wealth. In the Middle Ages, the structure of society changed and a new merchant class emerged between the very rich and the poor. This new middle-class prosperity was a key driver in the economy of the later Middle Ages which contributed to the demand for more diverse products and indirectly raised the lifestyles of the majority of the medieval population. Today's baby-boom generation, for the most part, moved into the workforce in the 1960s and 70s from humble beginnings, and over time accumulated physical and financial assets that will see the largest transition of wealth between two generations since the Black Death in the fourteenth century. Our contemporary attitude towards affluence is very different from our medieval counterparts, who often equated poverty with piety. As Lopez noted, 'the paupers were more acceptable than merchants: they would inherit the Kingdom of Heaven and help the alms-giving rich to earn entrance'.[100] Even though our contemporary attitude towards the accumulation of goods may be different, the desire to acquire goods as a reflection of status is the legacy given to us by our medieval forbears.

Today the Internet is redefining the structure of the relationship between consumers, middlemen and manufacturers, testing the very limits of the transactions that bond these groups into supply and retail chains. Many manufactures (or providers) are ill-equipped to offer the level of customer service that today's society demands. Therefore, the opportunity for middlemen (or brokers) is to provide a collection of value-added services that will enhance the products or services they are distributing. As the market continues to disintermediate and organizations which provide middlemen services consolidate, a new class of middlemen will emerge, delivering a combination of products and services.

As the new class of broker merchant emerges, there will be a 'reintermediation' of the retail markets due primarily to the end consumer's inability to contend with thousands of relationships with manufacturers and service providers. This market consolidation is represented today by Internet portals, places which bring together a suite of co-branded products and services. These portals can be anything from a loose association of products linked together by shared advertising fees, to orchestrated co-opetition ventures designed to establish a market between trading partners or even competitors.

In the Middle Ages, there was an advantage to being a citizen of more than one country (or swearing allegiance to more than one feudal lord) if you were engaged in trade across geopolitical borders. Having multiple allegiances was not considered dishonourable by medieval people. In many cases, geographic areas were controlled by several lords. Medieval peasants often had dual loyalties to both a king and a local lord as a matter of necessity in a town or district caught between two warring parties. This practice of dual allegiances was particularly true in Italy, where seaports maintained previously forged relationships with the Byzantine Empire after they themselves were conquered by the Lombards and the Franks.

In the sixteenth century, we can see the start of the formation of national states, that is, European states which were formed from the political coalition of different feudal states. The formation of national states was not completed until the nineteenth century, when Italy and Germany were finally consolidated into two political units. The modern concept of 'nationalism' emerges at this moment, when the pressure for unified territory met with the expansionist desire of some states (namely Germany and Italy) in their pursuit of rapid industrialization. Today, the concept of nationalism is under pressure as the effect of globalization takes place, virtually removing national barriers in order to allow a global economy to exist. The self-imposed barriers to trade, established along geopolitical boundaries, were originally formed to enhance trade but these are now an obstacle to Internet commerce. eCommerce gives us a chance to re-examine these fundamental socio-economic structures and question not only their function, but also their requirement. The primary goal of sales tax, for example, is the redistribution of wealth within a geopolitical boundary.[101] Is the method of taxation, its collection process and the bureaucracy that enforces it the important factor, or is wealth redistribution the essential element? The Internet is increasing our awareness of these impediments to commerce, raising even more compelling questions, such as: Can another, more efficient process perform the same function? Is a global organization such as Microsoft in a position to collect and distribute taxes to nation states more effectively than the thousands of separate regulatory authorities?

Microsoft as the Glue

During the early part of the Middle Ages, the city of Amalfi in what is now Italy was an autonomous merchant seaport closely linked to the local landowners. Fierce competition for trade existed between it and the ports of Naples, Gaeta, Salerno and others along the western shore of Italy. The prime export commodity was olive oil. Amalfi forged strong trading relations with Constantinople and Egypt which continued even after the Normans conquered it in 1073. In the course of the eleventh century, the continuous growth of its trade in the Levant and Africa was accompanied and fostered by the slower development of a network of extraterritorial enclaves or colonies, whose importance hinged on the rebates on tariffs granted to them and the opportunities offered by the surrounding region.[102] Today, hundreds of years later, the same business model of building a network of trading relationships occurs in today's Internet economy. Consumers trading directly with manufactures and service providers soon realized that comparison shopping is not easily performed without the aid of a third party. These new third parties (resembling the medieval trading enclaves) or relationship brokers offer direct links to producers and provide a host of services designed to facilitate the purchasing process. The attributes of the new class of middleman merchants will be a continual forging of relationships with shared service offerings (Figure 3.1).

The new merchants will filter producers by price, quality and availability of their products and provide the customer with that most valuable commodity: Time. However, modern marketing methods ironically still reflect the trading mechanisms used by their medieval predecessors by

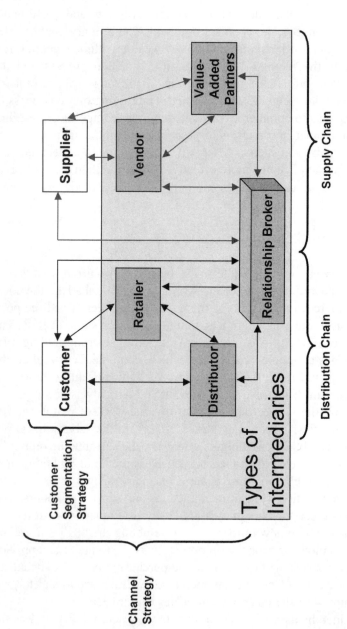

Figure 3.1 Intermediaries

offering customers rebates (or buying points) and governments tariffs (or taxes), acting primarily as a method of buying customers' loyalty. One could argue that ultimately this practice results in promoting customer disloyalty by encouraging customers to switch to the next merchant who offers a better deal. By linking these factors and marketing gimmicks to attract customers, trading portals must also provide a mechanism to filter good producers from lower quality or even bad producers. Without these trading incentives, customers will find switching portals easy and will examine their brand loyalty. Various new merchants acting as shopping portals will co-brand products simply by association on their website.

It is amazing to think of how commerce worked during the Middle Ages compared to how modern society is defining the ultimate consumer nirvana, that is, buying direct from a manufacturer. This transaction between product developer and consumer existed in the twelfth and thirteenth centuries with the beginning of an evolutionary process that continues today. If one examines the dynamics of medieval economics, one becomes aware of a set of dynamic elements working in a supply and demand cycle. In the early medieval period, luxury goods played a large part in influencing what was produced. Craftsmen or merchants were interested in enlarging the profits on a limited number of sales as opposed to enlarging the number of sales with a limited amount of profit. In the larger market of selling to the peasant population, the continual pressure on profits made it impossible to increase the volume of products manufactured without mechanization. The inability to mass produce products kept the medieval merchant focused on regulating the profit margin to a consumer base of the gentry that could afford his products.

Medieval retail exchanges were often delivered without the use of a middleman. Craftsmen simply displayed their products in the front window of their own shops and passing gentry (later the rising middle class) merely stopped, looked and purchased. Advertising and marketing consisted of simply presenting a product to a mobile or passing audience, which bears a striking similarity to watching customers in a twenty-first century shopping mall. However, when the socio-economic conditions developed in the later part of the thirteenth century, the merchant class was transformed into an economic force of great proportions. It is never prudent to overgeneralize the activities of an entire continent during any century. As in today's society, not all merchants and cities were created equal. In 1293, the volume of sea trade in Genoa was three times larger than the revenue of King Phillip the Fair's entire kingdom of France.

Another factor to consider in medieval trade was that the cost of transportation was high and had a greater influence on the price of goods. Each time the product changed hands or location road tolls and other levies were paid, so the price of the product rose to recoup the additional expense. The high cost of transportation tended to keep goods in a local or regional market to avoid additional transportation costs. The two key factors that changed the dynamics of medieval exchange were the improvement in transportation technology (that is, bigger ships) and the transportation infrastructure (that is, the improvement of roads). If we examine today's business-to-consumer eCommerce, the critical factor once again is controlling the transportation cost of the product as a percentage of the total price – a rising concern as products can be purchased from all corners of the globe.

Within the evolving cycle of disintermediation, Vikram Lund of the IBM Corporation noted that technology was making possible the formation of new classes of business interactivity:

> Three types of emerging business models: utilities, infomediaries and brokers. Each takes a different approach to consumer empowerment in applying agent technology technologies. Utilities enable customers to research and compare products in order to make faster and more informed purchasing decisions. Their value depends on the depth of their research. Infomediaries are consumer advocates that provide market information and advice for a narrower range of linked products and providers. Brokers offer advice and market information, and they facilitate complex transactions by matching qualified buyers with sellers.[103]

In sections 4.2 and 4.3, we will see that these three distinct forms of business activity (information utility, infomediary and transaction broker) can be applied to the three types of product/consumer behaviours emerging within cyberspace markets.

3.2   The Internet and the New Revolution of Communications

The torrent of marketing communications heralding the Internet as the greatest invention since the printing press is quick to point out that the initial intention of the technology is to foster new lines of communications. However, there is far less written (except in academic circles) on the effects of this technology on corporate value propositions in a greater historical context of socio-economic evolution and its relationship to international commerce. How technology alters the relationship between people, trade and the perception of value is a topic of continued debate among scholars and industry experts. The industry assumes that new communications technology will make the world a better place and commerce will flow as a natural extension of a perceived higher standard of living and increased socialization of the technology. This may indeed be true, but it would be naive to believe this scenario without first understanding the origins of technology's role in an information society.

To begin, Lopez reminds us of man's need to socialize: 'Whatever his personal inclinations, economic necessity made man a social being.'[104] As a species, humankind has an inherent need to be social. Communications between people as a means to exchange thoughts, ideas and other basic emotions has been the quest of many technologies throughout history. Greater communications between people is said to reduce the total amount of distrust between geographically separate cultures or socio-economic classes within a culture. Increased communication is said to promote good-will and a better understanding of the idiosyncrasies found in world populations, contributing to a higher degree of cultural tolerance. During the last one hundred years, more technological progress has been made along this front than ever before. Yet, this same time period produced some of the world's greatest political and social conflicts.

Since the Internet is quickly becoming an integral part of global commerce and business interchange, it is important to understand the intertwined roles of commerce, social structure and technology. These three converging forces have been labelled 'convergence', 'progress' and even 'globalization'. In order to develop a perspective of socio-technological evolution, it is crucial to examine the past behaviours of people, business and governments in order to project the next step in its development.

Roman administration demonstrated the effect of a strong central government on remote conquered locations by transplanting the values and social structure of Rome over the whole of the European continent. The fall of Rome and a return to isolationist groups of people created a void in socio-economic development and effectively thwarted technological advancement for centuries. The barbarian age of the high Middle Ages reflected a discontinued social contract that shifted the administration of governing people to local lords who remained cognizant of the decadence of central government. Within these medieval communities, powerful local lords emerged as a cohesive force to maintain order and provide a mechanism for social structure. In the later Middle Ages, the rise of town governments would compete with local lords by broadening the liberties of individuals.

The underlying characteristic of socio-technological progress is the relationship between the improvement in communications technologies and developments in the economic, educational and social systems. The efficiency of the Roman administration was a direct product of the Roman road system which provided an infrastructure for communications, commerce and military adeptness. The rise in trade and improved and more frequent communications were contributory factors to the social development of the later Middle Ages, which provided the foundations for the Renaissance. The winners and losers of technological advancement – from the perspective of individuals and skills – was discussed in section 1.6. Here, however, we focus on the quality of communications, data, information and knowledge as a product of simply conducting business (Figure 3.2).

In the twenty-first-century business, a high quality of data and information is essential to its ability to operate with an acceptable margin of profit and loss. Poor information and low quality data can effectively cripple a management team's ability to capitalize on the resources of the organization. Although the quality of the data used and generated by a firm is rarely correlated to a corporation's identity, balance sheets or income statements testify to the fidelity of information, thus placing an important role in understanding how a company functions.

The fidelity of corporate information is important because as technology changes, how we communicate and interact changes. In addition, alterations in our way of communicating influence the development of new products and services. As geographic boundaries disappear, economic activity becomes more intertwined, cultural aspects play a larger part in multinational product development and communications, and the issue of information fidelity is inescapable.

The industry speaks flippantly about the Internet's profound influence rivalling that of the printing press. This impact has typically been with reference to the speed at which information is disseminated, and rarely to the quality of what is being communicated, as we have seen in the example of the 'Wicked Bible' in section 2.2. The replicative properties of the printing press drastically reduced the cost of labour. To illustrate the quantitative nature of information fidelity, once again we turn to the printing press:

> The famous transition point in printing from the laborious handmade text to the low-cost mass production of the printed word occurred, of course, with the Gutenberg movable type press of 1440. It is important to note that this technological breakthrough was itself the product of several other technological breakthroughs – notably, low-cost paper and ink production and (introduced by Gutenberg himself) reusable molds for the type elements.[105]

Manuscripts which once took months of labour to create could be reproduced at a fraction of the cost. Seemingly, the majority of the cost was in

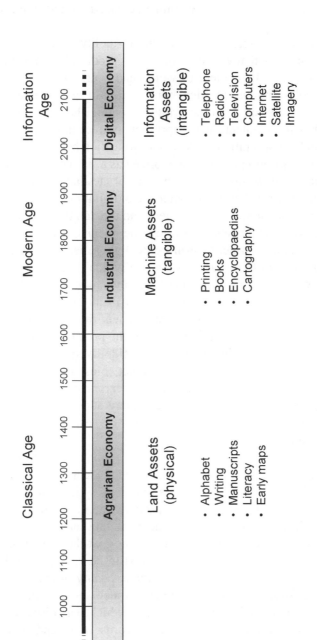

Figure 3.2 Technological economy time line

the initial set-up, and the cost per unit decreased as additional copies were pressed.

To illustrate the concept of information fidelity, one can examine a medieval manuscript that was subsequently reproduced in movable type. It becomes clear that the content or words had been reproduced, but the iconography, colouring and physical construction of each element on the original page are missing from the printed version. The words have been reproduced, but the elements which present indirect information on the context in which it was crafted are lost. This transition between manuscript and movable type printing is often categorized as a simple loss of aesthetic beauty. However, it is not only a matter of aesthetic beauty. Using advanced technology such as a computer and a digital microscope, one can examine the composition of the document and the details of each letter in order to develop an understanding of how the document was created and by what kind of author/scribe. Measuring the light reflectivity of the paper and assessing the density of the ink on an individual letter, one can infer, based on the way the ink ran down the letter, the angle of the table during the production of the manuscript, which can in its turn furnish us with information on medieval geometry. Similar scientific experiments can be conducted to provide a reasonable picture of the production process used by medieval scribes and illuminators. The fidelity of their production process was reflected in the finished product, most of which was lost during the printing revolution. Five hundred years from now, it would be interesting to try to understand how a company added value, developed products and fulfilled customers expectations by reading their quarterly and annual reports.

The goal of information in today's business climate is not to be able to reconstruct the past but to direct actions in the present and anticipate the future. That said, the fidelity of information plays a vital role in allowing organizations to put information into a proper context in which decisions can be made. Although the physical elements of data such as words can be replicated with astonishing mechanical precision, at the same time information must be placed into its proper context to be valuable. In the case of a medieval manuscript, the simple aesthetic beauty of the drawings in and around the borders of the words tells us much about medieval social attitudes, beliefs and craftsmanship, most of which was discarded when the new printing press merely replicated the words. In the end, it is important to say that regardless of losing the aesthetic beauty of old manuscripts (such as the *Book of Kells*), and a gradual loss of the knowledge about methods of medieval writing and manuscript illumination, the impact of the printing press had one undeniably positive effect: it allowed every sector of society to have access to books. What was lost in terms of beauty was gained in terms of dissemination.

The primary issue surrounding the accuracy of information is that as new digital communities are formed and culturally diverse people interact with greater frequency, the quality of information and its cultural context may determine a firm's success. Putting business information into its cultural, geographic or associative context is beginning to be recognized by firms such as the Hong Kong and Shanghai Banking Corporation (HSBC). The television commercials of HSBC in 2002 portray a firm which understands the cultural contextual significance of information, as they clearly point out the cultural significance of gestures that are indigenous to more than one country meaning different things in different cultures. A greater understanding of the context of information will be needed to avoid the temptation of developing one technological solution that can be applied to all people everywhere. More importantly, information fidelity has a direct influence on an organization's ability to collaborate with itself and becomes a critical factor when interacting with other global businesses. Collaboration between individuals inside the firm and, to a greater extent, outside the traditional organizational structure, is a key element in a long-term business strategy. The next evolution of business will thrive on individuals' participating in a connected cycle of business. Whether a firm is a supplier, an intermediary or simply a conduit for transactions, being connected and efficiently leveraging a bidirectional channel to other business enterprises is of paramount importance. During the last 25 years of technology implementations, it has been the primary goal of companies to employ technology in order to reduce operating cost and eliminate unnecessary steps in business operations. This method of using technology to automate business activities has given many organizations the desired results and in many cases a competitive advantage in their respective markets. Surprisingly, a large majority of technology projects failed to achieve their optimum implementation and, more alarmingly, an even higher percentage of these projects were labelled as failures for not reaching many of their business objectives for which they were designed. However, technologies such as the Internet, electronic commerce and innovations in desktop technology coupled with a convergence of communication technologies such as the telephone, television and the Internet are changing the way we transact business. Corporations who are early adopters to this fundamental shift in how business communicates are embracing these technologies and establishing digital pathways for customers and suppliers to engage them in new conversations. This establishment of a digital presence, which is discussed in section 4.1, and a new strategy for engaging customers in this new communications medium is similar to marketing organizations developing strategies in the early days of television, with one big exception: now geography, culture and demography do matter.

3.3 Changing the Boundaries of Geography-free Business

In order to address the impact of technology on business transactions that span geopolitical boundaries, it is necessary to define the basic premise of these technologies and their associated meanings; it is also necessary to readdress the definition of geopolitical boundaries. Without venturing into a long dissertation on the pros and cons of globalization, it is important to note the new roles that technology will play in facilitating commerce, communication, community and culture.

In *A Future Perfect*, John Micklethwait and Adrian Wooldridge put into perspective how popular culture is using the term 'globalization' as a scapegoat for larger socio-economic issues that are not being directly addressed by either world governments or business. While identifying the underlying problems associated with globalization, Micklethwait and Wooldridge dispel five myths which have been traditionally linked to this phenomenon: size trumps all, the triumph of universal products, economics needs to be rewritten, globalization as a zero-sum game, and the disappearance of geography. In their words: 'For most cultural conservatives, globalization is a code word for everything that perturbs them about the modern world, from broken homes to ubiquitous pop music.'[106] Their argument is clear, concise and puts the five issues currently associated with globalization in a perspective demonstrating how each item is linked to a hidden agenda such as national feelings of protectionism. More importantly, the authors argue that these myths are used to conceal underlying socio-economic problems. Because these issues have direct implications on how firms add value and, more importantly, will shape future value propositions, they will be examined here in more detail.

Micklethwait and Wooldridge remind us of the conditions that surround these myths:

■ *In many cases, size does not trump all*. Micklethwait and Wooldridge remind us that the history of western business is littered with large multinational firms that do not stand the test of time, citing: 'The title of world's largest bank changed hands at least six times in the twentieth century.'[107] This is but one of many examples which indicate that large bureaucratic structures in these changing business conditions are often too slow to remain viable in their own right over time. The trend of mergers and acquisitions will continue as industries redefine themselves and technology will play a larger role in facilitating that process.

■ *The triumph of universal products is predicated on a belief that everyone in the world wants to purchase products that are the same everywhere.* Here again Micklethwait and Wooldridge point out: 'Indeed, in recent years, marketing departments have become obsessed with segmenting customers rather than bundling them together. Companies err if they treat entire countries as single markets, let alone the whole world.'[108]

■ *Economics needs to be rewritten* is a myth that Micklethwait and Wooldridge addressed before the dot-com meltdown. With hindsight, their argument appears to be more than valid: 'Globalization means that competition can spring up anywhere. But the underlying rules of how to make money are the same as always.'[109]

■ *Globalization is a zero-sum game.* Here Micklethwait and Wooldridge strip away the issues that cloud globalization and address the underlying misconception: 'For some people to profit from globalization, others must lose to an equal degree.'[110] By taking a non-partisan view of the dynamics of the economics of globalization, the evidence clearly indicates that trade of all types fosters long-term economic growth. Erecting limits to trade by special interest acts only to reinforce the myth and does not make for a sound global strategy.

■ *The disappearance of geography as corporations continually search for cheaper labour.* Micklethwait and Wooldridge reveal that geographic clusters of business are needed to enable competition and that businesses operating in a global economy must weigh the savings in labour cost with the additional added cost associated with logistics.[111] Another aspect of moving business to remote geographies is that eventually the labour cost rises and one could argue that as the economies, industrial output and financial markets of the world become more and more intertwined eventually (too many years to estimate with any credibility) world labour costs will reach an operating parity.

If the role and application of technology is examined in each one of these globalization myths, it becomes understandable how technology can be associated with perpetuating them. Technology is so interwoven into the fabric of corporate activities it is often difficult to separate it from the effects seemingly attributed to it. Furthermore, the value proposition to a firm and, more importantly, how value is represented to its customers are linked to the five myths in the following ways:

- *Size trumps all* – Technology will be used to expand market presence by using customer-linking technologies to bring western products to all corners of the globe.

- *The triumph of universal products* – The Internet will bring the products of the world to our doorstep.

- *Economics needs to be rewritten* – Technology provides mechanisms to drastically reduce cost and expand revenues.

- *Globalization as a zero-sum game* – Technology enables a global work-force in which anyone can do anything from anywhere.

- *The disappearance of geography* – Technology will enable you to order globally branded products to the exclusion of local products.

Unfortunately, firms with global aspirations in the post-dot-com economy are still reciting the same technology mantra. However, since the number of total consumers who can effectively purchase goods is a relatively fixed number, there must be winners and losers in the new growth estimates of any technology company professing to decimate the competition in the emerging markets.

What is clear is that the *laissez-faire* attitude corporations are taking towards globalization can be viewed as exacerbating the issues raised by anti-globalization groups. Corporations operating in the global economy must develop a concise definition of their globalization policy in order to identify how technology will ultimately integrate into their value proposition with customers. A brief examination of the five myths isolates the role of technology in which corporations are basing value generation.

Firstly, the terms used by the technology community must be understood in the context of the technologies they represent and the actions which firms must take to employ them. 'Commerce', in its broadest sense, can be defined as interactions and activities that result in transactions between business entities, including but not limited to barter, exchange and transfer of materials or value between two parties. Terms such as 'eCommerce' denote that the transactions associated with commerce are now conducted with the use of a sophisticated telecommunications technology. If one considers that the same set of words could have been used during the early years of the twentieth century, when firms were first embracing electricity as a technology to improve productivity, slogans such as 'Powered by

Edison' or 'business at the speed of the electron' could have easily been applied. One could project that the 'e' in eCommerce is simply the new state in which business now operates. That said, the definition of Internet commerce redesignates the type of commerce as falling into two broad categories: commerce which has achieved a new level of efficiency by employing technology to facilitate transactions and new commerce resulting from the introduction of technology.

Secondly, the definition of geopolitical boundaries or, more importantly, the concept of nationalism, must be examined to ascertain the relative impact that factors have in the adoption and implementation of technology by various global cultures and nations. Nations or geopolitically bounded sovereign states as we know them today are a relatively new idea for mankind. Not that the geopolitical map is due to be redrawn in the near future, but, as we discussed in section 3.5, new technology is creating debates on what constitutes a nation state, fair and equitable taxation and the role of government in the emerging information age. These factors coupled with the cultural aspects of consumer taste must be an integral part of a firm's comprehensive management strategy when deploying brands, products, people and technology.

Regardless of the degree of cultural consumer loyalty that can be generated by technology for various businesses or market channels, organizations should develop scenarios of varying degrees of business activities and market conditions in order to react in a timely fashion to changing market conditions. A good example of technology-based scenario planning is demonstrated by the United States Air Force, which compiled a series of possible global economic scenarios to determine which type of response is warranted. These scenarios only provide a set of corollary conditions in which each could be considered in the next evolution of technology and its influence on global business activity. This type of strategic scenario planning which anticipates various permutations of future operating states is a crucial skill that corporations need to develop to stay competitive in a global market.

3.4 Collaboration and the New Global Marketplace

The Internet, intranet and extranet have one thing in common apart from the technological infrastructures: the ability to facilitate knowledge-sharing within the corporation and with external entities, what the industry calls 'collaboration'. Corporations have acknowledged in principle that people are their biggest asset. However, most companies have a tendency to treat

employees as easily replaceable commodities that can be added and sub-
tracted from business processes at will. Recognizing that employees do
possess process knowledge – or at least compartmentalized knowledge
associated with components within a larger process – firms are eager to
capitalize on information and draw it out of employees and into knowledge
management systems to record and effectively begin to commoditize
process knowledge.

What firms often overlook is that knowledge is not simply the recording
of information using sophisticated technology but the ability to associate
information acquired in the past and correlate it to an ever-changing set of
business conditions. Collaboration technologies such as IBM's Lotus
Notes, Microsoft's NetMeeting and Parametric Corporation's Windchill
present new avenues for interoperability between companies and external
business partners to reach mutually inclusive business objectives.
However, in the shadow of businesses that are starting to develop an appre-
ciation for collaborative efforts, society in some cases is viewing the
exchange of information as a cultural threat.

The cultural aspect of technology application and adoption is often
overlooked by businesses interested in establishing themselves in the
global marketplace. Elsewhere, I analysed the cultural aspects of brand
definition regarding financial services,[112] section 4.5 analyses brands in
relation to technology. Regarding the use and application of technology
itself, companies tend to develop an approach based on what they have
observed during years of research in their own countries. For example; a
US company wishing to establish itself in Ireland may depart from the
premise that consumers in Ireland tend to share the behaviours of North
American consumers. Nothing could be further from the truth. Yet the
underestimation of cultural aspects has been a problem for over a decade,
and is still so today. Governments and society itself tend to resist foreign
businesses especially when they show no respect for the nation's values,
language, religion, the 'habits of the heart' that make cultural diversity. If
disintermediation and globalization are translating into homogenization,
they are being translated wrongly. 'Cutting out the middle man' does not
mean overlooking local knowledge; it simply means making the best of
what international business has to offer. Collaboration is the way of the
future, the means to eliminate the intermediary through a close relationship
between international companies sharing knowledge of their consumer
behaviours, product advantages and so on.

One consequence of the lack of collaboration has been the growth of an
isolationist policy. For example, in 1999 the French government passed a
law that if a website (geographically located server) resides inside France,

the content of the website must be in French. This is not surprising when one remembers France's Centre for European Studies' 1995 motion with regard to the threat posed to French culture by the invasion of Anglo-Saxon Internet elements and the English language, in this case representing yet another foreign influence, that of North America.[113] The most important thing to remember is that although the world seems to be going through a process of globalization, it has never been more fragmented. In the late 1980s and early 1990s we saw Germany reunited, but at the same time we saw the collapse of the Soviet Union and Yugoslavia, single entities now reconfigured into separate nation states. Within countries such as the United States, cultural values have become so fragmented that the term 'culture of separation' has come to describe American culture better than any other term.[114] In a world where mass media apparently dictates values, fashion, religious and political stance, how to explain the diversity of electrical plugs that one needs to carry when travelling from the US to Europe? In their dream of homogeneous global values, business must not forget that globalization is not to be seen as a 'one size fits all' solution.

One company that is rightly evaluating local culture in order to establish a business internationally is the United Kingdom's Tesco. In their South Korean stores, the food chain employs local people and, realizing the importance of family values in South Korea, has 'culture centres' for mothers and their children at all their stores. While doing their shopping, mothers can take quick classes on how to cook, how to use the Internet and even how to draw.[115]

The issues of national sentiment and anti-globalization can also be found in the current debate on the Internet language. As we have already seen, France has reacted to the pre-eminence of English as the language in computer-based media. One could argue that the use of the English language on the Internet has come as close as anyone has ever got to the idea of a Tower of Babel, which ultimately seems to represent the intention of globalizing groups. However, as one can see from the growing research on multilingual websites, the issue is not going to be solved by simply accepting English as the new *lingua franca*. Governments and local companies are insisting that all websites should be translated or multilingual. The same applies to colours and iconography – certain colours, such as black and white, represent different meanings and sentiments in different countries. Certain icons and gestures are offensive in one country but extremely friendly in others.[116] An international company wanting to establish a venture in a foreign country needs to consider all this to avoid alienating online customers. As said above, the matter of culture is often underestimated by companies seeking to establish themselves internationally. The key thing to remember is to think global, act regional and look local, thus respecting local cultural values which must not be underrated.

3.5   Business Taxation and the Role of Governments

Internet technology has made one thing painfully clear: the way in which business activity is taxed in the world is too complex. As commerce crosses local, state, national and international borders, the question of how to tax commerce continues to be a topic of heated debate. In the United States alone there are approximately 30,000 recognized tax jurisdictions and within these delineated areas of commerce approximately 7,000 tax rates control the exchange of goods and services. Considering the number of local tax authorities worldwide and taking into account international trade agreements and other commerce-related regulations, the Internet and eCommerce has brought to the surface an outdated and arcane process that resembles a business process that has been made extremely complex by incorporating exceptions to the rule over a long period of time.

Government officials who once scoffed at the Internet as a viable medium for trade and commerce are now trying to determine how to tax transactions which continue to grow and cross international borders. Taxes are a levy imposed by the government on the income, wealth and capital gains of persons and businesses (direct tax), on spending on goods and services (indirect tax) and on properties. In the United Kingdom, taxes on income include personal income tax and corporation tax; inheritance tax is used to tax wealth and capital gains tax is used tax windfall profits; taxes on spending include a value added tax, excise duties and tariffs; taxes on property include council tax or local tax and the uniform business rate. Such taxes are used to raise revenue for the government and as a means of controlling the level of distribution of spending in the economy.

International taxation on goods and services will be the next big battlefield for economic supremacy. The traditional geopolitical boundaries drawn because of the invention of nationalism in the nineteenth century and subsequently redrawn after World War II become an impediment to global business if a taxation war breaks out.

In 1293, almost four million pounds (medieval currency unit, four Genoese pounds to one pound sterling used in England) of taxable exports flowed through the port of Genoa in Italy. Italy had four cities with populations over 100,000 (Venice, Milan, Florence and Genoa).[117] In comparison, taxable exports in England during the late thirteenth century were only a quarter of a million pounds. Taxation in the Middle Ages was not intended to level the playing field between geopolitical centres of power; rather, it was a mechanism for raising funds for local governing structures.

An examination of the basic premise of the American dream of home-ownership as an icon of freedom from a sovereign reveals that in reality the social contract has replaced a monarch (king or queen) with a faceless monarch embodied in the ever-growing layers of government. In order to illustrate this point, the reader can look at states that charge a property tax to homeowners. In later medieval society, an individual paid a tribute to the king *in lieu* of having to serve in military actions. This tribute was later transformed into a basic taxation mechanism to provide a ready source of funds. The land was entrusted to the sovereign and people rented the land from the sovereign. Modern property tax follows the same mechanism; people are simply renting the land from the faceless sovereign – the state/local government. In the United States, if property taxes go unpaid, the government can seize a property and place the homeowner into a state of receivership liquidating the property to settle the debt. In either case, you pay the king or the state to rent the use of land. Failure of payment has the same consequence; the mechanism is the same, only packaged into a readily accepted social contract that disguises its roots in a medieval past.

Medieval taxation is disguised in many of today's socio-economic trans-actions. The geopolitical structures of world governments rarely agree to the value, amount and level of taxation on goods and services. Adding to the complexity is the lack of agreement on what should be taxable or not taxable. Value added tax (VAT) comes with various different rates in different countries within the same geography. In the UK a single rate of 17.5 per cent is levied on goods and a few miles across the channel France has four different rates ranging from 1.5 per cent to 20.6 per cent. In another example, books and magazines are subject to VAT in some countries, but not in others.

To the dismay of local, state and federal governments, the World Trade Organization (WTO) is currently lobbying to establish the Internet as a tax-free zone. The countries of the European Community are not happy with the idea, and are trying to make sure that the appropriate tax is paid on goods bought over the Internet. Similarly, the United States has declared a moratorium on all Internet taxes until a government committee has finalized its report, which for now gives US companies yet another advantage over their European counterparts.

The Internet and eCommerce technologies give us a chance to re-examine the relationship between customers and manufactures and also the function of government and its services. In the United States, there is one central state government for the state of California, with a land area of approximately 158,000 square miles and a population approaching 34 million according to the 2000 US census. Located on the opposite side of the country, where state boundaries were drawn over two hundred years ago, a similar number of people (33 million) living in a smaller area of approximately 114,000 square miles is governed by the seven state governments of New Hampshire, Massachussets, Maine, Vermont, Connecticut, New York and Rhode Island. If government was viewed through the same lens as business, stockholders would be encouraging a consolidation of the states operating on the east coast to reduce operating cost. However, taxpayers seem oblivious to the cost of running seven governments compared to one and the potential savings of tax dollars in consolidating government functions into one state, say the state of New England. Alternatively, since many people identify with the lifestyles associated with each existing state, they could keep the basic structure of the governments in place and consolidate administrative functions such as purchasing and technological infrastructure as a way of achieving economies of scale.

Evidence of using technology in the same way that business employs it to reduce the cost of operating is the move towards interacting with government agencies electronically. The UK's Inland Revenue has made great strides in streamlining the filing of business taxes and payroll taxes by utilizing the Internet. Electronic filing of employer returns will become a universal requirement by the year 2010. What is important to note on the rising debate on Internet taxation is that it will ultimately result in world governments, local tax authorities and individual taxpayers reassessing the concept of taxation as a mechanism in the redistribution of wealth.

Electronic Voting

It is surprising that individuals have embraced eCommerce and Internet banking with its sometimes well-publicized security flaws, while being reluctant to exercise a digital right to vote, or eVote. In the minds of individuals, personal wealth requires security, privacy, fidelity and trust. The technology industry has demonstrated that commerce and banking can be conducted in this new medium within an acceptable margin of security. This must also be the feeling of the millions of people who regularly use home banking to pay bills and purchase goods online, thus providing merchants with their credit card numbers.

However, voting on the Internet remains as elusive as the medieval unicorn. The industry has created a technology that revolutionizes communications, allowing politicians to receive public responses to many of today's political issues. Yet, only pockets of experimentation are underway. There are two reasons for the reluctance – or resistance – to use technology in this way: fear of fraud, and voter behaviour (apathy and adoption).

The fear of fraud stems from the perception that elections are controlled and ballots manipulated. This fear is not directed towards the individual voter; it indirectly accuses the electoral process as being susceptible to indiscretions from within. Oddly, electronic ballots with an encrypted token could carry an individually generated authoritative key that would provide a greater ability to audit election results. For an electronic infrastructure to be a viable mechanism for a democratic process, it must demonstrate that it is trustworthy. The public must be convinced that eVoting prevents impersonation while maintaining a degree of anonymity, safe from computer terrorism or hackers and, more importantly, manipulation by individuals within the government.

Voter behaviour can be characterized as apathy and adoption. In the democratic nations where voting is not compulsory, voter turnout rises and falls as political, economic and military activities increase or decrease. Enticing people to take an active role in government is a problem that transcends technology. However, as discussed in section 2.3, technology literacy is on the rise. One could argue that the convenience and timeliness offered by eVoting may be the value proposition that will persuade voters to take a more active part in the electoral process. Theoretically, politicians could pose questions to their constituents and receive valuable feedback on the social attitudes regarding key issues, without having to depend on the media or other survey data. The value proposition to a political appointee is direct feedback versus data that may be broader in its coverage of voters. This is not to say that broad consensus data is invalid. However, using data as a source of comparison, a politician could correlate the relevance of an issue with the attitude of his or her constituents. Adoption of the technology as a legitimate medium for this type of exchange will come from creating an ethos of trust. In the UK, for example, individuals are fearful of identity cards and the possibility of votes being traced. Alternatively, votes could be cast and tabulated using existing banks and clearing networks, thus providing a new function for banks.

As Kevin Brown pointed out, another value proposition of eVoting is the fact that today's youngsters – who will soon be eligible to vote – are so used to doing things online that eVoting will perhaps be the most effective way to get them to participate in the election process.[118] It may come as a surprise that in today's society voting or not voting is a matter of personal preference rather than exercising one's right in one of the few truly participative elements of democratic societies. However, this is what voting has become, and therefore it is up to governments to make the best of the opportunities offered by technology to provide incentives and reinforce our civil rights.

CHAPTER 4

Customer Interaction

Technology has had a long-lasting relationship with bridging the actions of customers to various components of a company's business processes. These processes have typically been labelled 'customer order fulfilment', 'customer management', 'customer services' and, simply, 'order processing', which represented their basic functions. The application of technology has traditionally been focused on inwardly optimizing these processes with the express intention of reducing processing cost, increasing the number of transactions or improving customer service. Technologies such as the Internet permit these processes to be extended beyond the confines of the corporation directly to the customer. The initial focus of applying new technologies to these processes was to allow existing customers to place orders and thus lure new customers from competitors.

The new challenge for businesses using technology is to present a clear and definable value proposition to their customers. In his book *The Agenda*, Michael Hammer gets to the heart of the customer value issue: 'What customers care about is themselves, and from their point of view, your only excuse for existence is your ability to improve their lives and their businesses.'[119] Value propositions must be developed from the customers' point of view, and not from the product perspective. It is interesting to note that this seemingly straightforward statement – which most companies will attest to be their express objective – reminds us that companies rarely invite customers to help in the product development cycle or the reengineering of the customer services process. It could be argued that a company's most valuable asset is its existing customers.

Developing a customer-centric viewpoint has less to do with technology and more to do with resources, time and organizational attitude. Companies around the world are now using the Internet to establish a corporate presence, linking high-speed infrastructures to increase their customer

service capabilities and implementing customer relationship management
(CRM) technology, automating and recording every aspect of customer
interaction. Customer information, which at times is a subject of consumer
concern stemming from a lack of privacy (which will continue as a result
of more and more government intervention), is the primary source for
market intelligence and the development of customer segmentation. We
shall see in this chapter that companies must be aware of their corporate
presence and how it is interpreted by a wide variety of market segments,
and how the influence of technology categorizes products by distinct types
of purchase behaviour. This chapter will also explore how some organizations must unlearn their legacy of corporate behaviour in order to compete effectively in the new global marketplace.

4.1   A Sense of Presence

Unlike medieval people, we do not have a sense of presence in today's society. We are growing more and more detached from our families, workplace
and friends. The latest surveys of the millennium generation (post-
generation X) indicate that although teenagers are striving for individualism, they are searching for a sense of belonging to a social group. The
Internet has given many individuals a new sense of presence by connecting
them with people who share a common interest. In Zachary's words:

> Science and technology innovations are giving people the power to make over
> their identities, and they are using them. To what extent people can figuratively
> and literally reinvent themselves through a combination of computer simulations,
> computer-human mergers, biomechanics, bioelectronics and genetic engineering
> is more a matter of speculation that reasoned debate.[120]

We live in a world governed by our interactivity with the physical
elements of our daily life. Technology now permits interactions that are
representative of physical actions, such as controlling remote devices. Thus
technology offers interactions that are clearly detached from the physicality
of the action, such as creating an electronic agent that acts on one's behalf
in cyberspace. Actions, transactions and interactions that represent your
connection to the digital world reflect your cyberbehaviour and call into
question how an individual is present in the new digital information age.

Technology is enabling the average person to experience a new global
citizenship in which the traditional boundaries of geography, religion,

culture and government are undergoing a redefinition as a direct result of technological advancement. Using technology, our fundamental relationship with activities previously associated with work transforms our notion of *when*, *where* and *how* these activities are performed. Similar to the knights of the Round Table's quest for the Holy Grail, technology companies are striving to create the universal information appliance, a device that transforms information and access to and/or from any device. Using this device (conceivably wearable), interactions can be facilitated universally. That is to say, it is a device that acts as your primary interface between the physical and digital (or virtual) world.

In order to put this device into a greater context of how one is present in the digital information age, the characteristics of socio-technological behaviour must be addressed. Individual behaviour in the physical world (terraspace) and virtual world (cyberspace) can be classified into three broad categories of interactivity: public, private and personal, as depicted in Figure 4.1. Individuals in terraspace and cyberspace share a common set of actions as a result of their two-way interaction with others:

- *personal*, in which the action or infrastructure that surrounds the action is not to be shared, or shared only with a small, intimate audience

- *private*, where the interaction and data are shared with a selected organization or group of individuals

- *public*, where the action, data and other attributes are generally available to anyone.

Transactions are the product of a direct action or indirect initiation by a customer. Direct actions such as an individual actively making a purchase occur via interactive gateways such as PDAs, PCs, or bar-code scanners. Indirect actions are those carried out by an intelligent agent responding to a prescribed set of conditions laid down by an individual, such as triggering a stop loss order to your brokerage when a particular set of shares drop below your preset limit. Another type of indirect action is where a person is caught speeding by a camera and the fine is directly debited from their bank account. Both direct and indirect activities must be facilitated by a mechanism, a mode or a method of delivery, and usually are representative of a state of mind.

Of course, a person could easily behave in one way in the physical world, and yet behave in another way in the cyberworld. For example, a person could create a false identity on the Internet to purchase pornographic material digitally, not wishing to reveal his/her true identity, while

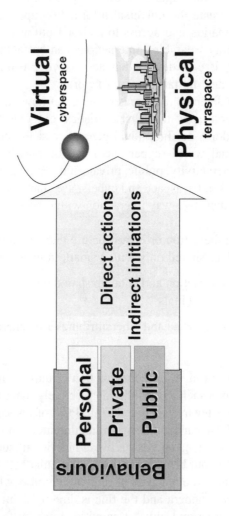

Figure 4.1 Categories of interactivity

in the physical world he/she would never dream of purchasing such material in a bookshop because of social pressure. The Internet reduces the physical distance to products, but can decrease the bond with society. It could be said that the Internet provides that same level of anonymity as living in a large city. The ability to construct your own identity on the Internet raises the question of ethical digital behaviour and the extent to which one develops a cyberworld reputation. Moreover, the virtual reputation carries the same or greater risk of being misused or misappropriated by persons unknown to you in the organization.

Apart from the potentially dark side of technological advancements such as the Internet, PDAs, biometric devices, wireless communications and other new high-tech toys, the value proposition they present to technophiles, technologists and the rest of the technology-adept world is clear and easily understood. These devices offer convenience, timeliness and simplicity in interacting with the ever-increasing plethora of digital products. The key is the seamless interaction with many devices, reducing the number of interfaces that an individual must learn. The transitional nature of technology, discussed throughout Chapter 1, means that each new generation of technologies – and indeed any manufacturer's device – will require learning how to use a greater number of commands, key clicks and set-up features. For those of us who have not yet mastered our VCR programming, the universality of these devices means they only need to be mastered once.

It is interesting to note how the designers of these technologies describe their use, as in the following scenario: while on holiday, sitting on the beach on a Caribbean island, you can use the device to instruct your VCR at home to record your favourite television show, check to see if your house is OK, and order milk and eggs from your local grocery shop to be delivered on the day of your return. The most striking aspect of this future scenario is that it is devoid of technological foresight, that is, it is designed to emulate only today's behaviour. Firstly, it subscribes to the notion of the old television broadcast model, where one must wait until a programme is transmitted by the network. In this day and age, one should be able to go to the TV network website and simply order the programmes one would like to watch. Secondly, it assumes that, while on holiday, one wants to be continuously connected to the environment from which one is actually escaping. Finally, it assumes that everyone waits until the last minute to do everything, while we are evolving into a society which plans nothing and seeks instant gratification. Cynicism aside, the promise of this technology is that it offers uniformity in the heterogeneous world of digital devices; conceivably, it will increase the rate of adoption in all technologies that subscribe to this universal protocol.

These devices enable an individual to extend themself by initiating activities, collecting information, collating data and conducting transactions on behalf of the user or in agreement with the user's intentions. For example, if the device recognized a behaviour pattern in the user (such as the type of book read), it could identify these books, rank them, search the Internet for the best prices and, based on these criteria, present the suggested books to the user for acknowledgement, and, after agreement, placing the order on his or her behalf, completing the transaction with credit/debit card information. The most integrating aspect of these devices is their ability to learn and record one's behaviour. It is through this process of feedback that an individual will modify his or her physical and virtual behaviours to reflect their connections in the digital society. The proliferation of mass media communications technology coupled with the Internet make market differentiations possible, allowing consumers greater choice in highly specialized areas of products and interest. This specialization of interest is fostering a narrowness of focus in special interest groups, comprising popular social movements like anti-globalization, nationalism and religion.[121]

Conversely, in the early media hype of the Internet one would have thought that cybersex was the greatest thing since the invention of electricity, until it was realized that the girls on the Internet were really male computer nerds logging on with female usernames. Their logic was that with a female username you would be more likely to engage another female in conversation and start the seduction process. The big joke was there were many 20–35-year-old men trying to seduce each other. On the other hand, pornography does have a presence on the Internet, but not as rampant as the media would like us to believe. A recent study concluded that the vast majority of pornographic sites required a major credit card to acquire anything that was not readily available on cable television. The role technology plays in providing seemingly transparent access to indecent material is discussed in section 5.4. The key may be in restricting *opportunity*, not *access*, by proactively making people aware of the consequence of their actions. For example, if you knew that whatever you watched on television would be printed in the newspaper the next day for everyone in your town to read, would you change your viewing habits?

Now that we have moved beyond the hype about Internet growth, corporations are starting to use the Internet as a viable medium of exchange, and a new sense of presence is needed. Individuals are less likely to attach their username to a piece of questionable correspondence travelling through a corporate firewall with the chance it could be traced back to the source. Developing an understanding of individuals' actions in cyberspace and their associated behaviours is key to assessing the types of product that can be enhanced, sold or merely facilitated by a combination of new technologies that have been categorized as eCommerce enabling.

4.2 Three Kinds of Product

Products are purchased according to an individual's needs, wants and desires. The problem is that the ability of products to fulfil these urges is only known to the individuals, which businesses can only guess at. Marketing, sales forecasting, demographics and a host of other science-based mechanisms are designed purely to assist in the guesswork.

In the latter half of the twentieth century, technology was applied to improve the art of guesswork, or to increase the effectiveness of the instruments measuring guesswork. A new value proposition has emerged for technology with the advent of the Internet; that of reducing or eliminating the guesswork in sales forecasting and other marketing activities. However, this seemingly exciting value proposition entails developing an in-depth understanding of the changing behaviours of customers around the world. Our current product/desire fulfilment behaviour is a result of sales and marketing efforts during the course of the twentieth century, most of which were heavily influenced by western culture. These efforts centred on making individuals aware of a product, then convincing them that the acquisition of these products or services was a necessity. What is or is not a necessity is at the heart of Internet technology's value proposition, requiring us to understand the buying habits of customers worldwide.

Necessity and luxury go hand in hand; defining one leads to a definition of the other. Werner Sombart puts the issue in the following context:

> Luxury is an expenditure in excess of the necessary. Obviously, this is a relative definition which becomes intelligible only when we know what constitutes 'the necessary.' This again may be determined in either of two ways. We may view 'the necessary' subjectively, with reference to some judgement of value (for example ethical or aesthetic), or we may attempt to establish an objective standard to serve as the measure of 'the necessary.' Such a yard stick is found either in man's physiological needs or in what may be called his cultural wants. The former vary according to climate; the latter, according to the historical period. As regards cultural wants, or cultural needs, the line may be drawn at will; however, this arbitrary act should not be confused with the above-mentioned subjective evaluation of 'the necessary.' In this case, luxury has two aspects: qualitative and quantitative.[122]

Sombart's discussion about the importance of culture in the context of purchasing is extremely relevant to firms which, because of the use of the Internet, now find themselves in a global environment in which North American models find difficulty meeting the expectations of customers in diverse geographies. Different types of product, such as commodities, luxuries and staples, are influenced to a greater or lesser degree by cultural idiosyncrasies. Table 4.1 combines the concept of necessary and luxury with implications of cultural differentiation.

Product types – or product classes – can be grouped by a variety of attributes related to the use of that product by customers within geographic or cultural boundaries. On the Internet, products and services fall into three broad categories of products, according to consumer behaviour:

■ Products you will buy because you already know them (such as stationery, airline tickets, CDs, books and so on)

■ Products you have to experience once, such as a shirt where you experience the attributes of the product (that is, quality of material, colour and so on) and you purchase the second item via the Internet

■ Products that you will not buy until you experience them (such as a car and so on) but you will price compare, search for features or options, make the final purchase decision once you have experienced the product and then use the Internet to facilitate the transaction (that is, register at the Department of Motor Vehicles, purchase insurance and so on).

Many important lessons can be learned from how consumers typically behave, and how products need to be structured. As I argued elsewhere,[123] the last few years of eCommerce revealed that consumers often migrate between these categories as their level of trust increases. Consumer product-selection behaviour can be correlated with product categories to design the overall customer experience or level of customer engagement. Each type of product can be purchased using Internet technologies: products you know, products you have to experience once using the Internet to resupply, and products that you may not buy, but the Internet will facilitate their purchase with information. Each type of product has an optimum corresponding level of customer engagement: interactivity, intimacy and immersion.

'Products you know' are products and services with which you are familiar (such as a book or a CD which you may want to purchase); in this case, you go to the Internet simply to make the purchase or place a future order. Retailers such as Amazon.com have found that product-linking presents the consumer with additional choices for cross-selling. For example,

Table 4.1 Luxury versus necessary goods

Culture		Necessary		Luxury	
		Physiological	*Cultural*	*Qualitative*	*Quantitative*
	United States	Means of transportation due to long distances between home and work	Basic car	Luxury car	Luxury car plus urban vehicle plus motorbike
	Europe	Means of transportation due to long distance between home and work	Train or car	Luxury car	Two luxury cars
	Africa	Distances between home and work are small	Bicycle	Car	Two cars
	Asia	Distances between home and work are small	Bicycle or old car	New car	Luxury car

when you buy a book, Amazon's website suggests other titles which you may consider buying. For financial services, this can be a powerful cross-selling tool in which a customer can be advised that other customers in the same income, lifestyle and/or financial position recently purchased a home and a certain insurance on the property, contents and liability, establishing a beneficial connection between buyers, owing to their common interests or purposes.

'Products that need to be experienced once' centre on developing a tactile relationship or, in the case of services, an experience in order to inform and make oneself acquainted with the product, for example purchasing clothes, shoes and other accessories. Given that the size and make of clothes vary from vendor to vendor, it is useful to try online shopping once, select one's size and then remember this size for future purchases (websites could help customers by always remembering their last purchases and sizes for future references). The UK's Top Shop and Debenhams have websites which do not allow much customer choice when online shopping. Past Times, on the other hand, has a much wider variety of products, which can be purchased in store or online, and the website provides the necessary information to make the customer confident in the purchase.

'Products you select and facilitate' require a longer consumer education process and typically characterize higher priced items in which visual examination and tactile experience of the product are essential to the purchase, but the decision to purchase can be helped by additional information, and the transaction of the purchase can be accompanied by the need for other services. For example, the purchase of a car does not necessarily require physical inspection. However, people often want to test drive a car before buying it. The Internet can be used to find the car of choice, limit the options and pinpoint a dealer or person wanting to sell the vehicle. Using the Internet, car registration with the national or local authorities can also facilitate additional transactions that support the purchase, car insurance policy can be obtained, and financing can be prearranged. Firms such as CarMax and Autobytel were pioneers in this process.

Product Types and Customer Experience

In summary, these three product categories relate directly to the customer experience in transacting with the providing organization, and are composed of a variety of customer-driven fulfilment preferences. Obviously, as the complexity of the product increases, the need to educate the customer rises, and the underlying technologies to deliver these products can be vastly different.

Organizations in the retail industry have developed 'click-and-mortar' strategies. Retail customers adopt technology at a rate slightly ahead of banking technologies, and their buying habits are more impulsive for low-cost items and planned for higher priced, durable goods. Consumer and small business transactions take place within three types of environments surrounding a transaction: the interactive, the intimate and the immersed. Each environment offers the background for the customer experience by providing details on the item to be purchased, communicating pricing, displaying shipping options and in many cases describing the way in which the product can be used or applied. The environment is divided into two distinct domains: cyberspace and terraspace. Let us now turn to the levels of customer engagement in these domains.

4.3   Three Levels of Customer Engagement

The Internet has provided businesses with a new look at how consumers behave beyond a simple transaction of buying a product or service. What is most important to learn from the retail markets is that the behaviour of consumers within both domains is surprisingly analogous to how the transaction is executed, and unlike the way in which the interaction occurs. Customer behaviour and engagement can be broken down into three increasing levels of engagement with the selling and fulfilment process within a firm: it starts as simple interactions or interactivity, intensifying to a higher degree of customization or intimacy, and finally evolving to complex customer relationships or immersion. These three levels of behaviour (or customer engagement) represent a challenge for retail firms because they are in conflict with the objectives of standardization of services to a generic one size fits all strategy, which retailers have been using for decades. For example, anyone can see how hard it is to choose an item of clothing when sizes are small (S), medium (M) or large (L) with no variation in between. The fact that retailers have been using this sort of strategy for years will make it harder for them to adapt to the levels of customer engagement which is, after all, what they should be aiming to conquer.

The first level of customer engagement is interactivity, or the simple act of facilitating transactions such as buying stock, ordering a book, or paying your bills with home banking. This level of interaction between buyer and seller is simple and relatively straightforward, being designed merely to sell commoditized products. The second level is intimacy, whereby a seller

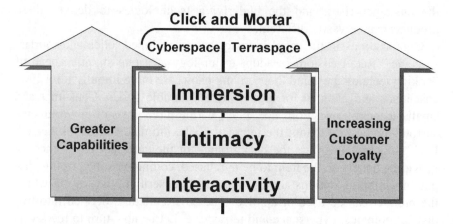

Figure 4.2   Click-and-mortar strategy

uses accumulated knowledge of the customer coupled with purchases made by other customers to recommend additional products or services. The third level is immersion, the encapsulation of multiple products and services into a suite of offerings which fulfil customers' immediate needs and anticipate future needs. In a click-and-mortar strategy, the more 'immersed' the customer becomes – as illustrated in Figure 4.2 – the more loyal the customer becomes.

Customer Experience: Interactivity

The first level of engaging a customer is interactivity. Interactivity means the act of transacting with the firm, the customer wants to buy an item and their request is quickly fulfilled. This level is best represented as a dialogue or exchange between a community, customer or an employee that results in a transaction of value. For example, browsing online and purchasing a book or plane ticket is the simplest form of interactivity. This level often represents the highest volume of customer interactions, in which regular purchasers are very price sensitive. It can be said that competition between websites tends to drive down the price of goods because customers are not loyal to one particular vendor. Customers who engage in an interactive relationship are often disappointed with the quality of the experience when using a company's website. Technologies such as Korean-based AvataSoft's T3 Studio can increase the overall customer experience by taking two-dimensional photographs and transforming them into three-dimensional images to enhance a product's presentation. This technology adds value to customers who are looking for additional information on the product. This type of software application strives to simulate the tactile experience of shopping which many people find missing from the cybershopping experience. It is naive to think that all shopping, even for mundane consumable items will be eventually replaced by Internet shopping. The physical act of shopping is a social phenomenon which people enjoy.

Customer Experience: Intimacy

The second level of engagement is intimacy, which places the customer at the heart of a total process of customized solutions or collection of products containing options and allowing the grouping together of components, to form a 'customized solution set'. This level is often represented by a community or affinity group that functions as a consolidation body and associates transactions. For example, on the US Airways website, a frequent flyer can select a preferred travel destination; this location will be monitored and when the prices change to the customer's advantage he or she will be informed via eMail on the reductions or special offers.[124]

Customer intimacy is not limited to big multinational corporations. From a micro-economic viewpoint, customer intimacy can be enhanced by simple delivery technologies which give the greatest flexibility in offering value propositions for small businesses. For example, PayCell is a wireless technology that allows a trader to be as mobile as a customer, disconnecting the sale of products from any physical infrastructure in order to conduct business remotely. The UK is known as a nation of shopkeepers and Keith Brasher of JusPerfick in Soham, Cambridgeshire, demonstrates how transaction-enabling technology greatly enhances the value proposition of a small to medium-sized enterprise (SME). Local outdoor markets offer local people and tourists the opportunity to make impulse purchases. Being able to facilitate credit card payments is vital in creating the perception of convenience which often closes the deal. However, a trader without a telephony-connected, card-processing device must use the traditional credit card process of making a manual impression of the card. The trader will not know if it is a fraudulent card user until late in the day when entering the credit card transactions into an attached reader. The value proposition of the PayCell to the trader is clear: a minimal risk of fraud and a reduced risk of robbery associated with carrying cash. These facts, coupled with the overall cost of a wireless device reaching parity with in-store technology, create a compelling reason for traders to migrate to this technology. For customers, the value proposition is equally compelling: it allows an individual to make a purchase with the same expressed trust as in a store connected with infrastructure, and the traders can create a more intimate experience by focusing time on the customer, while reducing the time spent facilitating the payment.

Customer Experience: Immersion

The third level, which is most difficult to achieve, is called immersion. In this level, the customer *is* the process and the firm provides a total environment to supplement a lifestyle with anticipatory services. Few retail firms have achieved this level of customer behaviour and many dot-com firms, such as Peapod.com and Streamline.com, who tried to apply this to the mass market, realized too late that most customers are not prepared to bear the expenses of this level of service. In fact, each market segment may indeed have a different idea of what is the immersion experience.

In all cases, the three types of interaction culminate in a complex set of relationships between the company and the customer. Technology can be used to discover the patterns of customer behaviour attributable to developing loyalty. Moreover, the behavioural patterns can be assessed to improve the customer relationship and linked directly back to profitability. This relationship analysis is instrumental in identifying customer attrition and improving customer retention.

One facet of the new customer experience will be the deployment of electronic 'valagents'. Valagents – or 'value exchange agents' – are intelligent agent technologies that provide a bridge between advice and action in financial services. Value exchange agent technology can be applied to any or all of the aforementioned levels of a customer experience because they can add value not only in facilitating transactions and negotiating on the customer's behalf based on predetermined rules, but they can also sense changes in market conditions and inform the owner of the new state of intended transactions, and wait for the owner's confirmation to proceed. Preist of Hewlett-Packard noted that:

> As the time and cost of making a contract drops rapidly, the nature of contracts will change. Contracts between businesses will no longer be things laboriously set up, lasting for months and years. Instead, they could last for as little as a single transaction. New electronic marketplaces, trading good such as bandwidth on

transatlantic cable connections, will come into being. Agent technology will form a central pillar of this new world of business.[125]

At the present time, agent technology is focused on the individual acquiring the agent, providing it with instructions (rules) and sending it into cyberspace to execute on the individual's behalf. The value proposition for companies providing customers with this type of technology is to enable a customer to perform basic functions and participate in predefined activities such as a news clipping service. A customer who uses a valagent issued by a firm providing intermediary services, such as America on Line (AOL) or Amazon.com, could be allowed to take part in product purchasing activities already in progress but with other agents, such as:

■ Standard agents: an individual defines the needed product, establishes the conditions or rules according to which the agent will act and determines the methods of payment and delivery.

■ Branded agents: allow the individual to define the needed product, provides predefined conditions or rules based on the customer who is looking for similar items, thus giving the individual options for the execution of the rules. This type of agent also provides aggregation services in which the agent collects information on the execution of this action and coordinates delivery with other agents which the individual has issued, or other agents that are part of the branded provider. For example, an intermediary service provider might allow users of a certain agent class to participate as a buying group and negotiate low price or combined delivery.

The second type of branded agent could be organized within an intermediary's market space. For example, Amazon could permit an agent to execute within the domain of Amazon's offering and with the product offerings plus its affiliates. This type of agent confined within the Amazon domain could have privileges such as special pricing and products not offered to free-roaming agents.

A third type of branded agent could be deployed externally or with an intermediary having a predetermined mission to seek information along a vertical industry. To illustrate: a customer wants to purchase a book, and the agent has to find the best price from booksellers and buying groups in that particular industry; this could occur horizontally across an industry in which a customer has a desire that is predefined by a brand definition. For example, I have £15,000 to spend on a car; I have two children and drive

20 miles to work every day. What is the best car for me? In this case, the valagent investigates the Internet or a collection of predetermined sites and negotiates, based on each criterion set by the individual, or else the valagent subscribes to criteria that others have developed for its use and executes only if the resulting agreement is within the original criteria. Methods of payment and logistical preferences could be selected at the time of execution by initiating confirmation transactions such as eMail. Preist also observes that:

> Agents will not only negotiate. They will also play an active role in all aspects of electronic commerce between businesses, from the decision of what to purchase to after-sales support. They may determine when to initiate purchases, by automatically monitoring inventories and making predictions about future stock requirements. They may keep track of customer accounts, determining which new products customers are likely to be interested in. They may monitor a product after sale, and inform the supplier when it needs servicing.[126]

One way in which valagent technology could be applied to the firm's value proposition to customers is by deploying agents that enable transactions at each level of the customer experience, as illustrated in Figure 4.3.

Valagent technology presents an opportunity to personalize a customer's experience to a high degree by fostering greater levels of interaction and, more importantly, *trust* (as the provider of the agent is inherently acting in the best interest of the customer).

Valagent technology is not confined to applications external to the firm; they could also be applied to support information consolidation and data exchange. Jim Eckenrode of TowerGroup Research and Advisory identifies a prime example of where an agent could be employed:

> To date, the complexities inherent in exchanging data between systems of different types have limited an institution's ability to understand the true nature of its relationships with its customers and to process transactions across systems as efficiently as possible.[127]

Internal valagents could be focused on complementing various activities within the organization and executing them in line with corporate goals and objectives. For example, within a large multinational firm which offers a wide variety of products globally, a new product launch could employ agents that combine the purchases of several types of products in order to develop a profile of what kind of individual is most likely to purchase the new product. The resulting information could be broadcast to agents already

Customer Engagement	Valagent Name	Goal
Interactivity	Commodity seeker	Find best price and find best delivery time.
Intimacy	Holistic acquirer	Determine selection; rank findings; find best price; find best service; find best delivery time.
Immersion	Market sensor	Sense market conditions; determine selection; rank findings; act on changes or trends; inform on results.

Figure 4.3 Valagents and levels of customer engagement

seeking alternative products and information exchanged on the new product. Theoretically this new product data could be created before the physical product is even in the production phase, and it may be used to assess market demand even before manufacture of the product. In theory, a firm could develop two classes of products: *real* and *proposed*, or 'imagined'. Products could be defined and developed virtually, with pricing data transmitted to agents who negotiate on future deliveries.

More immediately, internal valagents could be used to supplement applications such as CRM systems by providing information linking customer activities to tangible behaviours and actions. The customer behaviour data obtained from agent technology could be synthesized into information to develop market and channel strategies. It is to these that we now turn.

4.4 The English Channel and Demographics

In the medieval period, the concept of demographics and market channels was unknown. It is easy to say the English Channel was a boundary that not only separated geography, but created a barrier between cultures. Geography and natural boundaries have been the primary element in developing and maintaining individual cultures, now expressed as nationalism. However, nationalism is often revered as stemming from an ancient association or binding of people to a specific land. It is actually a modern invention stemming from the 1800s. Prior to that period, the allegiance of an individual was to a sovereign lord, not to geography.

It is difficult for today's marketing mavens to appreciate the simplicity and complexities of the medieval marketplace. However, the simplicity of those markets provides valuable lessons for today's global business. Medieval society comprised several broad categories: royalty, gentry, clergy, military, merchant class, peasant class and administrative class. Each class was ultimately defined by birth. However, they all vied for the same goods and services, such as clothing, weapons, food and spices such as pepper. It was the rising demand for new sources of spices that led to an explosion of trade with many parts of the world and the eventual discovery of the American continent. Medieval merchants did not have the analytical sciences of market segmentation, customer behaviour and demographics. They merely identified that people needed or desired certain goods from nearby markets and distant lands and brokered the exchange between parties. This value proposition is strikingly similar to that of the modern dot-com companies; it is simple, concise and relatively uncomplicated.

Technological innovations in transportation such as shipbuilding enabled these transactions to increase in volume, making necessary larger, more formalized organizational structures. In many cases merchants began financing their own expeditions and evolved into merchant bankers. Unlike their Internet-age counterparts, they were concerned with the preservation of resources and viewed growth as a series of opportunities independent of the entire enterprise. This pursuit of new market opportunities is centred on a timeless formula which sounds like our contemporary definition of a value proposition: people would pay a premium for goods which they cannot readily acquire locally.

However, the complexity of the medieval marketplace, which was a combination of religious custom and sovereign market rights or local guild controls, has now been replaced by technology, marketing, advertising, trade laws, licensing and legislation governing merchantability of products and taxation. The medieval catalyst for establishing and maintaining a market was, in most cases, religion, a cycle of fairs and festivals that is absent from contemporary western market capitalism. Not surprisingly, the religious influence and cultural aspects of markets and commerce is often overlooked by western multinational corporations expanding into areas less influenced by western capitalism. Global products need to incorporate regional idiosyncrasies that reflect the tastes of indigenous peoples into not just products, services and brands, but into their application of technology.

Technology plays a critical role in the ability to enhance a value proposition. Individual types of technologies such as wireless devices, biometric sensors and even the Internet need to be applied to a company's value proposition in accordance with the social adoption of each device by market sub-segments. However, companies often take concepts to their extremes, and many firms are needlessly creating more micro-market sub-segmentation than is actually necessary, which can result in customer alienation. As Wiersema puts it:

> Mere variety and multiple choices make choosing the right solution the customer's job. And that's a job they may not be prepared to handle.[128]

Therefore, organizations participating in a globally aware market space must strike a balance between providing customers with an ever-increasing range of products and organizing offerings into logical associations such as products that facilitate a customer's lifestyle. In any case, product offerings targeted to a specific market sub-segment must present a clear and discernable value proposition, regardless of the technology used to deliver it.

Technology should be viewed as the mechanism for product delivery and value realization.

Market Segmentation

Sales and marketing departments are realizing the value of information technologies as they apply powerful database engines to analyse customer transactions. This analysis centres on discovering the essence of customer behaviour in order to understand how a product's value is perceived during the buying process. This information is used to develop profiles of customer behaviours which indicate the type of individuals that are prospective new customers and identifies products that are likely to be purchased by existing customers.

One method used is that of market segmentation, the division of a market and its customers into homogeneous groups. Each segment reflects a group of characteristics separating one set of individuals from another. An individual's likes, dislikes and purchase behaviour can be used in a model of future behaviour, resulting in isolating specific buying trends. This approach to customer analysis was first used in the 1950s. Now technology enables the examination of customer behaviour with increasing levels of data granularity. This type of analysis becomes increasingly important when organizations are moving to a mass-customization marketplace. The value proposition for market segmentation and its related technologies is that:

- It can identify the needs of smaller groups of customers with similar characteristics sharing a common behaviour

- It identifies customers not receiving services or 'market niches', providing an opportunity to develop a new product or service

- It can correlate product data to identify low-volume buyers and customers who are unintentionally ignored

- It enables companies to classify segments by value, profitability and other criteria that can be matched to marketing campaigns, promotions and other distribution activities

- Simply, it avoids sending inappropriate information to certain groups of consumers.

Market segmentation was once limited to organizations with large budgets. Technology gives even the smallest company some level of market segmentation capability. How markets are segmented is a matter of the complexity of the product and the depth of the market offering, which varies from company to company and product to product. The most popular methods of segmentation are: demographic (age, income, education level, gender, occupation); geographic (location, population density); psychographic (personality traits, lifestyle, hobbies and attitudes) or behavioural (brand attraction, benefits sought, amount of usage and number of purchases). When combined with product types and the levels of customer engagement, these provide a powerful toolkit for pinpointing future customer activity.

4.5   King Richard II and Branding Strategies

One of the ways the Internet and related technologies are changing how we communicate is the notion of brands. Are brands simply a mechanism to entice consumers to select and purchase a product, or does our sense of who we are drive the selection of the products we buy and the companies we use? The answer is yes to both. How a product is branded influences not only its appeal to customers, but also how an individual feels about himself or herself. Brands are governed by three factors: quality, satisfaction and a meaningful distinction. These three factors must appeal to an individual's values and beliefs, or be relevant to facilitate a lifestyle. The value of a brand is its ability to comply with the desires, needs and wants of individuals who, in most cases, are similar to other individuals within a demographic group. Technologies such as the Internet, biometrics, PDAs and other ubiquitous devices are redefining not only our perception of brands, but the delivery and composition of products and corporate identities.

In this sense, brands add value when they possess a distinctive value proposition to a customer, fulfilling a customer's desire at the right price point. That is to say, that the price is reasonable with regard to a customer's perception of the product meeting his or her needs.

As I have argued elsewhere, the competitive landscape that has come about primarily as a result of technological evolution now demands a re-examination of the composition of brands and their relationship to products and services. Firms can reinforce existing products by developing a dual branding strategy for cyberspace and terraspace.[129] The Internet can be viewed as a channel to specific market segments in which old products

can be recast, new products can be introduced, and new niches can be identified. A brand must incorporate these factors in its strategy, as Clifton and
Maughan maintain:

> Whichever way you look at it, brands today are the most demonstrably power-
> ful and sustainable wealth creators in the world. The term 'brand' and the prac-
> tice of branding are not only being applied across the full spectrum of
> businesses; they are now being applied across any type of organization that
> seeks to create a relationship with its audiences over and above day to day
> process and cost.[130]

A click-and-mortar strategy addresses both terraspace and cyberspace,
presenting the customer with the perception of a new and exciting product
coupled with a stable and established firm. Stability was less important in
the early years of the Internet; however, as the channel matures and the
value of the goods purchased increases, consumers are more aware of the
need to service a product during its lifetime and are showing concern about
the increasing number of Internet business failures. Stability can be
achieved by creating a strong anchor brand that represents the values
expressed by the firm such as high quality, excellent customer service or
speedy delivery and reinforced by a physical presence and market awareness at the global and regional levels. The dynamic nature of today's
marketplace demands that brands quickly adapt to reflect changes in
customer requirements or market trends. Organizations that are increasing
their product offerings, participating in joint ventures or mergers, and
transacting business in global eMarketplaces will need a cohesive branding
strategy that shapes how global is their reach and how valuable their products are to the local markets which they serve. However, when rebranding
a firm or a product, it is important not to alienate customers during the transition period, instead efforts must be made to retain customers.

Contemporary brands that are increasingly dependent on technology for
their appeal, development and distribution – or are simply given new
access paths to market by technology – often have overcomplicated strategies. Striking the right balance between product/brand and customer/
market does not have to be a complicated process when developing a brand
that is technologically enhanced. As I argued elsewhere, insights into the
simplicity of a branding strategy can be found in Nigel Saul's examination
of England's King Richard II, who faced the problem of how to change the
perceived loss of royal power after the actions of the Appellants in 1387.
During the 1390s, Richard's reign was a resolute effort to reinstate royal
authority not by military action, but by a set of actions that bear a striking

resemblance to the elements used in a modern branding strategy. Oversimplifying, it could be argued that King Richard's methods could easily be employed by any advertising/marketing/public relations firm, because they address the fundamental nature of brand identity and perception management. In the case of Richard II, the use of language, ritual and iconography created the idea of what it meant to be regal, the brand being the sovereign himself. This use of imagery and language are still the fundamental building blocks of branding strategies today, in which the use of logos, images and words define contemporary products and link them to the corporate brands they represent.[131] Firms embracing the Internet today as a viable channel to market can profit from adopting the same basic methods employed by Richard II.

As Saul said: 'If he was to re-establish his authority and power, Richard needed not only to build up support and win friends, but also to do something more: to convince his subjects that he was mightier than he was.'[132] Richard's method was clearly to create imagery. Iconography, heraldic symbols and, most importantly, the use of language distanced the king from his subjects. In effect, the combination of the royal iconography and the introduction of phrases such as 'your highness' and 'your majesty' set the king apart from the rest of society. Richard's commissioning of portraits, heraldry and iconography provided the physical links that individuals could relate to and offered a relationship to the king.

The Image of Value

For most corporations, the branding of services must reflect the overall value proposition to customers and exemplify the values of the organization delivering the service. For example, the new value proposition for financial services is the customer's relationship with the bank and an advisor who guides customers through the plethora of financial product offerings. In a globally connected business environment, service firms will develop an image of value in three fronts. The first is the Internet or virtual world, which needs integrated service offerings that are easy and convenient to use. The second is the physical or local world, demanding a reinvention of the brand network targeted at all demographic sectors. The last is the interconnected partner network, which requires providing and receiving value from brokering services with affiliated organizations.

As previously said, in each distinct channel, a brand must carry a clear value proposition to customers, that is, a differentiated product that is indigenous to a geography or emerging market opportunity that must be formed in line with the overall objectives of the brand. Advice for developing a strong image of value is best expressed by San Jin Park of Samsung Electronics:

> I think a brand is an embodiment of the comprehensive promise made by the company to the outside world. It's a proposition of the value provided to customers by the company, and it's all the underlying corporate activities that support that proposition. All these constitute a brand.[133]

Therefore, traditional local businesses with aspirations of growth are challenged to reinvent themselves locally while engaging global channels and new market entrants. However, image and brand are only the first step in a solid value proposition; delivery technology, driven by a robust infrastructure, is the execution part of the value equation.

Richard II employed a calculated strategy to transform the image of the king. He did not just create a self-centred image by a complete reinvention of the relationship between the sovereign and his/her people; Richard realized that the development of the image of kings was the primary mechanism to improve the power of the monarchy. He was responsible for the creation of the first successful English brand.

Retailers could learn much from Richard II, as they clamour to build gee-whiz websites which often disappoint with a less than expected upturn in purchases by consumers. The introduction of the Internet as a legitimate avenue for facilitating purchases has turned established marketing channels upside down and the traditional lines of branding have become blurred. Establishing a brand based on quality and focused on customer service is the key to branding in the new economy. In the past branding was focused on the product, and good customer service was what separated two similar products. Global Internet shopping is still in its embryonic state with the United States clearly an early adopter of this new purchasing medium. US shoppers initially used the Internet for price comparison. Although price sensitivity has been a brand differentiator, as the market becomes saturated with eTailers, customer service will become the prime differentiator in branding strategies. Features such as free shipping, first time buyers' incentives, coupons and cash back offers constitute the bulk of the existing brands strategies.

However, firms selling products through a combination of physical retail outlets and virtual cyberstores have a bigger competitive advantage over pure Internet offerings. Retailers embracing this combination of sales channels have been dubbed 'click-and-mortar eTailers'. Consumers are looking for the best product at the best price and want a combination of offerings that make them feel like they are getting a good deal or saving money. One advantage of click-and-mortar organizations is that they can integrate both retail channels by allowing consumers to return goods purchased online at any one of their retail locations. In many retail organizations, this concept becomes problematic. The new online division gets the sales credit and the local branch's profit and loss statement reflects the returned merchandize, making them look less profitable. Organizations will need to develop a comprehensive design for their internal business processes, how those processes are measured and how the business operates under a combined digital retail – or eTail – strategy.

After highlighting the positive effects of Internet branding, we must mention a few of the negative aspects of it. One of the problems that companies are finding are those related to cybercriminals, people who abuse a certain aspect of the Internet, such as hacking, passing viruses and, more recently, stealing and abusing brand names. As Kehoe argues, one of the most common practices of the latter type of cybercrime is 'brand-borrowing'. It is not unusual to be, for example, searching for something on a well-known website (let us say, Nintendo) and be diverted to a porno-graphic site instead.[134] Sometimes, just changing the ending dot-com to dot-net may allow an individual or corporation to create a website with the name of a famous brand but offering a completely different content.

Together with the problems of brand-stealing, cybercrimes are the concerns which companies now express regarding the brand names dot-com. With the fall of the dot-com in the year 2000 as a means of doing busi-ness, came the fall of the terminology itself. 'Incubators' and 'dot-com' are no longer favoured when new companies choose their names. This is an important point which shows that no matter what the company's business is, the company always needs to protect itself and its brand from potential pre-conceived notions that society will employ when making a choice whether or not to do business with this or that company.

One last aspect of branding which cannot be ignored is the cultural one. As said above, even brands of large multinationals have to indicate a relationship with the local company in order to allow the business to succeed. One example of the poor application of a brand name in a foreign country was Coca-Cola's foray into the Indian market. Established in India in the early 1990s, Coca-Cola has not been a success, actually coming 41st on a list of customers' preferred drinks, despite its massive initial invest-ment.[135] The reasons for this range from a poor evaluation of the actual potential market for the beverage (the largest part of the Indian population is what can be described as 'rural poor'), dietary issues, income, consumption preferences, and the actual non-existence of something that can be called 'an Indian market' because of the existence of several different market segments. McDonald's, on the other hand, seems to have been much more effective in increasing consumer interest in its products: special sandwiches and a special menu in line with dietary restrictions have made the fast-food brand more acceptable to the Indians. In the end, as we have said, it is not how much you invest that matters, but how wisely you evaluate the potential market and how you brand your product in line with customers' needs and preferences.

CHAPTER 5

The Digitally Connected Renaissance

The eBusiness revolution, heralded by the ever-growing suite of communications technologies, has failed to deliver the quantum change in business operations. This significant shortfall in the delivery of perceived benefits is because of the overhyping of capabilities, a lack of action in addressing business transformation and a lack of a clear value proposition in which the technology would act as an enabler. The overestimation of capabilities, contained in the marketing hype generated by the technology companies and the media, failed to consider the rate at which companies can absorb the organization and procedural changes needed to accommodate the new capabilities that technology presented. Although the technology presented new opportunities for organizations to rethink themselves, the rate at which businesses redefined their internal and external business processes was much slower than the expectations of the customers. In most cases, it was because the investment required to redesign processes was not factored into the timely delivery of benefits. Internet technologies enable an organization to reduce business process latency by reconfiguring not only the processes themselves but the intervals between the process steps. The Internet also enables new distribution capabilities and reinforces communications with customers and suppliers.

One thing is clear, however: the new business models brought forth by the Internet gold rush demonstrated that all models, regardless of their inventiveness, must have a measurable value proposition and a sustainable return on investment. Many of the new Internet-based business models were based on future savings or the acquisition of new customers, not on sustainable earnings.

However, organizations which dismiss the potential long-term impact of the Internet on global business must rethink their position. The Internet demonstrated the need for international and domestic businesses to increase the level and frequency of information transfer in the execution of business operations. Customers' lifestyles are changing; this fact requires business to operate at a time which is convenient to the customer. Technology is the key in accommodating this new dimension of order fulfilment and customer expectations and, as we shall see, the continued redefinition of social behaviours will increasingly influence the construction of a business's value proposition.

5.1 Medieval Social Change and the Digital Renaissance

In many societies at different times, an event or series of events takes place that drastically alters the fundamental elements in the socio-economic balance between supply and demand. In the fourteenth century, the Black Death ravaged the population of Europe and Britain, and the sudden, drastic reduction of available labour changed the relationship between the gentry and the peasant class. Peasants who typically worked for a local lord realized their toil had intrinsic value. In many cases, peasants were lured from one village to another because of higher wages. Until this time, the lower rungs of the social hierarchy (that is, lower gentry, peasants, serfs, and so on) were given land by the local lord to produce crops to feed their family, a percentage of which was retained for the lord's use. As time progressed, the lower gentry who swore allegiance to the king and the upper levels of the aristocracy converted the time they pledged for military service in campaigns such as the Crusades to payments in kind to the royal treasuries. This became the primary building block of the medieval currency and because of the Black Death peasants and serfs began receiving various forms of wages. This sudden reduction in population, which ranged between 20–50 per cent in some areas and as high as 100 per cent in isolated areas, coupled with the innovations of new technologies, was the starting point of an irreversible change which resulted in the Renaissance. When social change is combined with new technologies, the resulting process leads people to develop misconceptions about the true nature of technology's effect on society, which Cooney noted is still true today:

> The way in which new technology, including information technology, affects our lives is one of the very complex problems at the limits of our understanding. Major innovations in technology eventually change the whole social and natural environment within which we live. The speed and complexity of change lay a burden of analysis on human intelligence which it sometimes seems that intelligence is not able to cope with.[136]

In effect, technology is blamed for many social problems to which it is only minimally connected and often the true nature of technology's influence is realized after the passage of time. The Internet and other communications technologies have the same disruptive force in reshaping today's society as the Black Death had during the Middle Ages. Cooney does not describe 'informatics technology' as a negative force, but as a mechanism for social evolution:

> New informatics technology will play a significant role in making self sufficiency an attractive option. At present [1985], most people are dependent on jobs or on the state for the income with which to buy the means to live. By enabling the present large scale technology to be miniaturized, simplified, and adapted to the home or local community, informatics will enable people to become relatively independent of the larger economy, of commercial pressure and of bureaucracy, none of which any longer provide everyone with income yielding jobs. In particular, by enabling communities everywhere to communicate quickly and cheaply about common problems, the micro communication technology will reverse the present trend towards greater and greater dependence on the central bureaucracy and its 'macro information technology'.[137]

Therefore, if one considers the arguments raised in Chapter 1 on the intention of technology and its ultimate results, one will place technology in the greater context of changing the global socio-economic environment, thus concluding that the post-dot-com era of business is the beginning of a renaissance in the application of technology. Nevertheless, there has been a reduction of Internet traffic which cannot be solely attributed to the dot-com failures, as Liikanen points out:

> The slowdown in the Internet revolution or more precisely the total number of people using the Internet for commerce is due to a variety of factors; the erosion of the technology's novelty, concerns of security especially in Europe, the slow proliferation of transmission medium such as broadband and a focus that has concentrated on the technology not the people using it.[138]

Conversely, digital communities are a new dimension of communications and intercultural exchange. It would be difficult and even imprudent to predict their total influence on humankind. However, they are now part of the greater human learning experience, and will usher in a new chapter in global business.

5.2 Medieval Communities and Their Digital Counterparts

In medieval society there were several hierarchical social infrastructures providing an unconscious framework in a loosely connected social contract. An individual belonged to a social class, religious persuasion and fiefdom with loyalties to a sovereign, allegiance to a local lord, and in the later Middle Ages, with the advance of merchants and town trade, with a socio-economic hierarchy. Many of these social structures were a fact of heredity, not a conscious choice made by an individual. However, there was on occasion the opportunity to alter one's place in these social structures, usually due to a special circumstance. The majority of the population was subjugated to the land on which they lived (serfs or villains), binding them to a specific task or set of tasks that through community need and not planning benefited the entire social order of the geographic community.

What was true in the Middle Ages is true today: the majority of the modern population is bound to working for a single corporate entity or employer. Traditionally, a career consisted of working for one employer throughout one's lifetime. However, in the United States during the last two decades, this changed as a result of a new feeling of self-worth (as opposed to Europe, where workers were forced to leave). Workers have been encouraged to be mobile and change jobs, seeking higher wages. The attitude of contemporary American society seemingly rejects the medieval notion of class; in reality, American society accepts and reinforces it. The notion of class is reinforced firstly at school, where children are taught that factory and manual labour workers need little education, whereas professional workers are smarter and require more education. The goal of labour, both manual and professional, is to add value, to fulfil a corporate need. Concepts such as 'free agent nation' are only starting to gain legitimacy in American society.

Knowledge workers can be found in both categories of labour, adding value by virtue of what they know and how they apply their knowledge. In designing business processes, it is often the experience of workers closest to the process that yields the breakthrough insight to a new process design.

Technologies such as the Internet now make it possible to revaluate the traditional socio-economic contract with employers. Knowledge workers – who are no longer bound by technology – are asking themselves: Do I still want to limit my value to one company? Will I get more satisfaction (and/or salary) by spreading my value across several corporations and minimize the risk of not having any work during times of economic downturn? Like the feudal barons of the Middle Ages, who came together to ward off invading enemies, the corporate elite has been practising this for decades. Corporate officers who sit on multiple corporate boards of directors, spreading their knowledge, receive from each company compensation packages less than a full-time employee. Yet, this type of cross-fertilization behaviour is frowned upon when applied to other levels of the organizational hierarchy.

Technology now gives individuals with specialized skills the opportunity to rethink this traditional relationship and develop a multi-organizational working state similar to an agent. Not to be confused with consultants, whose allegiance is to another corporate entity, the opportunity is for free agents to be connected in a new way to corporate entities, thereby establishing a new set of social contracts with profound implications. Analogous to having several part-time jobs, a specialist can perform a discrete activity for several employees during the course of a day or week. Tax codes, benefits, healthcare insurance, investments are just a few of the things that will have to be redesigned to fit a new social contract. Corporations are beginning to look at these phenomena with renewed enthusiasm, primarily because of the potential to reduce operating cost. Pay for the talent when you need it and use only the amount you need. At first glance, individuals will greet this change in the social contract with fear and anxiety because it changes some of our core beliefs in the social views of how we work.

The first group of individuals that will naturally gravitate towards the agent concept are people who have been downsized or outsourced – having felt the pain of corporate disloyalty, they will be less likely to pledge allegiance to a corporate entity. However, as an agent serving multiple companies, the individual learns a valuable new skill, that of business management, which will benefit all employees as a by-product of this work environment. In effect, the agent worker is running his or her own micro-business. The agent must master the practice of maintaining cash flow, record keeping, small office administration and customer services functions. The individual may never get an opportunity to master all these skills within a corporate framework; in order to survive as an agent, however, he must master them. Loyalty to a group of employers is directly proportional to the working relationship that the employers nurture with the agent worker. The one consolation for people going through this process of transformation is that there is a feeling of *controlling one's own destiny,* not being solely dependent on one employer. In addition, if an employer suddenly makes one redundant, the impact is less severe. This redefinition of the social contract between employer and employee means that a large majority of people will be unprepared for the new roles they must play and quickly realize the skills they are lacking. This once again

stems from an individual's foundation of learning and the need to reform
educational curricula to prepare individuals with adequate skills for the
new working environment. The reform in education is thus both the driving
force and the effect of the changes in the business environment and the
nature of work.

One argument for narrowing the curriculum differences in American
schools is that the introduction of intelligent environments will demand a
broader level of knowledge. Technology companies envision a world in
which every type of device is connected via an array of various networks
which will coordinate, inform and detect the actions of every individual
doing everything. Orwellian as this may seem, if the history of technology
offers one lesson, as we discussed in Chapter 1, if society finds a technology valuable, it will be adopted regardless of the implications to ethics
or privacy. One could argue that the increased paranoia over security since
the September 11 tragedy will accelerate the development of an environment that seeks security, and that will support technologies that foster
security because they bring a higher degree of safety.

Regardless of the social implications, or the preparedness of individuals
to engage in a connected society, a world where a myriad of devices all
communicate with each other presents business with opportunities to add
value in a variety of ways. The underlying premise of this new environment
is that technologies which traditionally were activated by the intervention
of a person (switch on, switch off) will now have the ability to exhibit
conditional behaviour. Businesses will construct their value propositions to
enhance and exploit this new ability. For example, in automotive technology, an individual can sense the state of his or her vehicle and assess the
conditions under which it is being driven. When a maintenance event is
approaching – such as oil change, tyre wear or vehicle inspection – the car
can deploy an agent to determine where the owner should take the car
based on price, availability or any other criterion. Using cellular eMail, the
car can send a message and make an appointment, conceivably logging into
the individual's electronic calendar to keep him or her informed. The same
could happen, for example, with a printer whose print cartridge is almost
out of ink; instead of telling the user of the computer, why not inform the
store where the computer user normally buys cartridges and get them
delivered, thus saving the individual time or the annoyance of running out
of ink? This technological scenario is predicated on technology 'sensing'
the physical state of the device's environment and anticipating changes in
its conditions.

Technology's ability to be both proactive and reactive coupled with its
influence on an individual's personal and corporate behaviour refocuses

our attention on the role of the corporation and its ability to generate value in this new technological environment.

5.3 Corporate Castles, the Bastions of eCommerce

In the Middle Ages, the local lord typically built a castle and installed a moat around it to defend the inhabitants from enemies or invaders. The presence of the imposing structure of the castle provided a psychological impact on the local population, travellers and rival factions. Today's corporate websites have taken a similar approach, constructing firewalls and other security measures to prevent the malicious intentions of potential hackers and provide a secure medium to transact business. However, a castle was more than a building or residence of a wealthy lord or king. It was a centre of administrative power; it provided defence capabilities, commerce and a sense of order. Whether the sense of order was motivated by fear or loyalty to a protector scholars have debated for centuries. It does bear a strange similarity to today's corporate culture. Employees have been attached to companies through fear of job loss, loyalty to past corporate performance and many of the same reasons that can be equated to medieval society.

As with medieval society, the corporate mindset (many times magnified by the technology organization) has moved from a protector-provider attitude to an exploiter commoditizing workers' activities into a very fluid workforce. For example, firewall technology was developed with one primary function in mind, to protect the corporate computing environment from hackers and other individuals that can harm, damage or manipulate corporate information. The technology is now being employed to monitor employees' activities, prevent employees from visiting questionable websites and censor information so that individuals are not wasting company time looking at material that is deemed inappropriate for them. This phenomenon began under the guise of filtering out pornography and is now branching into other material the company deems inappropriate. The next logical step is to stop people from seeing sports scores, the stock market, news broadcasts and so on because it wastes time. Yet employers are excited to know that employees are now working at home executing various tasks in order to keep up with the increased levels of communication on their own time. Maybe the next Internet filter software application will enable families to filter out parents doing work at home after working hours. However, while this does not happen – much to the chagrin of wives, husbands and children of businesspeople – some corporations are now using web-caching servers to copy from the net only those pages that are deemed appropriate and making them available on their intranet for employees. Although this sounds well intentioned, the implications are counter to the very nature of the World Wide Web. It does bring to mind a question: By exposing individuals to the vast amount of information on the Internet, will they become smarter or more informed? The decline of the Middle Ages can be attributed to the increase in knowledge and literacy beyond the aristocracy of the day. As people became more knowledgeable, they demanded more rights and self-government. As Michael Hammer put it:

> Corporate walls have traditionally been high, hard and heavily guarded. We can think of corporations as fortified castles that transacted arms-length business with each other. Typically, companies defined themselves in terms of a discrete set of products and services – making valves, distributing snack foods, or insuring middle-income clients. Their inputs included orders from customers, raw materials from suppliers, and various forms of market intelligence. Within the castle these inputs were processed to produce outputs that were tossed over the walls as products and services for customers and payments to suppliers. The company's processes were self-contained; they began and ended at the company ramparts. The classical strategy of integration was one of expanding the castle walls so as to encompass even more within it.[139]

Corporations will use technology at an ever-increasing rate to redefine their business process and endeavour to remove many of the internal walls of the corporate structure. The barriers are products of two intersecting structures: the transition between process steps – which is inherent in transferring work between functional groups – and the passing of information within the hierarchical bureaucracy. The second evolution will be to continue this process of technological transformation with processes beyond the confines of the corporation to external partners and other entities.

In the Middle Ages, a primary source of defence was to erect walls around a city or castle to repel an attacker's ability to conquer and lay siege to the population. Today corporations have embraced the fact that doing business and performing core business functions on the Internet or a private extranet is the new way business will be conducted. However, safeguarding corporate information from unwanted intruders is being done with the help of firewall technology. A firewall or information filter provides a sense that only legitimate users or trading partners have access to information. Some overzealous technology managers have tried to use firewall and filter technology on their corporate user's community to keep individuals from visiting sites on the Internet that they have deemed unsuitable. Resources would be better spent on providing users with self-servicing filters that allow them to establish filters to keep out the unwanted eMail traffic plaguing many users. Firewall technology can also be leveraged in a proactive manner to manipulate corporate data and make it available to individuals within the corporation in a variety of forms. Filters used in conjunction with intelligent agents can broker the exchange of corporate data on behalf of a user and provide information by which decisions can be made. Many user communities' initial reaction to the implementation of firewall technology is negative, seeming like big brother is looking through information that may be harmful to us or that individuals are not responsible enough not to visit questionable sites. An effective strategy should not attempt to restrict or monitor user behaviour and thereby alienate people. A comprehensive strategy is to create an environment so rich with information that individuals will not have time to look for information that does not enhance their job. The cold reality is that individuals who are bored at work and use the Internet during working hours to play will eventually find some other medium to play. So, why punish all users with gross impunity when social pressures in the workplace will correct unwanted behaviours?

If we consider the question of undesirable activities and corporate security, we can determine that there are two distinct operating philosophies:

- A reactive strategy (such as the erection of a firewall to thwart enemies coupled with the institution of software filters to govern behaviour)

- A proactive strategy of self-direction, in which the company outlines its expectations of individual behaviour and trusts people to act in a professional manner, self-policing the actions of their peers, in the same way corporations embraced casual work clothing.

These two operating philosophies can also be applied beyond the corporation to individual lifestyles with regard to the growing apprehension around the Internet's influence on family values and other social problems.

5.4 Parental Priories and the Quest for Values

In the Middle Ages, the Church acted as the primary control mechanism to influence social morals and structured the behaviour of individuals with ritual and dogma. The standards of conduct controlling society were implicit in the rules of chivalry and explicit in the guidelines expressed in the Bible and other church doctrine. These guidelines to societal behaviour evolved from the Roman-Judaeo-Christian legacy of morals and ethics passed down over the ages to the present day. These morals now influence the development of the Internet, in many cases without considering the long-term implications of the involvement of morals and technology. Nowadays, in particular, it is clear that cultures around the globe *do not* share the same ethical, moral or religious values; what will then happen if one nation's ethics and morals start hindering the development of Internet technology in another nation? Likewise, if the Internet has no limits and no parental guidance is available, how can one protect one's children from its potentially damaging contents?

The technology industry, the media and finally the government have all jumped on the high-profile media hype of protecting children from Internet pornography. Special interest groups and the government, each having very different motives, are all supporting their own particular agenda. Let us examine these motives and understand what the implications of these socio-economic behaviours are and how they are similar to a set of motives employed by medieval society to control the values of the population. It is crucial to understand this progression of moralistic behaviour from the Middle Ages to the present day as this behaviour continues to affect individuals today. Even if the majority of western society is distancing itself from religious values, the morals and ethics behind the religious doctrines are still very powerful. In eastern societies, this is even clearer, as the importance of religious values is more evident. In the western world, for example, the morals of one generation, and what is or is not 'socially acceptable', change constantly. What was considered pornographic in the 1950s is no longer thought to be so. What was considered outrageous behaviour in the 1960s is today perfectly acceptable. The question of what is offensive to society is relative, and is not only attributable to generational issues (as said above, geography and culture play a very important part). In a world that is constantly moving towards globalized values, how can we ensure that different levels of tolerance will not translate into censorship?

In the digitally connected world, media hypes are the single most important behaviour creators. The industry has the clearest motive: to sell software by latching onto the anti-pornography media hype. Companies get free advertising and sell a lot of software that caters to the need for an electronic babysitter, one which will prevent one's child or teenager from meeting a paedophile on a seemingly innocent chatroom. Frightened parents caught up in the fear of child abduction and moral decay seek to protect their children from visiting pornographic sites by using software filters and other censorship mechanisms. The early users of the Internet did not even know of or how to access pornography until it was reported by the media. As pornography was tucked away in obscure places that only a very experienced netizen (a citizen of the Internet) could find (that is, before search engines), the media was indeed responsible for creating the curiosity and the opportunity for children to access pornographic sites. Therefore, it could be assumed that most children discovered dirty pictures on the Internet thanks to the press coverage – which also reduced the pornographers' advertising costs. On the other hand, the media highlighted the easy access to *all* sites on the Internet. One could argue that making Internet pornography news is legitimate; however, encouraging parents to become frightened by using isolated cases as a general rule is mere sensationalism.

The other fear that the media brought to our attention was the phenomena of children meeting the lurking masses of rapists, child abusers and abductors waiting at every Internet service provider's (ISP) corner. Yes, there are reported cases. However, to prove any point anyone can find any number of isolated incidences that are statistically flawed. As a percentage of total crimes, the Internet abduction is miniscule in comparison with similar crimes in people's own neighbourhoods. The Internet, like any medium that gives children access to material that is objectionable to society, must be regulated by parents in the home. Parenting begins with the individual families, not with technology. If government, for example, passes a law that all pornographic sites are forbidden and anyone who looks at them will be prosecuted, this would rightfully be considered an invasion of civil rights. The responsibility to educate and promote individual choice – and choose according to one's values – belongs to the individual. More can be done by a parent playing an active role in a child's access to the Internet than any software you can buy.

We must not forget that pornography is a current preoccupation of western nations with regards to the Internet and the freedom of access to information that it promotes. In other nations, however, the issues of Internet freedom and censorship – either cryptically masked as protectionism or openly referred to as such – are quite diverse. In China, where traditional media outlets are censored, the Internet seemed off limits until recently, when the government punished three websites which were allegedly divulging 'harmful information' about China.[140] The fact that the punishment coincided with China's defeat in its World Cup football debut against Costa Rica, when members of Internet chatrooms expressed their frustration with the Chinese team, made it very clear that in China the Internet is not free from censorship – and in a matter which any western nation would find most trivial. As always, it is important to remember that different countries have different cultures and values, and not all nations will react the same way to the same threats and opportunities.

Protectionism

Individuals seeking to protect themselves and their children from disturbing contents on the Internet are gravitating towards solutions offered by
two avenues of thought. The first avenue is that of individualized censorship, or enclaves of similar values. A self-censorship or family unit regulation of information takes the form of purchasing software packages such
as Filtered Internet Solutions (FIS)[141] or WiseChoice.[142] In this type of
service, pornographic sources are identified and filtered from the viewer.
One could argue that the sales pitches used by the majority of these
vendors are not selling security, but capitalizing on fear, as indicated
by NetAngle:

> Unfortunately, there are dangers associated with allowing your children to surf
> the Internet unsupervised. Much like you would not allow your child to
> purchase alcohol or see an X-rated movie, you should not risk exposing them to
> the filth and evil that exists on the Internet.[143]

In some cases, search engines can be blocked. Needless to say, children
today are very clever and often more computer-savvy than their parents; to
bypass the rules and gain access to pictures or websites containing pornography is therefore as easy as finding one's uncle's hidden Playboy magazines. These intervention technologies work by using filters based on word
compositions, in which certain words can block certain websites, eMail
attachments and so on. In other cases, the technology works using algo-
rithms which analyse the physical contents of a file (for example searching
for photos with flesh tones) to determine its offensive nature and duly
delete it or prevent the opening of the file. A side effect of this particular
technology was suffered by a consultant who innocently eMailed his
PowerPoint presentation to a client, only to have it rejected time after time
by the corporate filtering software. An analysis of the presentation showed
its disgraceful content: one of the images used was of a woman's head
showing a significant part of flesh in the neck area. It happened to be a
scanned photograph of a £10 note and the reprehensible image was Queen
Elizabeth's neck.

To thwart the use of text-based filtering, pornographers in some cases
simply changed the names of files containing illicit pictures, calling them
'biologyhomework.jpg' instead of 'bignakedbreasts.jpg'. Filters that
employ photo analysis have been bypassed by adjusting colour levels and
placing text at the bottom of photos to indicate how to reset the colour back
to the original.

The second avenue is the establishment of enclaves of similar values, that is, locations on the Internet where the content is carefully controlled and prefiltered to support a specific ideology or set of common beliefs. Christianliving.com is an example of a social enclave which promotes a sense of protectionism by advocating a particular environment. As expressed on the Christianliving.com website:

> Rest easy: our tamper-proof, adjustable server-based 'Smart-Filter' system safe-guards your family from online pornography and other harmful influences, so you and your loved ones can surf safely. And our filter is optional, so you can also sign up with Christianliving.com without a filter.[144]

Clearly, the 'optional filter' is probably targeted at part-time Christians or people struggling with their own personal morality.

These technological solutions, regardless of moral motivation or simple profit incentive, do exemplify an individual's right to make a choice and reduce the need for government intervention. Scholars, theologians and industry experts have been engaged in the debate over promoting the regulation of the Internet by government. Although they are not united in a solution, they recognize that government-based censorship in one area leads society down a slippery slope from which it is often difficult to recover. Castells describes the paradox that the Internet brings to society:

> We are living in an age of 'informed bewilderment', in which the elasticity of the Internet only intensifies the contradictions with which we have to live. The Internet, to give one example, genuinely expands individual freedom and yet also enables corporations and governments to exercise more control and surveillance over what we do.[145]

The issue of the preservation of morals, the enforcement of ethics and the control of societal behaviour will continue to be the subject of great debate within national boundaries and become more intense as individual nations begin to realize that citizens in cyberspace can cross international boundaries in the wink of an eye. That said, the one shinning light through this dark cloud of Internet opprobrium is that it does reduce the amount of time children spend on other pursuits, as noted by Bridge:

> The internet, more specifically access to global information is significantly affecting the lives or at least the behaviours of children. Children use the inter-net mostly at home, and in many cases are reducing the amount of time spent watching television.[146]

Here again, the problems associated with the issue of access to materials is *not a technological problem* but a social one. The computer use and network security policy of Southern Utah University (SUU) addresses this problem and places the matter into the hands of the individual:

> The rights of academic freedom and freedom of expression apply to the use of university computing resources and university-hosted web sites of faculty and students. So, too, however, do the responsibilities and limitations associated with those rights. The use of university computing resources, like the use of any other university-provided resources and like any other university-related activity, is subject to the normal requirements of legal and ethical behavior within the university community. Thus, legitimate use of a computer, computer system, or network does not extend to what ever is technically possible. Although some limitations are built into computer operating systems and networks, those limitations are not the sole restrictions on what is permissible. Users must abide by all applicable restrictions, whether or not they are built into the operating system or network and whether or not they can be circumvented by technical means.[147]

Simply, the SUU is declaring that people using a public medium of communication within an academic environment must use common sense in adhering to the rules. If you want to engage in activities that might be considered offensive to some people in the community, you should go and buy your own computer and use your own service. The beauty of this policy is that it requires people to use the world's most advanced computing system to solve the problem: the brain.

The most upbeat policy on the use of the 'porn filled Internet' comes from the least likely source, the Holy See:

> And even though the world of social communications 'may at times seem at odds with the Christian message, it also offers unique opportunities for proclaiming the saving truth of Christ to the whole human family. Consider … the positive capacities of the Internet to carry religious information and teaching beyond all barriers and frontiers. Such a wide audience would have been beyond the wildest imaginings of those who preached the Gospel before us … Catholics should not be afraid to throw open the doors of social communications to Christ, so that his Good News may be heard from the housetops of the world'.[148]

The Vatican's policy on the Internet acknowledges that there is a darker side to how parts of society use the technology, but recognizes the enormous potential to influence and perhaps lead people in a different direction. That said, technology can be applied to address the social, moral or behavioural problems in two ways: by special interest groups wishing to impress hidden agendas on others, or in a benevolent manner, promoting personal choice.

5.5   Extranet Trading Partner Enclaves

The commercial revolution in the twelfth and thirteenth centuries was fuelled by a steady rise in the demand for more diverse products and the growth of the population. Until the rise of the middle class, the demand side was represented by a simple balance between two classes, namely the very rich (who had the means to acquire goods but seldom needed to purchase them) and the lower peasant class, who needed products but did not have the financial means to make purchases. Commercial growth was centred in towns where craftsmen were able to create a variety of goods and depended on trade to acquire everything else that they did not produce. The towns also provided a mechanism for early merchandizing by displaying wares so that other townspeople, visitors and rural dwellers could see what others were purchasing and desire those goods as well. As optimistic as this picture seems, there was still starvation, poverty and hunger – which despite great strides in technological advancement are still prevalent in twenty-first-century society.

Commerce and trade has always been constructed around a relationship of trust. Intermediaries act as a buffer between buyer and seller to broker the equitable transfer of goods and payments to each party with implied and expressed trust. The reputation, brand, and network of relationships represent an implied trust in which a new customer can measure the value of the relationship and compare it with the experience of others. The more pragmatic element of trust is that of an expressed trust such as a guarantee, warranty or insurance that the exchange will occur without detrimental effects to either party. This expressed social contract of trust in an exchange of value has typically been represented by a physical contract or deal. However, technology is now able to emulate and enable an expressed trust between parties that was previously squarely in the domain of the intermediary. However, *trust* is a mutual relationship between customer and intermediary, which in the new connected marketplace must also extend to manufacturers and suppliers, as indicated by Davidow and Malone:

> For its part, the manufacturer must reward this supplier support with trust. Until now, firms have protected their interests by lining up multiple suppliers that could fill in for one another in case of failure. Second sources were identified in case a primary supplier failed to perform. By the same token,

suppliers were proud of pointing out in annual reports how widely distributed their business was. Being dependent on a narrow customer base was considered to be a great risk.[149]

The closer compression of the traditional supply and distribution chains means that there must be an integrated set of relationships not merely to facilitate the transfer of goods, but to build a link to long-term commerce. The value of trust is proportional to the length of time in which business is conducted. The initial transaction requires a combination of an expressed trust and faith, subsequent transactions build on this and it becomes an implied trust. It is equally important to note that when organizations interoperate or become co-opetition partners, all members of the value chain must develop the same or at least a similar operating philosophy in order to reach an operational synergy, as described by Davidow and Malone:

> In the business model of the future, customers will have far fewer suppliers. The just-in-case supply philosophy will be increasingly obsolete. On the other hand, suppliers will be dependent on fewer customers. A customer's failure will be extremely damaging to the supplier's business.[150]

The key to creating this interoperability is to develop a robust and predictable technological infrastructure. The robustness of the infrastructure should be in its ability to provide a network that readily accepts a wide range of compatible technologies that interface using a standard protocol. A predictable infrastructure offers seamless integration of successive new technologies to everyone who is part of the network. Thereby, a technology infrastructure works at its optimum when it is invisible to the participants in the process. As I have argued elsewhere, one can extrapolate the broad use of these technologies to an end which infers that a technologically expressed trust may eventually circumvent the need for an implied trust.[151]

When the Internet was first viewed as a viable medium for trade, pundits heralded a new age of disintermediation, where consumers and manufacturers could be linked together thereby eliminating several layers of the distribution chain. Theoretically, the wholesale and retail levels of product distribution would disintegrate and consumers would simply order direct from merchants. In the spirit of unbridled capitalism, the grateful manufacturer would pass the cost savings onto the consumer. The manufacturers were ill-prepared to embrace this medium as a primary vehicle for doing business for fear of alienating their well-established distribution channels. Moreover, manufacturers were ill-suited to provide the level of customer service that consumers were accustomed to via retail channels.

Consequently, consumers were now faced with having to search through the millions of pages on the Internet looking for products and were frequently dismayed at their inability to make direct purchases. The wholesale and retail distribution channels were slow to embrace this technology and a new class of intermediaries emerged. Several early plays began as start-up companies raced to acquire capital to build their corporate infrastructures. Dismissed by many as unprofitable ventures, they were steadily developing not a shopfront for selling products such as books but creating distribution channels and defining an entire new market.

As the Internet moved from an embryonic collection of computer nodes to a network of interconnected companies with access by the public, the attitude of retail and wholesale trade chains began to change. Next the Internet established platforms to launch businesses and provide a home base for consumers. Trading platforms began to emerge as new virtual real estate in which corporations could show up in the market associated with other organizations. Consumers could access the Internet or these trading platforms via newly established ISPs which quickly metamorphosed into business portals.

Trading networks include partnerships, alliances, affiliations and exchanges (Figure 5.1). A partnership is a relationship between two or

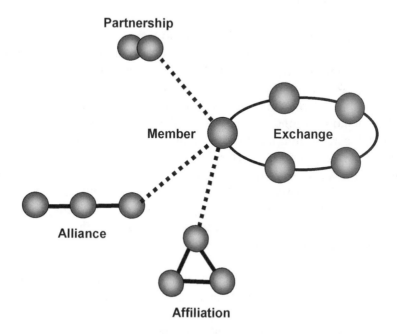

Figure 5.1 Elements of a trading network

more firms, characterized by cooperation to achieve a specific goal, provide a specific type of product or service a niche market. For example, computer hardware and software firms may bundle products to provide a solution to a niche market. An alliance is typically a formalized joining of firms to associate a product to a brand identity. For example, companies often link products together such as Intel Inside, which is used by various personal computer makers, or Powered by Hewlett-Packard, which is used by Apollo Consumer Products.[152]

Exchanges represent associations structured around giving and receiving items reciprocally. Members of an exchange often trade orders, customer data, monies, inventory and sales leads. Companies which mistake eCommerce for electronic data interchange (EDI) or subscribe to the notion that eCommerce is dead will be in for a rude awakening from the next wave of digitally enhanced commerce competitors. Countries such as China are in a unique position to provide a technological capability to business that surpasses most western nations, as noted by Peter Noland:

> The IT sector offers China an opportunity to 'leapfrog the Second Technological Revolution', which dominated the twentieth century, and rapidly become a leader in the new technologies of the Third Technological Revolution' in the early twenty first century.[153]

This 'leapfrogging phenomenon' is due to three key factors which many western businesses ignore or discount: firstly, many countries have less pre-existing infrastructure to undo in order to take advantage of newer technology. For example, smart cards offer superior capabilities over credit cards, but the replacement of infrastructure and POS devices has slowed its implementation. Secondly, the firms in these nations have eagerly read about and learned from the dot-com failures, so they will be prepared not to make the same mistakes. Thirdly, the rapid growth in highly skilled, often western university educated labour in the emerging nations enables them to provide technological services which are competitive in the global market. In the Chinese market, the primary issue which may limit the competitive threat that China could bring to the market is the depth of political bureaucracy, also noted by Noland:

> Despite great advances in its technical capabilities and important successes in aspects of industrial policy, it [China] was unable to truly separate itself from the operations of leading enterprises. Even after twenty years of reform, the Party remained deeply imbued with corruption, which seriously inhibited its efforts to implement a consistent, effective industrial policy.[154]

As discussed above, throughout history and across geographies organizations have gravitated towards any technology that reduces the cost and speed of operations in the exchange of value. The true value of these technologies is that they permit organizations to exploit unique business opportunities by enhancing their current business practices or creating new ones and entering new markets.

From a structural context, the firms' business processes are a complete system: processing orders, tracking inventory, making payments and a host of other discrete activities. Regardless of its type, make, model or version, technology adds value when it extends these functions externally to customers, trading partners, suppliers, distributors or employees. Extending the business processes adds value when the total output, cost of operation or some other meaningful measure is greater than the sum of the firm's internal processes. For example, when an organization uses the Internet to take customers' orders online, it is extending the order processing system to customers. In this scenario, a firm creates a value proposition in the following ways: allowing customers to perform the data entry previously performed by internal resources, thus reducing personnel cost, but increasing technology cost; extending the time in which a customer can order (24 hours a day, 7 days a week) without increasing internal staff resources. However, in some firms, an increase in weekend ordering makes for much higher volume on Mondays.

The above example did not include other factors – such as product quality, customer service levels, customer attitude and new channels to market – which are influenced in this scenario. However, the greatest implication of technology is not the measures we can associate with its implementation; it is technology's ability to change radically how business functions. The first generation of these technologies interpreted the radical change as a revolution in which one could jettison the fundamentals of businesses in the search for continuous growth. The second generation of the technological business transformation will be to redefine the business of business.

5.6 The New Structure of Business

Businesses are often founded on a simple premise, that is, the development of a product or service that represents a desire in a consumer group or opportunity created by a change in the business environment. A founder – or founding team – decides to bring a capability to the market and establishes an optimum process for fulfilling customers' orders for a product or a service. The founders create a value proposition for the business and carefully construct the optimum process or what is called a 'normative business model' for fulfilling the demand. All companies begin with a normative business model and strive through a series of organizational growth cycles to achieve the optimum operating state. This optimization occurs within the firm in two ways. Firstly, by continually streamlining business process steps and applying technology to achieve greater productivity in each step and secondly, by optimizing the intersections between the company's internal processes and its external, transaction-based processes with suppliers and distributors. One could argue that the ultimate optimization of business in the later stages of an organization's maturity is to establish control of a product from raw material to final distribution to customers, perhaps more clearly described as a monopoly or having monopolistic traits. Different types of business organize and address the process of adding value in various ways, often emphasizing the uniqueness of their process components, but these can be simplified into three prime functions, depicted in Figure 5.2.

Over time, people are added to the founding group and typically a hierarchical structure of organization emerges. Bushe and Shani remind us that:

> Structure is the division and coordination of labor. Organizations exist because there is something to do that requires more than one person; therefore, the work is divided up among several employees. Once the work is divided up, some way has to be found to coordinate the efforts of these individuals to ensure that the final product or service comes together. Structures are environments that affect how people behave. They channel effort and energy in a particular direction. When they are well designed, they support employees in accomplishing their tasks; when they are poorly designed, they can get in the way. Since they channel effort, changes in structure can lead to changes in how people behave at work.[155]

Coping with Changing Business Events

Business events invariably occur, such as customers requesting split deliveries of a single product in the order or fulfilment process which was not anticipated by the original business process. This triggers an exceptional state and the organization ultimately develops a method to address the anomaly. Organizations that reach this level of business maturity remedy this situation either by incorporating the rules and solutions for the exception into the business process, or else developing an external process

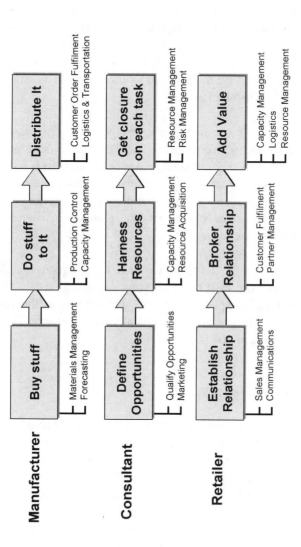

Figure 5.2 Business process activities

that deals specifically with the exception. In the latter, the preservation of the normative model is the desired goal, and the exceptions are not only corrected but also evaluated, feeding back information on the root causes of the problem to the appropriate group within the organization. For example, a product that is continually rejected by a customer may have a design flaw which the research and development group takes action to correct, instead of creating a new department to rework rejected products. Exceptions and modifications coming from customer input and changes in the business environment ultimately lead to alterations to a firm's business process, as noted by Tushman et al.:

> As competitive conditions change, fundamentally different organization forms are required. However, due to organization inertia, many organizations either do not effectively attend to environmental change or, if the threat is registered, act to bolster the status quo. This research indicates that both executive succession and strategic reorientations are important strategic levers affecting organization evolution. Those most effective organizations initiated proactive reorientations with no top executive succession.[156]

The primary factor in the development of business processes, ultimately influencing the structure of their supporting organizations, is the orientation of the combined output of the firm. Put simply, at the core of an organization's value proposition is typically an oversimplified, single intentional focus, as depicted in Figure 5.3.

The Influence of Technology

In recent years, technology has played an ever-increasing role in reshaping the structure of organizations, as business processes redefine themselves for greater efficiencies and individuals embrace new capabilities. In 1995, Rayport and Sviokla introduced the concept of a virtual value chain as '[...] the value that can be generated by exploiting the information generated by any stage of this process'.[157] This observation can be modified and applied to how enterprises are leveraging technology to enhance the structure of information and ultimately their organizations.

Technology is giving organizations new options on when work can be accomplished, where, how and by whom. In effect, technology is shrinking and expanding the effective time in which businesses can operate. Workers can execute activities from anywhere at anytime. In many cases,

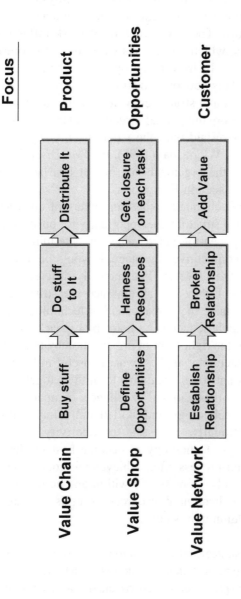

Figure 5.3 The process of value (adapted from Stabell and Fjeldstad)

the lines between work time and personal time are becoming blurred. The capabilities that technology brings to the act of working also introduce new issues including: a reduced amount of physical contact with co-workers; non-adherence to conventional rules; and a sense of loyalty to oneself, not to the firm. The new structure of work influences workers' renumeration systems, which are now assessed by their contribution to a collaborative project, not by the direct proportion of time spent working on any specific activity. This new organizational dynamism is giving birth to three distinct organizational structures: value chain, value shop and value network.[158] When the organizational structures identified by Stabell and Fjeldstad (1998) are overlaid onto the value discipline framework introduced by Treacy and Wiersema (1995) in *The Discipline of Market Leaders*, the focus of the organizational output can be correlated to its underlying structure as seen in Figure 5.4.

Since technology is continually redefining many of our traditional constraints to organizational structure, the opportunity for business is to reassess its structure as a component of added value and determine which structure provides the greatest competitive advantage. It would be unwise to assume that all organizations will develop fundamentally different structures, and even more naive to think they will all embrace one structure. Finding the right structure to maximize the convergence of technology and talent is a process of harmonizing these factors, as noted by Lipnack and Stamps: 'You can match the work to the right form of organization by understanding what teams can do, when hierarchy applies, what is useful in bureaucracy, what circumstances call for networks – and how to fit them together.'[159]

In order to achieve organizational excellence, companies need to align their processes with technology and skilled individuals into a coherent structure that continually assesses productivity and efficiency. Organizations that apply technology to become best in class in a single business process or sub-process often achieve their goal at the detriment of the overall process levels. Consistency within and across a process is, in many cases, a better application of resources, as it raises the aggregate level of performance, as Quinn points out:

> Companies seeking strategic advantage through significant technological innovation need to recognize the tumultuous, long-term realities of how this process operates, and design specific organizations and management practices to motivate it and guide it.[160]

Technologies such as the Internet amplify the need for a holistic approach to process management, especially when there is a requirement to integrate

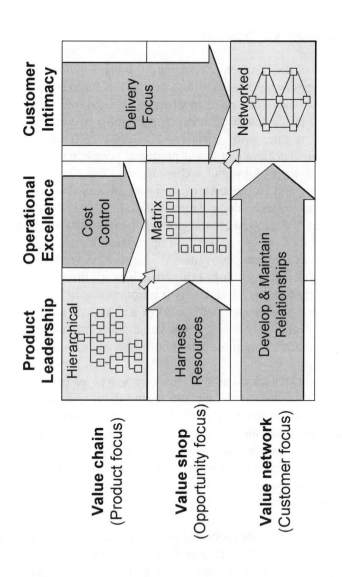

Figure 5.4 Organizational migration (adapted from Stabell and Fjeldstad)

new functions seamlessly. Firms often lose sight of the implications of
process changes which, in many cases, alienate customers during the
transition process.

The Influence of Virtual Products

The technologies of the Internet, telecommunications, databases and other
information processors have ushered in a new era of business in a global
marketplace. As we have discussed in Chapters 3 and 4, the definition of
what constitutes a product, a distribution channel and a customer is continually changing, in tune with social and cultural preferences. These
factors have brought technology-based products, people who understand
the application of technology and technology itself to the forefront of
strategic initiatives and to the core of business process design. Castells
notes the importance of technological prowess to a firm's value proposition:
'the new economy is organized around global networks of capital, management, and information, whose access to technological know-how is at the
roots of productivity and competitiveness'.[161] Customers are keenly aware
of the intrinsic value that technology brings to enhancing their lifestyles and
now, as the next generation of technology is introduced to the marketplace,
business will take the same approach. Davidow and Malone remind us that
the application of technology does not make us abdicate our own individual
responsibility to synthesizing information into strategic actions:

> The business revolution caused by virtual products will be led by companies in
> established industries that have recognized the potential of using some or all of
> the four kinds of information to reconstruct their business. They will be comp-
> anies that are observant enough to spot a technological crossover threat emer-
> ging in some distant industry and race to incorporate it. They will be the ones
> that develop multidisciplinary inventions themselves. In every case, technology
> will be subordinate to, not a substitute for, a complete understanding of the
> market and the business.[162]

Business entities across the globe are looking towards technology as the
primary mechanism for adding value to customers. However, Davidow and
Malone also point out: 'because many virtual products of the future will be
almost solely the creation of technology, there is a danger that business
executives will become overly reliant on it.'[163] Technology is only a part of
the value equation; people and process are the other two ingredients.

The Implications of the Virtual Organization

The collaborative influence of technology now presents business with the ability to fundamentally rethink its products, the relationship with customers and suppliers, the markets and the structure of the organization.

The value network is not simply connecting computers and sending eMails to each other, thereby increasing communications. It is a collection of collaborative technologies working with established business processes to distribute information to where it is most needed to support the horizontal process of business and the vertical hierarchy of organizational structure. The expressed goal is to increase the level of communications so that individuals can act intelligently and make decisions in a dynamic, competitive environment. However, the implied goal is not merely to subject everyone to an avalanche of detailed information (which is evident in corporate eMails); it is to provide data to individuals to participate in the business process effectively. Figure 5.5 presents a theoretical framework for a collaborative virtual healthcare system, in which the structure of the information centres on the patient, not on the individual organizations performing medical procedures.

The opportunity to share patient information and broker insurance trans-actions will fundamentally change the way healthcare is delivered in the next decades. A patient whose records are shared and accessed via loosely coupled servers may use a variety of dental specialists within or outside a specific insurance network with electronic co-payments and imaged records. So how can this type of system add value to healthcare customers and patients?

At the junction of the healthcare network is patient information. Coupling the healthcare network infrastructure with an existing Internet offering such as Minnesota's Medformation.com,[164] which acts as a destination for medical customers, creates an environment with significant potential savings for providers and patients. The value proposition of Medformation.com is twofold: proactive health maintenance (providing information on staying healthy) and reactive healthcare, enabling indiv-iduals to do a limited amount of simple self-diagnosis and brokering relationships for the patient to a variety of healthcare providers. The over-all value can be plotted into three distinct groups: patients or customers, healthcare professionals and healthcare administrators. Each group requires information that essentially stems from the patient but may only be loosely associated to specific data about the patient, such as a doctor may wish to know how many people used the hospital for cancer treatment in the last year. Patients will want to confirm their medical records, the

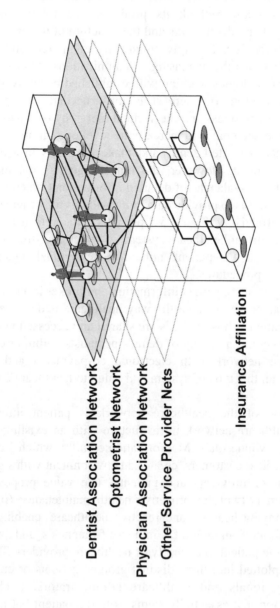

Figure 5.5 Collaborative virtual healthcare

status of any current procedures, reconfirm their benefits and look at general medical information. Physicians and other healthcare professionals will check the status of current medical tests, issue prescriptions, search patients' medical histories and schedule additional procedures. Healthcare administrators will review cases, coordinate benefits and other administrative functions.

The virtual networked organization has been defined as a network of organizations coming together in response to a market opportunity. These virtual organizations share skills, costs, and market access. Each member of the virtual organization brings a core competency to the group.[165] Key elements that define the virtual organization include opportunism, technology, excellence, trust and lack of organizational borders. The information technology supporting the virtual organization model is varied, ranging from simple communications technology such as teleconferencing to the sharing of databases, computer-aided design and manufacturing information and interorganizational linkages.[166]

Examples of virtual organizations include a variety of strategic alliances, partnering and outsourcing situations, as depicted in Figure 5.6, the molecular organization. This model emulates an example of a large multinational business engaged in joint product development and international market access with distribution partners. Small firms' models have included a number of consortia that bring together smaller manufacturers[167] using the same basic collaborative process and organizational framework.

The reasons for adopting the virtual organization model would be similar for the new venture and the existing enterprise, perhaps with a few differences in degrees of importance. The virtual organization offers the sharing of common infrastructure such as networks and expensive resources, collaborated research and development, shared risks and costs between partners. Another aspect of the virtual organization is linking complementary core competencies and other communities of practice to exchange ideas and designs. Reducing the time to market and gaining new access to markets is a by-product of the networked relationship, in that partners, associates and affiliates each bring to the network a link to other networks which act as gateways to other niche markets. Finally, the virtual organization brings an opportunity to build an associative brand, and can be leveraged to build customer loyalty to a corporation or product identity. The effectiveness of the virtual organization is proportional to the investment made in the corporate infrastructure. However, firms are now realizing that the change of structure from command and control to control and command needs to be accompanied by an equally drastic redefinition

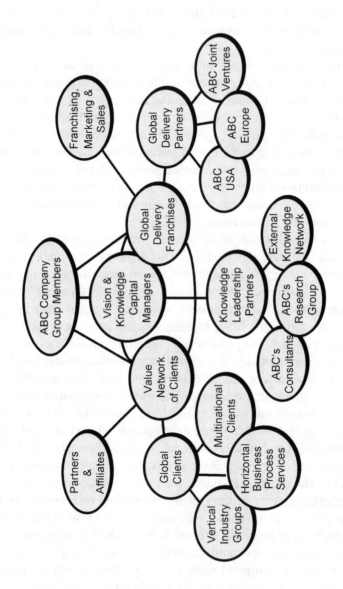

Figure 5.6 The molecular organization

of the way in which the organizational culture perceives strategic decision making, as Pacey observes:

> One way of expressing the issues raised by the technology-based bureaucracies, and by the big multinational companies, is to say that nations which are nominally democratic are finding that large sectors of decision-making have been taken over by totalitarian institutions.[168]

One clear aspect of the virtual organization structure and the hybrid organizations that it brings to life is a direct distribution of decision making and resource consumption. One could argue that this type of organization pushes the management of the company's business processes down to where the action is, that is, the process itself. The traditional senior management team now acts as a resource that is used by the individual operating processes, as needed in roles such as mentor, problem solver and other functions that require cross-process knowledge and industry expertise. Davidow and Malone detail the extent to which the emergence of the virtual corporation will influence our traditional notions of worker and employer:

> Several changes do, however, appear inevitable, given the increasing technological orientation of corporations, the distribution of decision making out to the rank and file, the less distinct boundaries between the company and its suppliers and customers, and the perpetually accelerating cycle times. These changes include the following:

- More sophisticated training will continue through employers' careers.

- Cross-disciplinary organizations, such as work teams, will have extensive decision-making powers.

- Hiring policies will select for adaptability to change.

- An unprecedented emphasis will be put on retaining existing employees in a shrinking labor pool.

- Unions (where they still exist) and management will enter into different, mutually dependent relationships.

- The traditional notion of career will be redefined.

- The potential will exist for a different form of worker alienation.[169]

Therefore, in line with the continued rate of technological advancement, organizations will transform into value chains, value shops or value networks and their technological infrastructure will enable a redefinition of the organizational structure to support a host of new and yet unimagined business processes. This is not merely a 'Brave New World' vision: it is a perfectly conceivable future, one that is becoming more and more real every day. As Stabell and Fjeldstad observe:

The business value systems reflect the activity interrelationships and drivers of the respective underlying value configurations. Value chains form sequentially interrelated value systems of suppliers, producers and distributors, each adding value to the output from the preceding chain. Value shops are linked and referred in a wheels-outside-wheels relationship to specialized problem-solving and implementation activities. Value networks form coproducing layers of mediators where one network may use a lower-level network as a subnetwork. In addition value networks form horizontal interconnected value systems of similar firms that extend the scope of the network by virtual mergers to gain mutual benefits from network externalities. The resulting scope is equivalent to the horizontal union of the vertical intersection of customer contracts. Most business value systems include firms representing all value creation logics.[170]

Technology's Impact on Global Business

One thing should be clear from reading this text: the fundamental methods through which people adopt and employ technology today follow a similar pattern throughout history and, more importantly, across cultures. The advance of technology merely reflects the ability of humankind to excel at applying physical devices to increase the quality of life and the efficiency of business. What can also be observed is that technology creates a condition in which our social, moral, ethical and business values are tested, and our perception of what is valuable to society is sometimes dictated by culture and personal choice. Throughout history, technology has played an important role in shaping our society, beliefs, values and business activities by continually giving us cause to re-examine them and understand their inter-relationships. Pacey reveals the paradox of our relationship with technology:

> Modern man, it often seems, is divided man. There are no universally agreed goals, no wholly comprehensive systems of values: 'the modern mind is divided – in tension'. Again and again there are attempts to resolve the tension by suggesting a rejection of high technology and reversion to a simpler, more rural way of living. But many of the finest achievements of western culture are the products either of high technology or of the virtuosity values that have impelled it. One thinks of the idealistic engineering of medieval cathedrals, the work of Renaissance artist-engineers, the constructions of Brunel and Eiffel, and the marvels of microelectronics or of space exploration. To disown all that would be both Luddite and Philistine. But to assert the importance of meeting basic human needs, and using technology to that end, is an inescapable obligation.[171]

It is from this paradox of socio-technological behaviour that business must create a compelling value proposition to engage customers and return some reasonable degree of profit. What technologies such as the Internet bring to light is that people no longer can enjoy the insular effects of technological isolationism of the past. Although we believe in technology, our inclination is to resist it in conscious and subconscious ways.

The bureaucracies within business, for example, complicate the process of adding value by emphasizing governing activities rather than the execution of the process. One could argue that no amount of technology will resolve the fundamental problems of bureaucratic behaviour; however, technology can be employed to minimize its effects. In the 1960s, organizations developed a method of anticipating future activities called 'strategic planning'.[172] This form of centralized annual planning allowed firms in many cases to establish rigid operating conditions that were designed to reinforce their hierarchical organizational structures. The structures simply reflected the compartmentalization of the business processes into functional areas. Paul Strassmann observes that simply providing poorly designed structures adds little long-term value:

> The amount of office work done in a bureaucracy is determined by organizational design. However, the closer one examines the details of office work the less understandable it becomes. Office work reflects the way power is distributed. Automation can be used to increase the autonomy of individuals or to strengthen the control of the hierarchy. Office automation should be attempted only after work has been simplified to respond to customer need. Productivity is improved by simplifying organizations rather than by speeding them up.[173]

The technologies of the twentieth century have proved effective in transmitting the image of western values to all parts of the globe in a serial broadcast method such as television. The Internet, unlike previous mass media technologies, is a two-way synchronous means of communication which will facilitate a greater awareness of the cultures, morals, ethics, beliefs, religions and all other aspects of society to be freely exchanged multi-directionally. Technology's potential lies in its ability to enable firms to conduct business globally in a competitive marketplace that continually strives for process optimization, higher quality goods and better returns for investors. This potential is realized not as a technology project aimed at improving customer services but in the creation, development and execution of the firm's value proposition.

A benchmark for a firm's success is not an increase in profitability, but the success of its customers. Competition acts as a catalyst for the continuous redefinition of customer's needs, wants and desires. Technology plays an integral but not exclusive role in meeting the customers' expectations and achieving customer centricity in our process designs. However, this transition to a business model which places the customer at the centre of a relationship requires a shift from traditional thinking, as reflected by Earle and Keen:

> Here are just a few of the many implications of the difference between a business model centered on relationships and one on transactions:
>
> ■ Relationship-centered business models generate very high incremental operating margins for repeat business and positive cash flows even when the firm is as yet unprofitable; in contrast, transaction-centered business models have lower infrastructure costs. Yet they must build high conversion rates – that is, build up the fraction of hits on the site that turn into purchases.
>
> ■ Relationship centered business models have high risk and potentially very high payoff; in contrast, transaction-centered business models are heavily reliant on price-cutting, discounts, and payment to portals.
>
> ■ Relationship-centered business models succeed when they offer a superb operational performance in fulfilment and reliability; transaction-centered business models, even when they perform superbly, remain vulnerable to online players who give away their service or goods to attract relationship business.
>
> ■ Relationship-centered business models are creating new power brands; transaction-centered business models face loss of product equity to strong Internet relationship brand players.[174]

A shift to a customer-centric perspective demands that corporations develop a clear understanding of who or what constitutes a customer and what are the associated demographic attributes to which the firm delivers value in its products. To conduct business globally, organizations will need to assess the relativity of the value propositions of their products and services with the cultural preference of indigenous people. This global proliferation of goods, services and technology generates a new set of issues which businesses must monitor. Businesses also need to develop clear and concise policies to address each matter as it gains momentum. In order to be an effective global business, organizations need to be aware of a number of issues that have been identified by the Global Internet Policy Initiative, such as: transparency, telecommunications 'liberalization', tariffing/universal service, technical standards/licensing, eReadiness guides, eCommerce/electronic and digital signatures, content controls/ISP liability/freedom of expression, privacy, intellectual property, cybercrime/cybersecurity, taxation of eCommerce, jurisdiction, domain names and international governance.[175] Moreover, these issues also bring a new set of opportunities for corporations to add value.

The advance of technological innovation is greeted by society with open arms. Society will use technology for purposes that are malevolent or benevolent or both; this is the choice of people who use it. Hopefully, technology users will choose to use technology wisely and benevolently. The Internet is a two-edged sword that is a vehicle for intellectual enlightenment through cultural exploration and at the same time exposes and magnifies the darker side of human behaviour. It is the ultimate representation of humankind's conundrum of gaining consensus in a world of celebrated differences, and portrays the human spirit at its worst and its best. Business technology's express goal is the same now as it was in the time of the Medici: to make operations more profitable and facilitate commerce between all parts of the world. The incorporation of new technologies into corporate value propositions is inevitable and must be now achieved by the proactive determination of senior managers who can lead business into a connected global environment. In this environment, business processes will ultimately be part of a synergistic socio-economic relationship linking cultures, not devouring them.

NOTES

1. G. Rochlin, *Scientific Technology and Social Change* (San Francisco: W. H. Freeman, 1974) p. 68.
2. Ibid., p. 148.
3. R. Foster, *Technology in the Modern Corporation* (Oxford: Pergamon Press, 1986) p. 35.
4. L. White, *Medieval Technology and Social Change* (Oxford: Clarendon Press, 1962) p. 28.
5. J. DiVanna, *Redefining Financial Services: The New Renaissance in Value Propositions* (Basingstoke: Palgrave Macmillan, 2002) pp. 127–8.
6. R. Bacon. *De secretis operibus*, c. 4 (c. 1260), as cited in L. White, *Medieval Technology and Social Change* (Oxford: Clarendon Press, 1962) p. 134.
7. A. Koyré, *Du Monde Clos à l'Univers Infini* (Paris: Gallimard, 1962) pp. 98–102.
8. P. Israel, *Edison: A Life of Invention* (New York: John Wiley and Sons, 1998) p. 423.
9. J. Gimpel, *The Medieval Machine: The Industrial Revolution of the Middle Ages* (London: Pimlico, 1998) p. viii.
10. T. A. Stewart, *Intellectual Capital: The New Wealth of Organizations* (London: Nicholas Brealey, 1998) p. 85.
11. R. Buckminster Fuller, *Critical Path* (New York: St Martin's Press, 1981) p. 148.
12. J. DiVanna, *Redefining Financial Services: The New Renaissance in Value Propositions* (Basingstoke: Palgrave Macmillan, 2002) pp. 37–8.
13. R. S. Lopez, *The Commercial Revolution of the Middle Ages, 950–1350* (Cambridge: Cambridge University Press, 1995) p. 40.
14. L. White, *Medieval Technology and Social Change* (Oxford: Clarendon Press, 1962) p. 87.
15. P. Jaffe, *Regesta pontificum romanorum* (Leipzig, 1888), no. 17,620, to Archdeacon Betrand of Dol in Brittany, in L. White, *Medieval Technology and Social Change* (Oxford: Clarendon Press, 1962) p. 88.
16. L. White, *Medieval Technology and Social Change* (Oxford: Clarendon Press, 1962) p. 88.
17. Ibid.

18. N. Postman, *Technopoly: The Surrender of Culture to Technology* (New York: Vintage, 1993) pp. 16–19.

19. W. G. Collingwood, *Northumbrian Crosses of the Pre-Norman Age* (Lampeter: Llanerch, 1989, [1927]) p. 172.

20. D. Knoop and G. Jones, *The Mediaeval Mason: An Economic History of English Stone Building in the Later Middles Ages and Early Modern Times* (Manchester: Manchester University Press, 1949) p. 79.

21. Speech given to the Royal Institute for Foreign Affairs. London, March 20, 2001.

22. See Digital Divide Network. Available at http://www.digitaldividenetwork. org/content/sections/index.cfm, April 2002.

23. I. Burkett, 'Beyond the Information Rich and Poor; Future's Understanding of Inequalities in Globalising Information Economies'. *Futures*, Vol. 32, Number 7, (2000) p. 679.

24. J. Micklethwait and A. Wooldridge, *A Future Perfect: The Challenge and Hidden Promise of Globalization* (London: William Heinemann, 2000) p. 325.

25. J. Stanovnik, 'Global Problems and the Role of Science and Technology in their Solution'. In J. Gvishiani (ed.) *Science, Technology and Global Problems* (Oxford: Pergamon Press, 1979) p. 42.

26. Ibid., p. 43.

27. J. Micklethwait and A. Wooldridge, *A Future Perfect: The Challenge and Hidden Promise of Globalization* (London: William Heinemann, 2000) p. 32.

28. See C. Christensen, *The Innovator's Dilemma: How Disruptive Technologies can Destroy Established Markets* (Cambridge: Harvard University Press, 1997).

29. D. A. Norman, *The Invisible Computer: Why Products Can Fail, the Personal Computer is so Complex, and Information Appliances are the Solution* (Cambridge: MIT Press, 1998) pp. 233–4.

30. P. Barwise, 'The Value of the Digital Prophets', *Financial Times*, April 23 (2002) p. 5.

31. N. Negroponte, *Being Digital* (London: Hodder & Stoughton, 1995) p. 48.

32. TiVo is a digital video recording system equipped with a hard disk that automatically finds and records broadcasted programmes for playback at a later time. Available at http://www.tivo.com.

33. N. Postman. *Technopoly: The Surrender of Culture to Technology* (New York: Vintage, 1993) pp. 16–19.

34. J. DiVanna, *Redefining Financial Services: The New Renaissance in Value Propositions* (Basingstoke: Palgrave Macmillan, 2002) p. 237.

35. M. Treacy and F. Wiersema, *The Discipline of Market Leaders* (Reading: Perseus Books, 1995) p. xii.

36. See PricewaterhouseCoopers, value proposition calculator (VPR). Available at http://www.pwcglobal.com/pam/solutions/valpropcalc.html.

37. N. Postman, *Building a Bridge to the Eighteenth Century: How the Past Can Improve our Future* (New York: Alfred A. Knopf, 1999) p. 46.

38. Ibid.

39. Ibid., p. 48.
40. L. B. Rasmussen, 'Consequences of Information Technology. The Design of Inquiring Systems and Culture'. In L. Yngström, R. Sizer, J. Berleur and R. Laufer (eds) *Can Information Technology Result in Benevolent Bureaucracies?* (Amsterdam: Elsevier Science, 1991) p. 64.
41. R. L. Meier, 'Late-blooming Societies can be stimulated by information technology', *Futures*, Vol 32 Number 1 (2000) p. 168.
42. C. Freeman, 'The Learning Economy of International Inequality'. In D. Archibugi and B. Lundvall (eds) *The Globalizing Learning Economy* (Oxford: Oxford University Press, 2001) p. 156.
43. F. Czerniawska and G. Potter, *Business in a Virtual World. Exploiting Information for Competitive Advantage* (Basingstoke: Macmillan – now Palgrave Macmillan, 1998) p. 22.
44. Ibid.
45. A. Pacey, *The Culture of Technology* (Oxford: Blackwell, 1983) p. 25.
46. F. Capra, *The Web of Life* (London: HarperCollins, 1996) pp. 29–30.
47. S. Cooney, 'Maximizing the Benefits from New Technology'. In L. Yngström, R. Sizer, J. Berleur and R. Laufer (eds) *Can Information Technology Result in Benevolent Bureaucracies?* (Amsterdam: Elsevier Science, 1991) p. 133.
48. Y. Doz, R. Angelmar and C. K. Prahalad, 'Technological Innovation and Interdependence. A Challenge for the Large, Complex Firm'. In M. Horwitch (ed.) *Technology in the Modern Corporation: A Strategic Perspective* (Oxford: Pergamon Press, 1986) p. 15.
49. G. R. Bushe and A. B. Shani, *Parallel Learning Structures. Increasing Innovation in Bureaucracies* (Reading, Mass.: Addison-Wesley, 1991) p. 5.
50. M. Hammer, *Beyond Reengineering: How the Process-centred Organization is Changing Our Work and Our Lives* (London: HarperCollins, 1998) p. 189.
51. R. Petrella, 'In Search of … the Benevolent Bureaucracy'. In L. Yngström, R. Sizer, J. Berleur and R. Laufer (eds) *Can Information Technology result in Benevolent Bureaucracies?* (Amsterdam: Elsevier Science, 1991) p. 20.
52. Ibid.
53. J. Lipnack and J. Stamps, *The Age of the Network: Organizing Principles for the 21st Century* (Essex Junction, VT: Oliver Wight, 1994) pp. 71–3; citation on p. 72.
54. J. Berleur, 'The so-called "Information Society"'. In L. Yngström, R. Sizer, J. Berleur and R. Laufer (eds) *Can Information Technology result in Benevolent Bureaucracies?* (Amsterdam: Elsevier Science, 1991) p. 23.
55. J. Naisbitt and P. Aburdene, *Re-inventing the Corporation. Transforming Your Job and Your Company for the New Information Society* (London: Macdonald, 1985) pp. 40–1.
56. See F. M. Lea, *The Chemistry of Cement and Concrete* (New York: St. Martin's Press, 1956), Chapter 1.
57. F. Andrews, *The Medieval Builder and His Methods* (New York: Dover, 1999) p. 8.

58. See J. Morgan. 'Event-Process View of Project Management' Computer Sciences Corporation, UK Division (1995).

59. M. Hobart and Z. Schiffman, *Information Ages: Literacy, Numeracy and the Computer Revolution* (Baltimore: Johns Hopkins University Press, 1998) p. 134.

60. D. Cleland, 'Borderless Project Management'. In D. Cleland and R. Gareis (eds) *Global Project Management Handbook* (New York: McGraw-Hill, 1996) p. 10.

61. M. Hammer, *Beyond Reengineering: How the Process-Centered Organization is Changing Our Work and Our Lives* (London: HarperCollins, 1998) pp. 238–9.

62. M. Hammer, *Beyond Reengineering: How the Process-Centred Organization is Changing Our Work and Our Lives* (London: HarperCollins, 1998) p. 234.

63. W. Wilson, *Strategic Business Transformations: Achieving Strategic Objectives through Business Reengineering* (Maidenhead: McGraw-Hill, 1996) p. 211.

64. Ibid., p. 212.

65. E. Eisenstein, *The Printing Revolution in Early Modern Europe* (Cambridge: Cambridge University Press, 1996) p. 51.

66. J. McCarthy, 'Information'. In G. Rochlin (ed.) *Scientific Technology and Social Change* (San Francisco: W. H. Freeman, 1977) p. 221.

67. N. Postman, *Building a Bridge to the Eighteenth Century: How the Past can Improve our Future* (New York: Alfred A. Knopf, 1999) p. 98.

68. W. H. Davidow and M. S. Malone, *The Virtual Corporation. Structuring and Revitalizing the Corporation for the 21st* Century (London: Harper Business, 1993) p. 187.

69. P. Conceição and M. Heitor, 'Universities in the Learning Economy: Balancing Institutional Integrity with Organizational Diversity'. In D. Archibugi and B. Lundvall (eds) *The Globalizing Learning Economy* (Oxford: Oxford University Press, 2001) p. 87.

70. F. Andrews, *The Medieval Builder and His Methods* (New York: Dover, 1999) p. 9.

71. J. Naisbitt and P. Aburdene, *Re-inventing the Corporation. Transforming your Job and your Company for the New Information Society* (London: Macdonald, 1985) pp. 141–3.

72. Ibid., pp. 127–8.

73. See www.bicnow.com.

74. J. Naisbitt and P. Aburdene, *Re-inventing the Corporation. Transforming your Job and your Company for the New Information Society* (London: Macdonald, 1985) pp. 83–4.

75. See Celemi, available at http://www.celemi.com.

76. P. Israel, *Edison: A Life of Invention* (New York: John Wiley and Sons, 1998) p. 272.

77. G. Pascal Zachary, *The Global Me* (London: Nicholas Brealey, 2002) p. 70.

78. Ibid., pp. 214–15.
79. M. Castells, *The Rise of the Network Society* (Oxford: Blackwell, 1997) p. 204.
80. M. Hammer, *Beyond Reengineering: How the Process-Centred Organization is Changing Our Work and Our Lives* (London: HarperCollins, 1998) p. 101.
81. M. Quennell, *The History of Everyday Things in England* Vol. 1 (London: B. T. Batsford, 1976) p. ix.
82. C. Wiener, *Trades and Crafts* (London: Wayland, 1972) p. 41.
83. Ibid., p. 42.
84. See www.bicnow.com.
85. J. S. Brown and E. S. Gray, 'The People Are the Company', *Fastcompany*, February (1997).
86. M. Hammer. *Beyond Reengineering: How the Process-Centred Organization is Changing Our Work and Our Lives* (London: HarperCollins, 1998) p. 204.
87. M. Hammer and J. Champy, *Reengineering the Corporation. A Manifesto for Business Revolution* (London: Nicholas Brealey, 2001) p. 89.
88. E. Hunt and J. M. Murray, *A History of Business in Medieval Europe 1200–1550* (Cambridge: Cambridge University Press, 1999) p. 166.
89. S. Davis and C. Meyer, *Future Wealth* (Boston: Harvard Business School Press, 2000) p. 42.
90. J. Micklethwait and A. Wooldridge, *A Future Perfect: The Challenge and Hidden Promise of Globalization* (London: William Heinemann, 2000) p. 325.
91. C. Rawcliffe, *Medicine and Society in Later Medieval England* (Stroud: Alan Sutton, 1995) pp. 32–4.
92. M. Hammer and J. Champy, *Reengineering the Corporation. A Manifesto for Business Revolution* (London: Nicholas Brealey, 2001) p. 35.
93. M. Tampoe, 'Don't Downsize – Improve Performance', *Strategy*, November (2000) p. 23.
94. N. Machiavelli, *The Prince* (Oxford: Oxford University Press, 1998) p. 8.
95. Ibid., p. 10.
96. Ibid., p. 10.
97. See Computer Sciences Corporation, financial services product offerings, available at http://www.csc-fs.com/offerings.
98. J. A. Hobson, *The Evolution of Modern Capitalism.* (London: Walter Scott, 1926).
99. U. Eco, S. J. Gould, J.-C. Garrière and J. Delumeau, *Conversations about the End of Time* (London: Penguin, 2000) p. 144.
100. R. Lopez, *The Commercial Revolution of the Middle Ages 950–1350.* (Cambridge: Cambridge University Press, 1995) p. 60.
101. For a detailed discussion, see section 3.5.

102. R. Lopez, *The Commercial Revolution of the Middle Ages 950–1350*. (Cambridge: Cambridge University Press, 1995) p. 64.
103. V. Lund, 'Virtual Agents: Expanding the Definition of "Customer Centric"', IBM's *Building an Edge*, September 6 (2001).
104. R. Lopez, *The Commercial Revolution of the Middle Ages 950–1350*. (Cambridge: Cambridge University Press, 1995) p. 48.
105. W. H. Davidow and M. S. Malone, *The Virtual Corporation. Structuring and Revitalizing the Corporation for the 21st* Century (London: Harper Business, 1993) p. 32.
106. J. Micklethwait and A. Wooldridge, *A Future Perfect: The Challenge and Hidden Promise of Globalization* (London: William Heinemann, 2000) p. 100.
107. Ibid., p. 101.
108. Ibid., p. 104.
109. Ibid., p. 106.
110. Ibid., p. 109.
111. Ibid., p. 114.
112. J. A. DiVanna, *Redefining Financial Services: The New Renaissance in Value Propositions* (Basingstoke: Palgrave Macmillan, 2002) pp. 101–4.
113. See M. de Kare-Silver, *e-shock. the new rules. e-strategies for retailers and manufacturers* (Basingstoke: Palgrave – now Palgrave Macmillan, 2001 [1998]) p. 90.
114. See R. Bellah, R. Madisen, W. Sullivan, A. Swindler and S. Tipton, *Habits of the Heart. Individualism and Commitment in American Life* (Berkeley: University of California Press, 1996) pp. 277–9.
115. R. Taplin, 'Tesco racks up a Local Success', *Financial Times*, April 18 (2002).
116. J. Perkin, 'Multilingual Websites Widen the Way to a New Online World', *Financial Times*, February 7 (2001).
117. See R. Lopez, *The Commercial Revolution of the Middle Ages 950–1350*. (Cambridge: Cambridge University Press, 1995).
118. K. Brown, 'An Electronic Electorate', *Financial Times*, 24 April (2002).
119. M. Hammer, *The Agenda. What Every Business Must Do to Dominate the Decade* (London: Random House, 2001) p. 38.
120. G. Pascal Zachary, *The Global Me* (London: Nicholas Brealey, 2002) p. 16.
121. Walter Truett Anderson, 'The Self in Global Society', *Futures*, Vol. 31, Number 8, (1999) p. 804.
122. W. Sombart, *Luxury and Capitalism* (Ann Arbor: University of Michigan Press, 1967) p. 59.
123. J. DiVanna, *Redefining Financial Services: The New Renaissance in Value Propositions* (Basingstoke: Palgrave Macmillan, 2002) pp. 201–3.
124. US Air Group. See www.usair.com.
125. C. Preist, 'Economic Agents for Automated Trading', Hewlett-Packard Company, (1998) p. 1.
126. Ibid., p. 6.

127. J. Eckenrode, 'Is Internet Technology the Path to Banking Efficiency?' IBM's *Building an Edge*, November 29 (2001) p. 3.

128. F. Wiersema, *Customer Intimacy: Pick Your Partners, Shape Your Culture, Win Together* (London: HarperCollins, 1997) p. 29.

129. J. DiVanna, *Redefining Financial Services: The New Renaissance in Value Propositions* (Basingstoke: Palgrave Macmillan, 2002) pp. 51–3.

130. R. Clifton and E. Maughan (eds) *Twenty-five Visions: The Future of Brands* (Basingstoke: Macmillan – now Palgrave Macmillan, 2000) p. xiii.

131. J. DiVanna, *Redefining Financial Services: The New Renaissance in Value Propositions* (Basingstoke: Palgrave Macmillan, 2002) pp. 101–5.

132. N. Saul, *Richard II* (London: Yale University Press, 1997) pp. 238–9.

133. S. J. Park, 'The Future of Brands'. In R. Clifton and E. Maughan (eds), *Twenty-five Visions: The Future of Brands* (Basingstoke: Macmillan – now Palgrave Macmillan, 2000) p. 47.

134. L. Kehoe, 'Leading Brands on the Run', *Financial Times*, October 11 (2000).

135. D. Gardner, 'Slim Pickings for the Global Brand in India', *Financial Times*, October 11 (2000).

136. S. Cooney, 'Maximizing the Benefits from New Technology'. In L. Yngström, R. Sizer, J. Berleur and R. Laufer (eds) *Can Information Technology result in Benevolent Bureaucracies?* (Amsterdam: Elsevier Science, 1991) p. 127.

137. Ibid., p. 144.

138. E. Liikanen, *The European Commission for Internet Policy*.

139. M. Hammer, *Beyond Reengineering: How the Process-centred Organization is Changing Our Work and Our Lives* (London: HarperCollins, 1998) p. 170.

140. R. McGregor, 'Websites Punished as China Acts to Control Content', *Financial Times*, June 6 (2002).

141. Filtered Internet Solutions, available at http://www.filteredinternet solutions.com.

142. WiseChoice pornography filtering software, available at: http://www.wisechoice.net/.

143. NetAngle anti pornography ISP, available at http://www.netangle.com.

144. See www.Christianliving.com.

145. M. Castells, *The Internet Galaxy: Reflections on Internet, Business and Society*. (Oxford: Oxford University Press, 2001).

146. S. Bridge, 'The New Generation', *eBusiness*, Vol. 6, May (2000) p. 19.

147. Southern Utah University, computer, use and network security policy, Available at: http://www.suu.edu/pub/policies/, May 2002.

148. Vatican Policy on the Internet. John Paul II, Message for the 35th World Communications Day, n. 3, May 27, 2000, as cited in Pontifical Council For Social Communications, The Church And Internet, available at http://www.vatican.va/roman_curia/pontifical_councils/pccs/documents/rc_pc_pccs_doc_20020228_church-internet_en.html.

149. W. H. Davidow and M. S. Malone, *The Virtual Corporation. Structuring and Revitalizing the Corporation for the 21st Century* (London: Harper Business, 1993) p. 153.

150. Ibid.

151. J. DiVanna, *Redefining Financial Services: The New Renaissance in Value Propositions* (Basingstoke: Palgrave Macmillan, 2002) p. 2.

152. Apollo Consumer Products Ltd, available at: http://www.myapollo.com/.

153. P. Noland, *China and the Global Economy: National Champions, Industrial Policy and the Big Business Revolution* (Basingstoke: Palgrave Macmillan, 2001) p. 172.

154. Ibid., p. 93.

155. G. R. Bushe and A. B. Shani, *Parallel Learning Structures. Increasing Innovation in Bureaucracies* (Reading, Mass: Addison-Wesley, 1991) p. 3.

156. M. L. Tushman, B. Virany and E. Romanelli, 'Executive Succession, Strategic Reorientations, and Organization Evolution'. In M. Horwitch (ed.) *Technology in the Modern Corporation: a Strategic Perspective* (Oxford: Pergamon Press, 1986) p. 215.

157. F. Czerniawska and G. Potter, *Business in a Virtual World: Exploiting Information for Competitive Advantage* (Basingstoke: Macmillan – now Palgrave Macmillan, 1998) p. 68.

158. C. Stabell and fl. Fjeldstad, 'Configuring Value for Competitive Advantage: On Chains, Shops and Networks', *Strategic Management Journal*, Vol. 19, Number 5 (1998) p. 413.

159. J. Lipnack and J. Stamps, *The Age of the Network* (Essex Junction: Oliver Wight, 1994) p. 20.

160. J. B. Quinn, 'Innovation and Corporate Strategy'. In M. Horwitch (ed.) *Technology in the Modern Corporation* (Oxford: Pergamon Press, 1986) p. 169.

161. M. Castells, *The Rise of the Network Society* (Oxford: Blackwell, 1997) p. 471.

162. W. H. Davidow and M. S. Malone, *The Virtual Corporation. Structuring and Revitalizing the Corporation for the 21st Century* (London: Harper Business, 1993) p. 85.

163. Ibid.

164. Medformation.com is a community service of Allina Hospitals and Clinics, a hospital and clinic system serving Minnesota and western Wisconsin. See http://medformation.com.

165. J. A. Byrne, R. Brandt and O. Port, 'The Virtual Corporation', *Business-Week*, February 8 (1993) pp. 98–103.

166. See S. L. Goldman, R. N. Nagel and K. Preiss, *Agile Competitors and Virtual Organizations: Strategies for Enriching the Customer* (New York: Van Nostrand Reinhold, 1995).

167. See W. H. Davidow and M. S. Malone, *The Virtual Corporation. Structuring and Revitalizing the Corporation for the 21st Century* (London: Harper Business, 1993).

168. A. Pacey, *The Culture of Technology* (Oxford: Blackwell, 1983) p. 134.

169. W. H. Davidow and M. S. Malone, *The Virtual Corporation. Structuring and Revitalizing the Corporation for the 21st Century* (London: Harper Business, 1993) p. 187.

170. C. Stabell and fl. Fjeldstad, 'Configuring Value for Competitive Advantage: On Chains, Shops and Networks', *Strategic Management Journal*, Vol. 19, Number 5 (1998) p. 435.

171. A. Pacey, *The Culture of Technology* (Oxford: Blackwell, 1983) p. 120.

172. M. Hammer. *Beyond Reengineering: How the Process-Centered Organization is Changing Our Work and Our Lives* (London: HarperCollins, 1998) p. 210.

173. P. Strassmann, *Information Payoff: The Transformation of Work in the Electronic Age* (London: Collier Macmillan, 1985) p. 242.

174. N. Earle and P. Keen, *From .com to .profit. Inventing Business Models that Deliver Value and Profit* (San Francisco: Jossey-Bass, 2000) p. 11.

175. Global Internet Policy Initiative, available at: http://www.gipiproject.org.

BIBLIOGRAPHY

W. T. Anderson, 'The Self in Global Society', *Futures*, Vol. 31, Number 8, (1999).

F. Andrews, *The Medieval Builder and His Methods* (New York: Dover, 1999 [1922]).

P. Barwise, 'The Value of the Digital Prophets', *Financial Times*, April 23 (2002).

R. Bellah, R. Madisen, W. Sullivan, A. Swindler and S. Tipton, *Habits of the Heart. Individualism and Commitment in American Life* (Berkeley: University of California Press, 1996).

J. Berleur, 'The so-called "Information Society"'. In L. Yngström, R. Sizer, J. Berleur and R. Laufer (eds) *Can Information Technology result in Benevolent Bureaucracies?* (Amsterdam: Elsevier Science, 1991).

S. Bridge, 'The New Generation', *eBusiness*, vol. 6, (2000).

K. Brown, 'An Electronic Electorate', *Financial Times*, 24 April (2002).

J. S. Brown and E. S. Gray, 'The People Are the Company', *Fastcompany*, February (1997).

R. Buckminster Fuller, *Critical Path* (New York: St. Martin's Press, 1981).

I. Burkett, 'Beyond the Information Rich and Poor; Future's Understanding of Inequalities in Globalising Information Economies', *Futures*, Vol. 32, Number 7, (2000).

G. R. Bushe and A. B. Shani, *Parallel Learning Structures. Increasing Innovation in Bureaucracies* (Reading, Mass.: Addison-Wesley, 1991).

J. A. Byrne, R. Brandt and O. Port, 'The Virtual Corporation', *BusinessWeek*, February 8 (1993).

F. Capra, *The Web of Life* (London: HarperCollins, 1996).

M. Castells, *The Rise of the Network Society*. (Oxford: Blackwell, 1997).

M. Castells, *The Internet Galaxy: Reflections on Internet, Business and Society* (Oxford: Oxford University Press, 2001).

C. Christensen, *The Innovator's Dilemma: how disruptive technologies can destroy established markets* (Cambridge: Harvard University Press, 1997).

D. Cleland, 'Borderless project management'. In D. Cleland and R. Gareis (eds) *Global Project Management Handbook* (New York: McGraw-Hill, 1996).

R. Clifton and E. Maughan, *Twenty-five Visions: The Future of Brands* (Basingstoke: Macmillan – now Palgrave Macmillan, 2000).

W. G. Collingwood, *Northumbrian Crosses of the Pre-Norman Age* (Lampeter: Llanerch, 1989 [1927]).

P. Conceição and M. Heitor, 'Universities in the Learning Economy: Balancing Institutional Integrity with Organizational Diversity.' In D. Archibugi and B. Lundvall (eds) *The Globalizing Learning Economy* (Oxford: Oxford University Press, 2001).

S. Cooney, 'Maximizing the Benefits from New Technology'. In L. Yngström, R. Sizer, J. Berleur and R. Laufer (eds) *Can Information Technology result in Benevolent Bureaucracies?* (Amsterdam: Elsevier Science, 1991).

F. Czerniawska and G. Potter, *Business in a Virtual World. Exploiting Information for Competitive Advantage* (Basingstoke: Macmillan – now Palgrave Macmillan, 1998).

W. H. Davidow and M. S. Malone, *The Virtual Corporation. Structuring and Revitalizing the Corporation for the 21st Century* (London: Harper Business, 1993).

S. Davis and C. Meyer, *Future Wealth* (Boston: Harvard Business School Press, 2000).

J. DiVanna, *Redefining Financial Services: The New Renaissance in Value Proposition.* (Basingstoke: Palgrave Macmillan, 2002).

D. C. Douglas, *William the Conqueror* (London, Yale University Press, 1999).

Y. Doz, R. Angelmar and C. K. Prahalad, 'Technological Innovation and Interdependence. A Challenge for the Large, Complex Firm'. In M. Horwitch (ed.) *Technology in the Modern Corporation: A Strategic Perspective* (Oxford: Pergamon Press, 1986).

N. Earle and P. Keen, *From .com to .profit. Inventing Business Models that Deliver Value and Profit* (San Francisco: Jossey-Bass, 2000).

U. Eco, S. Jay Gould, J.-C. Garière and J. Delumeau, *Conversations about the End of Time* (London: Penguin, 2000).

J. Eckenrode, 'Is Internet Technology the Path to Banking Efficiency?' IBM's *Building an Edge*, November 29 (2001).

E. Eisenstein, *The Printing Revolution in Early Modern Europe* (Cambridge: Cambridge University Press, 1996).

J. Fitchen, *The Construction of Gothic Cathedrals: A Study of Medieval Vault Erection* (Chicago, University of Chicago Press, 1981 [1961]).

R. Foster, *Technology in the Modern Corporation* (Oxford: Pergamon Press, 1986).

C. Freeman, 'The Learning Economy of International Inequality'. In D. Archibugi and B. Lundvall (eds) *The Globalizing Learning Economy* (Oxford: Oxford University Press, 2001).

D. Gardner, 'Slim Pickings for the Global Brand in India', *Financial Times*, October 11 (2000).

J. Gimpel, *The Medieval Machine: The Industrial Revolution of the Middle Ages* (London, Pimlico, 1998).

S. L. Goldman, R. N. Nagel and K. Preiss, *Agile Competitors and Virtual Organizations: Strategies for Enriching the Customer* (New York: Van Nostrand Reinhold, 1995).

M. Hammer, *Beyond Reengineering: How the Process-Centered Organization is Changing Our Work and Our Lives* (London, HarperCollins Business, 1996).

M. Hammer, *The Agenda. What Every Business must do to Dominate the Decade* (London: Random House, 2001).

M. Hammer and J. Champy, *Reengineering the Corporation. A Manifesto for Business Revolution* (London: Nicholas Brealey, 2001).

M. Hobart and Z. Schiffman, *Information Ages: Literacy, Numeracy and the Computer Revolution* (Baltimore: Johns Hopkins University Press, 1998).

J. A. Hobson, *The Evolution of Modern Capitalism* (London: Walter Scott, 1926).

E. Hunt and J. M. Murray, *A History of Business in Medieval Europe 1200–1550* (Cambridge: Cambridge University Press, 1999).

P. Israel, *Edison: a Life of Invention* (New York: John Wiley and Sons, 1998).

M. de Kare-Silver, *e-shock. the new rules. e-strategies for retailers and manufacturers* (Basingstoke: Palgrave – now Palgrave Macmillan, 2001 [1998]).

L. Kehoe, 'Leading Brands on the Run', *Financial Times*, October 11 (2000).

D. Knoop and G. Jones, *The Mediaeval Mason: An Economic History of English Stone Building in the Later Middles Ages and Early Modern Times* (Manchester: Manchester University Press, 1949).

A. Koyré, *Du Monde Clos à l'Univers Infini* (Paris: Gallimard, 1962 [1957]).

F. M. Lea, *The Chemistry of Cement and Concrete* (New York: St Martin's Press, 1956).

J. Lipnack and J. Stamps, *The Age of the Network.* (Essex Junction: Oliver Wight, 1994).

R. S. Lopez, *The Commercial Revolution of the Middle Ages, 950–1350* (Cambridge: Cambridge University Press, 1995 [1976]).

V. Lund, 'Virtual Agents: Expanding the Definition of "Customer Centric"'. IBM's *Building an Edge*, September 6 (2001).

N. Machiavelli, *The Prince* (Oxford: Oxford University Press, 1998 [1531]).

J. Manley, Canadian Foreign Affairs Minister, speech to the Royal Institute for Foreign Affairs. London, March 20 (2001).

J. Markham, *The Future of Shopping* (Basingstoke: Macmillan – now Palgrave Macmillan, 1998).

J. Martin, *Information Engineering* (Carnforth: Savant, 1986).

J. McCarthy, 'Information.' In G. Rochlin (ed.) *Scientific Technology and Social Change* (San Francisco: W. H. Freeman, 1977).

R. McGregor, 'Websites Punished as China Acts to Control Content'. *Financial Times*, June 6 (2002).

R. L. Meier, 'Late-blooming Societies can be stimulated by information technology', *Futures*, Vol 32 Number 1 (2000).

J. Micklethwait and A. Wooldridge, *A Future Perfect: The Challenge and Hidden Promise of Globalisation* (London: William Heinemann, 2000).

J. Morgan. 'Event-Process View of Project Management' Computer Sciences Corporation, UK Division (1995) (unpublished).

J. Naisbitt and P. Aburdene, *Re-inventing the Corporation. Transforming your Job and your Company for the New Information Society* (London: Macdonald, 1985).

N. Negroponte, *Being Digital.* (London: Hodder & Stoughton, 1995).

P. Noland, *China and the Global Economy: National Champions, Industrial Policy and the Big Business Revolution* (Basingstoke: Palgrave Macmillan, 2001).

D. A. Norman, *The Invisible Computer: Why Products can Fail, the Personal Computer is so Complex, and Information Appliances are the Solution.* (Cambridge: MIT Press, 1998).

S. J. Park, 'The Future of Brands'. In R. Clifton and E. Maughan (eds), *Twenty-five Visions: The Future of Brands.* (Basingstoke: Macmillan – now Palgrave Macmillan, 2000).

R. Petrella, 'In Search of … the Benevolent Bureaucracy'. In L. Yngström, R. Sizer, J. Berleur and R. Laufer (ed.) *Can Information Technology Result in Benevolent Bureaucracies?* (Amsterdam: Elsevier Science, 1991).

N. Postman, *Technopoly: The Surrender of Culture to Technology* (New York: Vintage Books, 1993).

N. Postman, *Building a Bridge to the Eighteenth Century: How the Past can Improve our Future* (New York: Alfred A. Knopf, 1999).

M. Quennell, *The History of Everyday Things in England* Vol 1. (London: B. T. Batsford, 1976 [1929]).

J. B. Quinn, 'Innovation and Corporate Strategy'. In M. Horwitch (ed.) *Technology in the Modern Corporation* (Oxford: Pergamon Press, 1986).

L. B. Rasmussen, 'Consequences of Information Technology. The Design of Inquiring Systems and Culture'. In L. Yngström, R. Sizer, J. Berleur and R. Laufer (eds) *Can Information Technology Result in Benevolent Bureaucracies?* (Amsterdam: Elsevier Science, 1991).

C. Rawcliffe, *Medicine and Society in Later Medieval England* (Stroud: Alan Sutton, 1995).

G. Rochlin, *Scientific Technology and Social Change* (San Francisco: W. H. Freeman, 1974).

N. Saul, *Richard II* (London: Yale University Press, 1997).

W. Sombart, *Luxury and Capitalism* (Ann Arbor: University of Michigan Press, 1967).

J. Stanovnik, 'Global Problems and the Role of Science and Technology in their Solution'. In J. Gvishiani (ed.) *Science, Technology and Global Problems* (Oxford: Pergamon Press, 1979).

T. A. Stewart, *Intellectual Capital: The New Wealth of Organizations* (London: Nicholas Brealey, 1998).

P. Strassmann, *Information Payoff: The Transformation of Work in the Electronic Age* (London: Collier Macmillan, 1985).

M. Tampoe, 'Don't Downsize – Improve Performance.' *Strategy*, November (2000).

M. Treacy and F. Wiersema, *The Discipline of Market Leaders* (Reading: Perseus Books, 1995).

M. L. Tushman, B. Virany and E. Romanelli, 'Executive Succession, Strategic Reorientations, and Organization Evolution'. In M. Horwitch (ed.) *Technology in the Modern Corporation: a Strategic Perspective* (Oxford: Pergamon Press, 1986).

L. White, *Medieval Technology and Social Change* (Oxford: Clarendon Press, 1962).

C. Wiener, *Trades and Crafts* (London: Wayland, 1972).

F. Wiersema, *Customer Intimacy: Pick Your Partners, Shape Your Culture, Win Together* (London: HarperCollins Business, 1997).

W. Wilson, *Strategic Business Transformations: Achieving Strategic Objectives through Business Reengineering* (Maidenhead, McGraw-Hill, 1996).

G. Pascal Zachary, *The Global Me* (London: Nicholas Brealey, 2002).